DYNAMICS OF GLOBAL CRISIS

DYNAMICS OF GLOBAL CRISIS

Samir Amin, Giovanni Arrighi,
Andre Gunder Frank, and
Immanuel Wallerstein

Monthly Review Press
New York and London

Copyright © 1982 by Samir Amin, Giovanni Arrighi, Andre Gunder Frank, and Immanuel Wallerstein

All rights reserved

Library of Congress Cataloging in Publication Data

Main entry under title:

Dynamics of global crisis.

    1. Depressions—Addresses, essays, lectures.
2. Business cycles—Addresses, essays, lectures.
3. World politics—Addresses, essays, lectures.
I. Amin, Samir.
HB3711.D93   330.9'048   81-84739
ISBN 0-85345-605-4   AACR2
ISBN 0-85345-606-2 (pbk.)

Monthly Review Press
62 West 14th Street
New York, N.Y. 10011

Manufactured in the United States of America

10 9 8 7 6 5 4 3 2 1

CONTENTS

Introduction: Common Premises   7

1. Crisis as Transition
   Immanuel Wallerstein   11

2. A Crisis of Hegemony
   Giovanni Arrighi   55

3. Crisis of Ideology and
   Ideology of Crisis
   Andre Gunder Frank   109

4. Crisis, Nationalism,
   and Socialism
   Samir Amin   167

Conclusion: A Friendly Debate   233

Notes   245

INTRODUCTION: COMMON PREMISES

Throughout the 1970s, "crisis," became an increasingly familiar theme: first in obscure discussions among intellectuals, then in the popular press, and finally in political debates in many countries. Few seem to doubt that, compared with the splendid postwar decades of world economic expansion, which at their height many proclaimed to be eternal, today large numbers of people live less well, and, more important, live in fear that their immediate future portends even worse.

Hence, once again, as frequently in history, bad times seem to have succeeded good times, and unease is pervasive. Of course, those with long historical memories remember worse times. But few people have such long historical memories. A large majority of the living world has in fact been born since 1945.

What then has brought on this change? There seem to be some popular villains in the general public discussion. Perhaps the commonest view is that the problem is an "oil crisis," which is the responsibility of OPEC. The oil-producing states, it is said, have since 1973 acted as a cartel and increased their prices outrageously, thus launching worldwide inflation, which in turn has brought on unemployment and declining standards of living. We reject this analysis. No doubt the OPEC producers have raised their prices; whether this is outrageous depends on one's perspective. However, not only does the onset of many of the world's current difficulties predate the price rise, but the crucial question is how it was possible for OPEC to raise world oil prices substantially in 1973 and not in 1963 or 1953. The answer lies outside the realm of the political decisions of the OPEC states.

A second favorite villain, at least in the Western world, is the USSR—expansionist, untrustworthy, and repressive. The USSR, it is said, has been able to impose its politics on an

7

ever larger part of the world—directly or via intimidation (so-called Finlandization). We do not deny the considerable increase in Soviet military strength; nor do we enter at this point into an analysis of the nature of the USSR as a socialist state. A close look, however, at its internal economic constraints, the political problems within and among the countries the USSR labels the socialist camp, and the growing reservations shown by world left movements toward the Soviet regime makes it clear that the image of a Soviet juggernaut is misplaced and that it should instead be thought of as a paper tiger, or at least a giant with clay feet. In any case, as the reader will see, we do not believe the USSR's actions can be said to account for the present state of the world.

A third villain is the governments of the industrialized countries. These are said to have grown too large and to have pursued foolish policies, particularly foolish economic policies. Some say these have been too inflationary; others say too deflationary. Some say they have been too directive and wasteful; others say that they have not been directive enough. That such opposite analyses are made, with such contrary implicit prescriptions, indicates the doubtful utility of focusing upon immediate economic policies. These are only a vacillating reflection of greater underlying difficulties, which are not the mere consequence of the fallibility of the people in power.

Other villains are suggested by smaller numbers of people, whose partisanship is all the more passionate. One group sees the wasting of nature as the great villain. The world is said to be in a profound ecological crisis, accelerated in recent years but the culmination of centuries of squandering our natural resources. We do not doubt that the squandering is real, but we doubt whether the proposed solutions (more natural technologies—sunpower in place of nuclear power—or so-called appropriate technologies as a mode of economic development) can play more than auxiliary roles.

Finally, there are those who believe that our current dilemma is the result of a worldwide degradation of mores, as long in the making as the economic dilemma. The content of this moral protest is variable. As in the case of ecology, it focuses on the ambiguous benefits of the changes of the past several hundred years. Yet although there is no doubt that much has changed at the level of social values, and perhaps at an accelerated pace, or that these changes have affected the political and economic arenas, we suspect that locating our ills in this arena is another distortion of vision.

We reject all these popular explanations of the crisis, even if each is not without an empirical basis and is relevant to understanding the current situation. Nonetheless, all of them deal with "intervening variables," the elaboration of which does not result in a cohesive or coherent explanation of what this crisis is, what brought it on, or where it is heading.

We think, nonetheless, that such a cohesive and coherent explanation is possible. While each of us does not present exactly the same picture, as will be clear to the reader of the four chapters, we share a number of important premises. These mark off our mode of analysis, our approach to the subject, from many (quite probably most) other analysts in the world today, and so it is important to present them at the outset.

1. We believe that there is a social whole that may be called a capitalist world-economy. We believe this capitalist world-economy came into existence a long time ago, probably in the sixteenth century, and that it had expanded historically from its European origins to cover the globe by the late nineteenth century. We believe it can be described as capitalist in that endless accumulation is its motor force. We believe that the appropriation by the world bourgeoisie of the surplus value created by the world's direct producers has involved not merely direct appropriation at the marketplace, but also unequal exchange, transferring surplus from peripheral to core zones.

2. We believe that we cannot make an intelligent analysis of the various states taken separately without placing their so-called internal life in the context of the world division of labor, located in the world-economy. Nor can we make a coherent analysis that segregates "economic," "political," and "social" variables.

3. We believe that, throughout the history of this capitalist world-economy, there has been increasing organization of oppressed groups within the world-system and increasing opposition to its continuance. The capitalist world system has

never been under greater challenge. Despite, however, the unprecedented political strength of the world's working classes and peripheral countries, both the praxis and the theory of the world socialist movement are in trouble.

4. After World War II, the United States was the hegemonic power, having commanding power in the economic, political, and military arenas, and able to impose relative order on the world system—a fact which correlated with the world's unprecedented economic expansion. We believe that this hegemony is now in a decline, an irreversible (though perhaps slow) decline—not, we hasten to add, because of any weakness of will among U.S. leaders, but because of objective realities. This decline is manifested in many ways: the increased competitiveness of Western European and Japanese products, the frittering away of the old Cold War alliance systems and the emergence of a Washington-Tokyo-Peking axis, and wars among states in the periphery, including states governed by Communist parties.

5. We do not believe that the struggle between capitalist and socialist forces can be reduced to, or even symbolized by, a struggle between the United States and the USSR, however much the propaganda machines of both assert this. Nor do we think the analysis of the crisis can be made by looking at the core countries alone, as though the crisis were located only there. What is going on in the USSR, Eastern Europe, China, etc. is not external, or in contraposition, to what is going on in the rest of the world. The "crisis" is worldwide and integral, and must be analyzed as such.

These premises laid out, it remains only to indicate our prejudices and our visions. We are all on the left. That is, we all believe in the desirability and possibility of a world that is politically democratic and socially and economically egalitarian. We do not think the capitalist world-economy has done very well on any of these counts. We all believe that capitalism as a historical system will come to an end. While our prognoses for what will replace it (and when) vary somewhat, we all remain committed to the historical objectives of world socialism: democracy and equality.

CRISIS AS TRANSITION

Immanuel Wallerstein

Crisis is a word that comes easily to the lips. We seem always to be in some crisis or other. The coin has become devalued, and therefore the vision has become blurred. If every problem presents a crisis, then none does. Yet the fact is that the world is in the midst of a crisis—structural and therefore fundamental, very long term and therefore one that lends itself not to a "solution" but to an "unfolding." We are also simultaneously in the midst of world economic stagnation, which is what many call the "crisis." A stagnation, however, is nothing new (since the pattern of economic ups and downs has been cyclical for centuries) and this current stagnation is not the crisis, although it accentuates it and brings it to our collective attention. Overcoming the stagnation (and renewing world economic expansion), which will require a decade, will not end the crisis. It will in fact make it more severe—a seeming paradox, but not really, once we know what the crisis is about and what its mechanisms are.

The crisis of which we are speaking is the crisis of the demise of the capitalist world-economy. Just as this economic-political system came into existence five centuries ago in Europe as the end point of the unfolding of the "crisis of feudalism," which was the lot of Europe between 1300 and 1450, so this historical system, which now covers the globe and whose technical-scientific achievements go from triumph to triumph, is in systemic crisis. It has been in this crisis since 1914/1917, and the crisis will no doubt continue through the twenty-first century. It seems to be a crisis of transition from a capitalist world-economy to a socialist world order. The prognostications we can reasonably make are in fact our subject, since it is only by analyzing the underlying secular trends of our present structures that we can make extrapolations on the basis of which we can act, in order to shape our world (within the limits of our individual and joint powers).

11

1. THE PROCESSES OF THE SYSTEM

To appreciate the crisis of our historical system, we must understand how it functions now, and how it has functioned historically. But there is another thing we must understand, something to which we are psychologically very resistant: the crisis of our historical system derives not from its failure, but from its success—success in its own terms, of course. The capitalist world-economy has been predicated on the cease-less quest for accumulation. Each time the economic forces within the system (the entrepreneurs, private and collective) have encountered a bottleneck which has caused a slowdown in accumulation—a bottleneck which these same forces had, to be sure, collectively created by their prior actions—they have engaged in behavior, efficacious behavior, to open up or bypass the bottleneck and resume the onward march of global accumulation. Each time individual actors have desisted from the prime economic task—accumulation—they have been pushed off center stage by others who have proved more loyal to the task or more hungry for its rewards. In short, the contradictions of the system have been constantly overcome. They are still being overcome. The economic stagnation which the world-economy has known since about 1967 will almost certainly be overcome by 1990, and the world is likely to know a period of seeming prosperity. It is this very "strength" of the system, its recuperative power, its ability to resuscitate the engine of economic expansion, that has created, and is deepening, the structural crisis, so that a system which has functioned and thrived for five hundred years is disintegrating at the very moment that it is at its strongest and most efficient.

What is this system we call capitalism, which has taken shape within the framework of a world-economy, a world-economy that has had as its political framework the interstate system composed of so-called nation states, presumably sovereign? It is a system based on a peculiar illogic, one which makes accumulation an end in itself. It seems reasonable to believe that our motive for working, individually and collectively, is in order to consume, in the widest sense of the word. But consume when? Even squirrels know that in order to consume evenly over time, they must not consume immediately all that they produce. "Saving" is thus an elementary prudence. Joseph advised the Pharaoh to save for the seven lean years, and our ecologists are warning us about the potential exhaustion of virtually all nonrenewable resources. Man the toolmaker added to the concept of saving the concept of investment. Some consumables were transformed into fixed capital, means of producing still other (and more) consumables. Land that has been transformed in some way—cleared and/or fertilized and/or fenced—is basically the first great variant of such investment, and was for millenia the central depository of accumulation. Once consumables are saved and *a fortiori* invested, it then becomes relevant to know who has legitimate access to them, whose property they are.

Savings, investment, and property have been part of every known system for a very long time; they are not inventions of the modern world. And they do not define capitalism, any more than technological change defines it. Inventions and innovations have been continuous in human history, if created at a slower pace in the past than in modern times. What is peculiar to the modern world is the stabilization of a particular structure, a world-economy, a social division of labor whose boundaries are greater than those of any political entity. Political structures do not contain "economies"; quite the contrary: the "world-economy" contains political structures, or states. It is only within the framework of such a historical system that persons or groups who give priority to the ceaseless accumulation of capital have been able to flourish. The problem for the accumulator has always been the state, the controller of weapons, for the state by definition can appropriate and redistribute wealth. The necessary condition for *ceaseless* accumulation is therefore a seemingly contradictory one: a state that can help the accumulator appropriate from others, but cannot easily appropriate from the accumulator.

This magical combination is possible only under one condition: the *single* economy within which the accumulator operates must be made up of *multiple* states. Then the various states may be induced to aid the accumulator—by repressing the workforce, by creating monopolistic advantages over other accumulators. But to the extent that any particular state interferes with the accumulator's security of property or privilege, they can have recourse to the protection of other states. Once such a system was in place, capitalism could "take off," which is exactly what happened.

The illogic of this system is that accumulation for its own sake makes no social sense whatsoever, since collectively people wish to consume and enjoy, not to accumulate. It is not merely that accumulation for its own sake implies an unequal distribution of consumption, but that it implies a far *greater* maldistribution than the previous historical pattern of nobles and warriors appropriating from peasant producers within the framework of imperial economies (or world-empires), and hence an ever greater polarization—and this amid the emotional disequilibrium of a system whose *raison d'être* is the treadmill of ceaseless accumulation.

This illogic has been covered over, and to some extent legitimated, for several hundred years by the fact that limiting the power of individual states to appropriate (not so much by internal constitutional constraints as by those of the interstate system on the real power of any single state) has meant removing the constraints on invention and innovation which existed prior to 1500 and which enormously slowed down the pace of technological progress. Once the creation and stabilization of this new genus, the capitalist world-economy, lifted these political constraints, technological change became simply one more weapon in the accumulators' arsenal, and the world entered a new epoch of the substitution of mechanical for human energy.

The results were so spectacular that we have tended to ignore how few profited by these technological achievements, and in particular how the use of machines has meant an *increase* in the average expenditure of human energy per person per lifetime. For along with "scientific progress" went (1) the hierarchization of space (the creation of an increasingly spatially polarized division of labor, of cores and peripheries, in an increasingly integrated capitalist world-economy); (2) the creation of a worldwide, polarized two-class structure (dividing the accumulators, or bourgeoisie, from the direct producers, and creating in its wake corresponding household structures to ensure the reproduction of the class structure); and (3) the creation of states operating within an interstate system, states of unequal strength corresponding to the hierarchization of space in the economy (and creating in their wake "peoples"—nations, ethnic groups—in uneasy relationship to the states).

This framework—core and periphery, bourgeoisie and proletariat, states and peoples—was already in place in the capitalist world-economy of the sixteenth century, whose boundaries encompassed only a part of the globe, although the structures were less clear in their form than they are today. How this world-economy came into existence is not our subject, but how it functioned once it did exist is, since only by analyzing its normal mode of functioning can we appreciate the nature of the present crisis, understand its origins, and make some informed guesses about how it is likely to unfold. The capitalist system, like all systems, has contradictions, which simply means that the mechanisms that are useful for achieving one set of objectives *simultaneously* undermine or contradict the achieving of that objective. Let us start by looking at one such contradiction, perhaps the fundamental one.

The primary desideratum, the defining characteristic, of a capitalist system is the drive for ceaseless accumulation. The formal structuring of the system—a single world-economy of multiple states linked in an interstate system—serves this end in the best way possible, since it facilitates the ability of each "enterprise" to make its production (and allied marketing) decisions in order to maximize profits over some middle run. Given a system that facilitates this ability, most entrepreneurs (we repeat, private or collective) will make rational decisions from their self-interested point of view. The totality of their decisions makes up world supply at any given moment. As long as there is a market somewhere for additional goods, world supply will tend to expand via Adam Smith's "invisible hand," each entrepreneur (or many of them) will find it worthwhile to expand production, and the structure of the world-economy will make it politically possible to do so. At one time, there prevailed the optimistic delusion that production created demand, but bitter experience has demonstrated that this is not true: demand is a function not of production but of how the revenues of enterprises are distributed, which is the intervening factor that determines demand.

And how is this distribution determined? Here there are no automatic, or impersonal, rules. To the extent that there are at least two groups involved in any enterprise—those who control the accumulated capital and those who perform the ongoing work—there are an infinity of possible divisions of revenue and therefore an inevitable and eternal tug-of-war concerning it. This tug-of-war occurs at the level of the enterprise, but is conditioned (limited, constrained) by political decisions taken at the level of the state. There are, however, many states, no one of which can control the totality of the world-economy, and each of which seeks a certain stability. Furthermore, political decisions on the parameters of distribution are the outcome of political struggles, and are not changed easily. Hence these state decisions tend to remain fixed for intermediate lengths of time. And therein lies the contradiction: world demand, the sum of the consequences of political decisions taken in each state, tends to remain stable over the middle run while world supply is hurtling toward ever greater production. Sooner or later, usually after about twenty-five years, there comes a point where there are insufficient buyers for the additional supply and the capitalist world-economy finds itself in one of its recurring "bottlenecks of accumulation." We are in the most recent such bottleneck today, and have been since about 1967.

Once the world-economy is in a state where, globally, current supply is outstripping current demand, there occurs a global "discomfort." The times seem out of joint, prosperity a thing of the past. It is, to be sure, not that everyone is suffering the same economic difficulties: for some—perhaps for many— "bad times" are the times of highest profit. Nevertheless, in such periods there are two major sources of pressure for change. On the supply side, those who are producing goods that they find difficult to market seek to discover new customers, new products, or new ways to reduce the costs of production (and thereby maintain their absolute profit level, or at least their rate of profit); on the demand side, those for whom bad times are translated into lowered purchasing power seek to renegotiate the political contract of distribution both at the level of the enterprise and of the state.

The resulting turmoil may last for up to twenty-five years, until a series of "adjustments" have taken place. But what is there to "adjust"? The world-economy is built upon a spatial hierarchization, in which there is a correlation between the degree of capital intensity of productive processes in given countries, the real wage level of ordinary workers, and the percentage of people who control "human capital" (but not necessarily real capital) and hence have medium-high incomes—a correlation in which there are zones that are high in all three characteristics ("core" zones), those that are medium ("semi-peripheral"), and those that are low ("peripheral"). There are thus at least three phenomena that can be "adjusted": the location of production activities, the level of remuneration (wages of workers, numbers of persons who live off "human capital"), and the size of the world-economy as a whole. In the past, changes have been made in all three phenomena in order to overcome the "bottlenecks of accumulation."

It is usually the products of the "leading industries" that have the most difficulty in finding sales outlets since it is these which, precisely because of their profitability, have attracted an increasing number of producers and therefore output. As many entrepreneurs scramble to get on the bandwagon in "good times," the wagon becomes overloaded. One solution is for some producers to go bankrupt, permitting both an increased world concentration of ownership and a reduction in world production. A second solution is to increase the capital intensity of production which reduces the wage bill. This, however, requires that the cost of the new capital be less than the savings in wages, and that the resulting "technological unemployment" be politically possible in the states in which the "leading industries" are located; this has not always been the case, particularly in the states in which the "leading industries" are located, because of the strength of the organized workers' syndical structures. A third solution is to relocate the production site to a zone where the level of wages is significantly lower, usually from core to semiperiphery, or (less often) from semiperiphery to periphery. But while relocation and further capitalization represent solutions for an entrepreneur, they tend to worsen the dilemma in terms of the world-economy as a whole, since they may represent a global reduction in demand. Sooner or later, bankruptcies (and concentration) must occur, reducing global supply, but also, via unemployment, reducing demand.

Another solution is to strike out on new paths altogether, with major technological innovation leading to the creation of new "leading industries" in core zones. Since the initial investment level is very high (including the financing of the invention process itself), this usually requires the use of social capital (that is, government funds), both as subsidies (open and hidden) for the entrepreneur and, perhaps even more important, as a major initial customer for the product. Still, in global terms the "new" demand primarily involves a reallocation of existing global demand, and while this may once again resolve the problems of the entrepreneurs involved in the new "leading industries," it does not necessarily provide a solution for the world-economy as a whole. Therefore the technological advance that each period of global stagnation brings on is not itself a solution to the problem of renewing the process of global accumulation: it may reshuffle the global geography of production, and hence the global distribution of power (without impinging in any significant way on the spatial hierarchization of production, and hence on the unequal development of the world-economy), but it probably will not solve the problem of global demand.

Global demand could of course be expanded by expanding global production (the old premise that production creates demand), but this presumes a buoyant world-economy, not one in which the existing level of world production is *already* too high for existing demand. In such a situation, which is precisely that of the recurrent stagnations, the only real solution is to expand demand by redistributing the surplus. But here we come up against another contradiction of the system: since the object of the economic exercise is ceaseless accumulation, redistribution of the surplus involves a diminution in global accumulation because it diminishes profit. Nevertheless, it is essential to permit a new expansion of global production, which alone holds out the promise for an increase in profit.

No wonder the entrepreneurs are dismayed, caught betwixt and between, reluctant to give up profits, avid to obtain them. But the direct producers are not so caught: they care little about the global buoyancy of the world-economy. What they care about is their own survival, which is threatened by the global stagnation.

The result is a period of acute political struggle over the issue of distribution. This can take multiple forms: in the workplace, with work stoppages or property seizures; in the consumers' marketplace, with food boycotts or riots; at the level of the state, with demonstrations, uprisings, revolutions. It can also take the form of acute interstate struggles, which can range from the use of mercantilist practices to the outbreak of local conflicts to the launching of those global civil wars we call world wars.

The process of acute struggle is something which requires the expenditure of accumulated capital on immediate consumption and thus helps to increase the effective world demand in the short run, while decreasing supply through the destruction and interruption of production. But the effect of this should not be exaggerated, since it can only operate in the short run and is countered by a decline in demand through death and privation. In the middle run, however, an acute phase of class struggle in the core zones has usually resulted in an increase in the real income of the regularly employed sector of the fulltime proletariat, which provides a new base for real demand. In addition, the partial transfer of industries, formerly leading but now second level, to semiperipheral areas has two relevant consequences. First, the entire stratum of middle-level technicians, professionals, and so on, in the states to which these industries are relocated, is significantly enlarged. For the individuals involved, this means a social promotion and a rise in real income. Second, the workers in the relocated industries represent a group that is transformed from part-lifetime proletarians. And while their wage level is significantly lower than that of analogous workers in core zones—that is, after all, the whole point of the relocation—this wage level still represents a significant increase, in cash terms, from their previous income as semiproletarians. (Since, however, this is not necessarily an increase in *real,* as opposed to *cash,* income for the new fulltime proletarian families, it is often by force or by *force majeure* that these workers are recruited to this, often less pleasant, work.) For entrepreneurs in the semiperipheral zones, the costs of the wage labor are bearable, since the overall cost of production is very competitive on the world market, or at least within that geographic segment of it located nearby. The competitive opportunities are often increased by the existence of acute conflicts between core states which improve the terms of trade of the semiperipheral states.

Globally, therefore, the various mechanisms that operate in these longish periods of stagnation *end up* by expanding global effective demand. When this is combined with the various mechanisms that have slowed down the rate of expansion of global supply, the world-economy once more finds itself in a situation of "buoyancy," when there are ready buyers for what is being produced and the possibilities of further accumulation once again seem great. The redistribution of surplus that has permitted the rise in global demand has necessarily, however, been at the expense of the world bourgeoisie (although of some segments more than others, to be sure). This, as we have noted, runs counter to the primary objective of ceaseless accumulation. There must be compensation, and one compensation is the expansion of production: even if the rate of profit is lower globally, the absolute level may remain stable or even increase.

There is a second mechanism that can operate to restore the global rate of profit, however: the incorporation of new zones, into the world-economy. These were mostly zones at the edges of the world-economy, although some were "internal frontiers" in remote or ecologically difficult areas. The transformation of such zones into new areas of peripheral production, usually of raw materials, involves the *creation* of an appropriate labor force, which can operate not only the new "export"-

oriented productive enterprises, but also the food-production enterprises needed to sustain those working on agricultural cash-crops or in the mines, and the expanded subsistence production in "labor-reserve" zones. From the point of view of world capitalism, the incorporation of new zones makes sense in the short run not because they will become loci of new demand but—quite the opposite—because they will become loci of cheaper supply, thereby creating a new source of increase in the global rate of profit. In order that these be zones of cheaper supply, however, the real wage levels of the export-oriented industries must be significantly lower than those in other parts of the world-economy, and the mechanism *par excellence* to achieve this is to extend the boundaries for income-pooling households, enabling employers in the export-oriented sector to pay wages below the minimum required for the survival of such a household over a lifetime. The wage-workers survive, but they do so *by virtue of* being embedded in these "semiproletarian" extended households, benefitting from the income earned or goods produced (subsistence production, petty commodity production, rent) by other members of the household or by the wageworker at other times. This involves the "super-exploitation" of these wageworkers ("super" by comparison with wageworkers elsewhere in the world-economy, since these are wages which are insufficient for the reproduction of the labor force), and also masks the fact that the employer of the wageworker is obtaining the surplus produced by the other members of the wageworker's household. The additional fact that the actual raw materials needed because of expanded world industrial production are there as well is almost secondary to the fact that the new locus of production permits a restoration of the world rate of profit. This is why stagnations generally lead to an expansion of the boundaries of the world-economy.

Capitalism has thus overcome its periodic difficulties, the bottlenecks of accumulation, in a cyclical pattern. Neither the leading industries (in terms of profitability) nor the leading countries (in terms of power and concentration of accumulated capital and wealth) have remained the same over time. Strong products and strong states seem to have passed through patterns of growth and relative decline, each succeeded by another—and the world-system has far from exhausted the list of products or states that could play those roles. But this merry-go-round has always occurred within the framework of a single historical system that has retained the same defining structure (a world-economy with a correlative interstate system) and the same *leitmotiv* (endless accumulation). This structure and this *leitmotiv* have survived all the cyclical changes which, however important they may be to subgroups, have not affected the *global* functioning of the system. Where the big money is (whether it be in textiles, steel, electronics, microprocessors, or biotechnology) is a matter of indifference to accumulators as long as *some* product plays that role and money can be invested in it. Whether Holland or Britain or the United States is the hegemonic power is a matter of indifference to accumulators as long as there remain strong core states (and occasionally a hegemonic one) to ensure the political viability of the search for profit.

2. THE STRUCTURAL LIMITS OF RENEWAL

Yet this cyclical pattern cannot go on forever, because in fact it is not truly cyclical but spiral. In terms of the underlying economic mechanisms, there are some built-in limitations to the process of renewal, and it is these limitations that have played a major role in creating the crisis of our historical system. The two fundamental recuperative mechanisms— proletarianization and geographical expansion—have built-in limits: their curves tend toward asymptotes. The lesser but more obvious problem is that of geographical expansion. The incorporation of new direct producers, "super"-exploited part-lifetime wageworkers embedded in semiproletarian extended households, in effect gives the world-economy a perpetual supply of immigrants from outside the system (except that the system expands spatially to incorporate them, rather than the other way around), immigrants who always come in at the bottom of the global pay scale to replace these who have "moved up." Yet this presumes a perpetual supply of workers, which is simply not there. By the late nineteenth century, the capitalist world-economy had expanded its outer boundaries to cover the whole of the earth; by the late twentieth century, it had reached most of its inner geographical frontiers as well. There are now virtually no populations left to incorporate, and the structure must begin to collapse.

Nevertheless, the system can continue for some time before the inability to incorporate new populations is felt in a slow decline in the global rate of profit. The real crunch will come in the process of proletarianization, or, more generally, in the process of commodification—the quintessential way in which the success of the system is in fact its main destabilizing factor. Since commodification, however, appears as "success" to both the defenders and the opponents of the system, it is seldom noted that it is a "success" that is breeding failure. I am speaking here of what neoclassical economists call the "free flow of factors of production" and what Marx called the realization of the "law of value."

Capitalism is referred to glibly as a system of free enterprise based on free labor (and, of course, alienable land and natural resources), and we often fail to recognize the most obvious of all historical facts about the capitalist world-economy: that, in the five hundred years of its existence, at no time have the factors of production been fully "free" nor the law of value fully realized. Indeed, the most evident empirical fact is that capitalist entrepreneurs have always operated *and flourished* in an arena in which some factors were "free" but others were not (or were less so), in which the law of value was dominant in some but not in all sectors of the "economy." Even today, in the core zones of this world-economy, such as the United States, Western Europe, or Japan, all land and natural resources are not alienable, all labor is not performed for cash remuneration, all products are not sold and exchanged through a money market, and gigantic barriers limit the free flow of commodities, capital, and labor between states. Indeed, any definition of capitalism that requires the *full* freedom of these factors, or even the freedom of a large majority of them would lead us logically to the conclusion that the world-economy is not yet capitalist but is still "feudal" or "pre-capitalist."

That would, however, obviously be absurd. Such a conclusion fails to take note of how central to the functioning of the capitalist world-economy is the *partial* freedom of the factors of production, the *partial* realization of the law of value. This "partial" phenomenon *is* capitalism. Nonetheless, capitalism, through its internal processes, pushes toward the fuller freedom of the factors of production, the fuller realization of the law of value. And it is this "success" that is causing the crisis, and will be the undoing of the capitalist system.

Each advance in technology pushes us to extend the commodification of real goods: for example, in the last thirty years many within-household transactions have become commodified for increasing numbers of people in the core zones—fast-food places cook meals, laundromats wash clothing, nurseries care for small children. And in the next thirty years we shall undoubtedly see the commercial sale of sunpower, under the pressure of anti-establishment ecologists, but for the profit of someone. Further, as the earth's land mass becomes increasingly commodified, we will move toward the commodification of the seabeds; and as we once sold bullion, then paper money, and then checks, we have now moved to a further commodification of credit through the medium of plastic identification cards, telephone communications, and more. Most important of all, we have moved steadily toward the commodification of labor power, the transformation of semiproletarian households into full-lifetime proletarian households, primarily for the reasons suggested above. At the same time, property claims to capital are being transformed from "heavy" forms difficult to transmute (such as land, machinery, and even bullion) to the most rapidly transmutable form of all, current cash income attached to positions that are not dependent on productivity achievements and access to which can essentially be bought (via the purchase of "education").

Nothing is new in this. But two things should be noted. First, the further commodification of transactions is for the holders of capital a *pis aller* in that it *reduces* the global ability to accumulate by reducing the existence of *super*profits and the security of existing capital for the current largest accumulators. Yet it is these very accumulators who regularly set in motion the increasing commodification in order to overcome the bottlenecks of accumulation, sacrificing increasing the rate of profit to increasing its absolute level. Second, there is an inbuilt limit to commodification—100 percent—and while we are still far from that, we have reached the point where that limit is visible, if remote.

3. STATES, PEOPLES, AND CLASSES

The two asymptotes of geographical expansion and commodification have reached the level where they have begun to act as structural constraints on the survival of capitalism as an historical system. And since the crisis operates through the consciousness of the people who live under these constraints, this brings us to the political and cultural arena. In order, therefore, to understand the ways in which the crisis has presented itself, we must look first at the politico-cultural superstructure of the capitalist world-economy.

The first political reality of capitalism is polarization. Over time and within the expanding space of the world-economy, the distribution of reward—as measured in material goods, life chances, quality of life, and total work effort—as a percentage of total time (by day, by year, by lifetime) between the smaller group, at the top (increasingly identical with accumulators, or bourgeoisie) and the largest group, at the bottom (the direct producers) has widened. While it is perfectly true that particular groups of people (as defined by physical location and work task) have improved their position over time (sometimes dramatically), this only means that in an expanding world system there is always some room at the top (or in the middle). But viewed globally, the "more at the top" is far smaller than the "more at the bottom," and the gap has grown steadily greater across the centuries. It is undoubtedly the case that few sixteenth-century rural producers worked as hard and long for so little as do rural producers in today's Third World—and this leaves out of account the increasing differentials in life expectancy, both as measured from birth (as is commonly done) and as measured from age 1 or 5 (which is almost never done, and which would show an even wider gap). If there is a crisis in the world-system today, this fundamental reality cannot be omitted from any account of its precipitating factors.

The social expression of this polarization has been the development of class consciousness. Class consciousness is a much misunderstood concept. It is not a badge one wears, an incantation invoked in every conversation; it is a solidarity and an interest to be invoked when it is important and possible to do so. The criterion of "importance" implies that class consciousness, for both accumulator and direct producer, for both bourgeois and proletarian, lies latent most of the time, surfacing only rarely, in major confrontations. The criterion of "possibility" implies that its evolution can take many forms: it can be overt, nominal, or tactically used under the guise of the claims of "peoples" or "states"; it can be evoked by state, local, or (up to now very rarely) trans-state organizations. Since overt class conflict most directly undermines the structural bases of the world system, it is no wonder that so much energy is mobilized against its concrete manifestations—even to the point of denying its existence. *Eppur si muove!*

The political impact of global class polarization has been obscured and channeled for a long time, rather effectively, by the existence and structure of the interstate system. Modern states are the creation of the modern world. Some claim to be modern incarnations of ancient world-empires; others claim vaguer continuities with previous political and/or cultural entities; still others claim similar longevity only by far-fetched ratiocinations. The fact is that all were molded in the tumultuous crucible of capitalist competition, with various groups of accumulators seeking political assistance in two central objectives: (1) the creation of nonmarket advantages over competitors through monopolies, subsidies, mercantilist protections, provision of infrastructure, and the destruction of the political supports of competitors; and (2) the containment of the demands of the working classes. Thus accumulators in core zones have generally wanted strong states at home, but they have also wanted states in the peripheral zones—states weak enough that the peripheral states do not have the power to set the terms of the flow of factors of production, yet strong enough to guarantee this flow against the interference of local potentates or the resistence of the local workforce. Thus, one by one and bit by bit, these states were constructed or reconstructed, honed to an ever finer edge to play their institutional role in the elaboration of an overall political framework that could contain the world market and its multiple state structures. This framework is the interstate system, which has been elaborated and rationalized since the sixteenth century.

As is well known, the fundamental principle of this interstate system is not national sovereignty (largely a fiction, if a convenient one, parallel to the fiction of the equality of citizens in a modern state) but the so-called balance of power. What is a balance of power? It is the name given to the fact that in a system in which there are multiple core zones, as well as a few semiperipheral ones wanting to change position, coalitions will always form so as to constrain the ability of the stronger military entities to conquer the world—for the simple reason that the recreation of a world-empire as a superstructure for the social division of labor would undermine one of the crucial supports for the functioning of capitalism as a world system, the ability of groups of accumulators to constrain even the strongest state structures by playing one off against the other. Constrain them against whom, one asks? Against the temptation of power holders to give primacy to the maintenance of order (and hence give concessions to the direct producers) rather than to sustain a structure that promotes the ceaseless accumulation of capital (which requires partial order but partial disorder as well).

The boundaries a state comes to have are often arbitrary and frequently unstable. They are the result of the intricate give-and-take of world power politics. Their very arbitrariness and instability, the fact that a modern state is a creation—perhaps not *ex nihilo*, but a creation nonetheless—means that state-structures need a social cement to function adequately. This cement is nationalism. But whereas state boundaries are both juridical and physical, the boundaries of nations are socio-psychological—they can be drawn wherever one wishes to draw them—and constructing a "people" is a bilateral process, bringing into concordance the self-image of the people concerned and the other-image of other peoples. Thus the construction of a people is far more tenuous than the construction of a state, and it is no accident that a perfect congruence of the boundaries of state and nation does not exist. Furthermore, those who control state structures are constantly trying to create and recreate peoples, as well as to destroy others, creating a political maelstrom that has absorbed much of the collective political energy of the modern world. Peoplehood is a powerful political claim, one that determines economic privilege, but it is built not on rock but on sand and must be constantly reasserted if it is to survive the cyclical economic processes of the world-economy. We must always remember that the relative stability of capitalism as a historical system is the consequence of the precariousness of particular groups of accumulators. For individuals, all is risk and power is often passing, but the polarized hierarchy of productive relations, of spatial specialization, and of the distribution of rewards has remained constant despite (or because of) individual and group mobility (up and down).

This construction of peoples, or nations, has not been haphazard. Just as states are placed in a hierarchy of power, reflecting a spatial hierarchy of the production processes and of the concentration of capital in the world-economy, so peoples are located in a rank order of "superiority" and "inferiority." Anthropologists may talk of "cultural relativity," but every street urchin knows the difference between the supermen and the "minorities." Racism is not merely endemic to the modern world-system; it is intrinsic to it. And beneath the basic fault line (white versus nonwhite) lie a thousand more subtle distinctions which demonstrate the importance of the pecking order despite its occasional fuzziness and despite the ability of some world castes to win minor adjustments in their position.

There is a crude version of racism which justifies privilege overtly and is a convenient tool in dividing the world's population, allowing middle-ranked groups the honor of repressing lower-ranked ones. This version is cruel as well as crude, but it is efficacious. There is, however, a more sophisticated version which thrives not on hatred but on polite scorn, which appeals not to the emotions but to the intellect. This is the assertion by intellectuals in the core zones that their ideas, their theses, are universal, transcending time and space, disinterested and secular. The shift from God's law to natural law may have been touted as a liberation and liberalization, but in fact it provided logical basis for a cultural imperialism that has dressed itself in scientism and categorical imperatives.

Racism, of both the crude and sophisticated variety, has inevitably evoked an ambivalent reaction among its victims. They have sought to escape its consequences, on the one hand by assimilating the values and symbols of the superior group, and on the other by posing claims (weakly sustained by real power) to counter-superiorities. This mode of combatting the cultural premises of the world system has helped sustain its development, for the low-ranking peoples have been pushed to create state structures that conform with the processes of the interstate system (if not to assimilate to it, then to organize a counter-power of some sort) and to mold their production processes so that they become better integrated into the world division of labor (again, if not for one reason, then for the other).

4. THE RISE OF ANTISYSTEMIC MOVEMENTS

Our subject, however, is the crisis of this system. The creation of states, of peoples—like the creation of classes and their basic element, households—has been integral to the construction and functioning of the capitalist world-economy. But just as purely economic mechanisms have moved toward asymptotic limits, so the broader social, political, and cultural processes have involved fundamental contradictions which, as they have played themselves out, have contributed to the onset of crisis.

The first such contradiction has long been evident. It is that the desire to reduce costs of production as much as possible leads to the creation of units of production that concentrate direct producers, in workplaces (factories, plantations, mines) and residences (urban agglomerations). Furthermore, the technological advances intrinsic to the world-economy in transportation and communication further sociopolitical as much as purely economic transactions. Hence, the very process that permits the extension and intensification of capitalist development *per se* also facilitates the organization of social movements opposed to it.

The second contradiction is that the transformation of political entities into states linked in an interstate system, and the systemic pressure to conduct all social transactions in the political arena in the separate states, has concentrated attention on the usefulness and importance of achieving world systemic power by achieving and strengthening state power, particularly in the weaker states. Ergo, the very superstructure that was put in place to maximize the free flow of the factors of production in the world-economy is the nursery of national movements that mobilize against the inequalities inherent in the world system.

These two forms of antisystemic movement—the social movements of the working classes and the national movements of the weaker peoples—already had emerged in the nineteenth century and had begun to play an important (if still secondary) role on the world political scene. The continuing "successes" of the world capitalist system deepened, not lessened, the contradictions of the system. By the twentieth century, social and national movements had emerged everywhere and had become collectively stronger. Furthermore, whereas social and national movements were at first rivals, they became increasingly interconnected, thereby tending to close the gap between antisystemic forces that had originally loomed so large. By the first quarter of the twentieth century, not only were there a series of well-organized workers' movements and socialist parties in the core countries of the world-economy, but serious nationalist movements had begun to take shape in China, India, Mexico, Turkey, and the Arab world, as well as of course in much of Europe. The Russian Revolution of 1917 crystallized this ferment because, although it reflected all the ambiguities of the world's antisystemic movements, its vigor was spectacular and it seemed the first concrete evidence of the possibility (quite different from the reality) of a new world order. If we date the crisis of the capitalist world-system from this event, it is not because it created a new world, or even in any real way an improved one—one could plausibly make the opposite case—but because it shook one of the pillars of any historical system, the certainty of its rulers and cadres that it is eternal. In that basic sense, October 1917 was a world revolutionary moment whose effect no subsequent event or development has undone, and it was therefore a threshold in the history of the modern world-system.

If the twentieth century has seen the strength of antisystemic movements reach a level where they are collectively serious contenders in the political arena, it has also seen a less spectacular, subtler, but no less important decline in the strength of the defenders of the system. Here too we find an in-built contradiction in how the system operates. In the precapitalist world, rulers needed cadres (mostly armed men) to enforce their will, but they did not need many. The disparity in strength between soldiers and ordinary people was so striking that internal repression was relatively easy—especially since control was seldom intended to reach into the work process itself. Direct producers were allowed relative work autonomy, provided they paid their rent or tribute at the required intervals. But this changed dramatically with the advent of our historical system. A capitalist world-economy is a complex mechanism to administer. It involves an integration of very disparate production processes, which in turn requires close control of the workplace. We speak glibly of enterprises "responding to the market," seldom realizing how much discipline and organization such a response requires. The elaborate machinery of states linked in an interstate system has led to the construction of bureaucracies, of which we are all quite conscious.

In short, in one field after the other, the capitalist rationalization of the world has led to the growth of an increasingly large stratum of intermediaries—technicians, managers, professionals, engineers, service personnel—who are essential to the operation of the system and who live off a segment of the surplus value that others create. The striking feature of this stratum is that its claim to recompense is based not on the possession of real capital but on the possession of human capital, and its ability to transmit status is based not on bequeathing property (since its members tend to consume virtually all of their current income) but on arranging access to the training program which creates the "human capital."

The contradiction of the system is that the great accumulators need an ever larger stratum of this kind in order to keep the system profitable. Since, however, the only source of recompense for this intermediate stratum is the same surplus from which entrepreneurial profits—and hence accumulation—comes, the growth of this stratum threatens to reduce these profits. It does so in two ways: because it becomes larger (as a percentage of world population), and because as it does so it also becomes politically stronger, especially vis-à-vis the owners of capital, and can operate the parliamentary mechanisms—direct negotiation and welfare-state redistribution—of the core states to its advantage, exacting an ever greater percentage of the surplus. Once again, to maintain the absolute expansion of the system, those who operate it sacrifice relative expansion.

Although this constant "buying off" of the intermediate cadres by the accumulators of capital has deferred political crisis for the past two hundred years and strengthened the world bourgeois front against antisystemic revolt, it has an asymptote. For, while the decreasing percentage of the surplus reserved for the private accumulators of capital may satisfy the needs of the intermediate cadres and ensure their collaboration, it will also affect the will and ability of the great capitalist classes to operate. Indeed, as the intermediate strata have gained strength, they have begun to reproach the upper strata for their "failure of nerve." Are they so wrong? Thus, not only have the antisystemic movements taken collectively become stronger, but the defenders of the system have become weaker; this is one of the political foundations of the contemporary crisis of the system.

5. THE UNFOLDING OF THE CRISIS

We are now ready to discuss the crisis itself. I have insisted on spelling out in some detail what has brought it about, and have emphasized the ways in which it is the ongoing development of the capitalist world-economy—its "success"—that has brought it on, by the contradictions inherent in the system. If I have taken a long detour, it is because most discussions of the crisis are too cataclysmic in tone, and fail to take into account the fact that, despite the crisis, the capitalist world-economy continues to follow its internal logic and hence is *still* developing, is still (in its own terms) "succeeding." Analyses of the crisis are too full of illusion and hence inevitably breed disillusion; they are too full of triumphalism and unwilling to recognize how the antisystemic movements themselves are caught in the contradictions of the system. They tend to use a language of propaganda *pour encourager les autres,* but have fallen prey to their own simplifications and misapprehensions. And finally, in the atmosphere of collective insecurity which is the outward symptom of the crisis, these analyses offer pablum instead of more painful medicine, thereby responding to warranted impatience with a treatment that has prolonged rather than reduced the long trial. Our collective need is surely not for an olympian disdain of the crisis, but rather for a cool commitment, an incessant pursuit of those political effects that will hasten the transition accompanied by a constant reflection on the long-term possibilities that condition our collective will.

The political turmoil of the twentieth century has been the central expression of the crisis. By political turmoil, I do not mean the United States–German "world war" (1914–45), since the capitalist world-economy has at least twice previously been embroiled in such a world war—the Anglo-French (1792–1815) and the Dutch-Hapsburg (1618–48) conflicts. To be sure, the world war of 1914–45 was immensely destructive in material and moral terms, and its protagonists became partially embroiled in the ideological clothing of the crisis, but the most salient point about it was that it did *not* coincide with the dominant ideological cleavage of the time. The political turmoil of which I speak is rather reflected in the series of revolutions—socialist and/or nationalist—that have been successful throughout the periphery and semiperiphery of the world-system. Among them I include such rather different historical examples as Russia, China, Vietnam, Yugoslavia, Mexico, Cuba, and Iran—a list that is by no means exhaustive, because one of the features of this chain of events is the fluidity of the form and length of the process in different states. There is no model of a contemporary "revolution." One must add to this series of political events the many vaguer but nonetheless quite real politico-cultural modes of rejection: the civilizational "renaissances," the pan-movements, the assertion of the claims of "minorities," the women's movement.

All of these have the same starting point: the long-lasting acute oppression of a group which suffers from the mode of operation of the capitalist world-economy. These are movements of victims, and their central activity has been mass mobilization, achieved by different means (not always party structures) and in varying contexts. This mass mobilization has tended to focus on immediate enemies (what Mao Zedong liked to call the "principal contradiction"), and relatively concrete and realizable political objectives, which almost always involve obtaining power in a given state structure. While an antisystemic ideology has underlain each of these movements in its period of mobilization, it was seldom permitted to interfere with the creation of the necessary coalition or "front" required to achieve state power.

The result of this global activity has been twofold. On the one hand, the successive mobilizations have built upon each other. They have channeled sentiment into political will and created a force capable of competing with the well-armed state structures that defend the system. John Foster Dulles' metaphor of states as dominoes that will fall before a revolutionary wave was too simplistic, but it was not devoid of a certain reality. What it neglected was the other side of the coin. The wave of falling dominoes has been halted not only by strong counter-force, but also by the cooptative effects of the achievement of state power.

The partial or total achievement of state power by a revolutionary movement forces a clarification of the tension between the long-run objective of fundamentally transforming the world-system and the middle-run objective of achieving specific improvements for specific groups. As long as a movement is in the mobilizing phase, its internal contradictions can remain blunted. But power forces decisions as to priorities, and the priorities of today tend to win over the priorities of tomorrow—especially since the priorities of today imply the rewards of today. The reforms, however radical, of those in power can be accepted by the world's dominant forces as a redistribution of global revenue that has the beneficial aspects of augmenting global demand and enlisting new intermediate cadres in the further development of world forces of production. The pill turns out to be less bitter for the upholders of the status quo than they had feared.

Nonetheless, the cooptation of revolutionary movements has at most been partial, precisely because they are not separate entities but segments of a global movement. Just as cooptation is the result of the fact that the states in which such movements come to power are not truly sovereign but are constrained by an interstate system, so mobilization is rendered easier and solidarities are rendered obligatory by the fact that each particular antisystemic movement (socialist and/or nationalist) is constrained by the global political field in which it finds itself. (I deliberately use the image of a magnetic field to suggest the idea of a force which is real even if it seems to have no visible organizational structure.) Movements in power have often lost the will to solidarity with movements not in power—this is the result of cooptation—but they have offered reluctant solidarity nonetheless. This is the result of the pressure of the network of movements within which they continue to operate. The ambivalence of movements in power towards those not in power is matched by an ambivalence toward the forces of the status quo, since their cooptation offers them only relative insurance against organized attempts to remove them from power.

Movements in power have thus found themselves increasingly on the defensive. They lose the advantage of certainty and the aura of hope and approbation of the mobilizing phase.

Sooner or later they discover that their policies meet active, popular internal opposition. And as more and more of these regimes come to exist, the cumulative effect of their successive demythologizations begins to weigh upon the intermovement network itself. This affects the ideological expression of these movements more than their existence or their force, which are the consequence of the objective contradictions of the system. However contradictory the behavior of the movements during this long crisis, the factors which sustain the intermovement network are unlikely to change in any basic sense, and hence the successive mobilizations will continue to dominate the world political arena.

But the tone, the flavor, of these mobilizations is beginning to change. The mobilizations of the nineteenth and early twentieth centuries were very much children of the Enlightenment—nationalist, oriented to the work ethic and the state, universalizing in doctrine. In short, despite the fact that such movements sought to be antisystemic, they reflected in their formulation of long-term objectives middle-range methods that reinforced the mechanisms of the capitalist world-economy. However, under the impact of successive mobilizations that have recruited elements only marginally culturally integrated into the world-system, and successive demythologizations that have questioned the Enlightenment values, we have seen a search for new modes of expressing rejection of the existing world order, and these have drawn their strength from a belief in the existence of multiple "civilizations." It is thus that, throughout the period of crisis, the "cultural nationalist" component of these mass mobilizations has grown stronger, and "nationalism" is today seen less as a "bourgeois" response to workers' movements than a popular response to capitalist universalistic ideology.

The shock of the 1914-18 war permitted a volcanic upsurge of revolutionary movements, most notably that of the October Revolution in Russia. This upsurge was Europocentric, urban-industrial, insurrectionary; except in Russia, it failed. It was in part defeated by brute force, and in part preempted by counter-revolutionary populist Fascist movements. Beginning in the early 1920s, the USSR was increasingly constrained by its participation in the interstate system, forced to accept a strategy of "socialism in one country." The antisystemic forces, which had regarded the first phase of the United States–German struggle for hegemony in the world-economy as of no intrinsic concern, were drawn directly into it when the German regime took on the aberrant and virulent form of Nazism. This increased involvement in the intra-bourgeois struggle served as a final capping of the Europocentric upsurge—as could be seen in the Spanish Civil War, and in the de facto decisions of the French and Italian Communist parties to renounce insurrectionary strategies.

Meanwhile, as Sultan-Galiev and others predicted, the focus of antisystemic activity moved to the "East," or, as we would say today, to the more peripheral regions of the capitalist world-economy. The physical ravages of the 1939-45 war were no doubt as great in the European theater as in the Asian one, but the political consequences were quite different. A second volcanic upsurge was felt in China and in Southeast Asia, and this was not as easily capped as the earlier one had been. It has rumbled and spread throughout the peripheral areas ever since. The most striking thing about this second upsurge is that it has continued despite the renewed expansion of the world-economy and the extent of U.S. hegemony in the 1945-67 period. While the world capitalist system underwent a period of intensified development that was greater than any previous such period (as was to be expected, since practically every successive expansion has been more intensive than the previous one for over four hundred years), the factors that had caused the system to be in crisis had become so extensive that the global network of antisystemic movements went from strength to strength. Alongside the "Internationals" that emerged out of nineteenth-century European socialist movements grew up new organizational forms linking both states (Bandung Conference, Group of 77, OPEC, etc.) and movements (Tricontinental conferences, Afro-Asian Peoples' Solidarity Organization, etc.). But these formal structures were feeble shells compared to the expression of those forces in terms of concrete "protracted" struggles in specific areas.

The most extraordinary thing, however, about the 1945-67

period was that it was a time of almost universal and un-guarded optimism, in part the response to the acute pain and pessimism (at least for some) of the 1914-45 period. In 1945-67, dominant forces in the United States perceived an "Ameri-can century." However much official propaganda screamed of a world Communist menace, the psychology of the leadership was pervaded by a certainty that the existing world hierarchy promised a virtually eternal existence. This optimism was shared in Western Europe and Japan, where rapid postwar reconstruction made possible not only a restoration of their role as the location of core activities in the world-economy, but, by the early 1960s, a state of greater prosperity than ever before. Meanwhile, the USSR also saw the situation as posi-tive too. The power of the state had been reinforced by its military development, its ability to construct a significant in-dustrial network, the zone of influence it had carved out in Eastern Europe, and the beneficial side effects of the suc-cesses of the world revolutionary movement (accounting in part for the diplomatic recognition and integration that went under the label of détente). And, finally, the antisystemic forces of the peripheral states went from success to success, dragging in their wake many local bourgeois forces.

It is not that these various causes of optimism on the part of the various groups were not contradictory. Obviously, what was a plus for one was often a minus for the other. It was rather that the persistent expansion of the world-economy created rose-colored glasses which everyone wore: the nega-tive elements in the objective situation were seen as less important than they really were. All this changed however, after 1967, after the cyclical downturn or stagnation of the world-economy had set in (the so-called Kondratieff B-phase, usually lasting about twenty-five years). This period of stagna-tion, as we have already noted, is not "the crisis," but, occur-ring in the midst of the crisis, it highlights it for all.

One basic element of this stagnation, as of all such stagna-tions, is the worldwide "overproduction" of highly mechanized goods (electronic equipment, steel, automobiles, and also wheat). Overproduction is a deceptive term, however, because it does not mean producing more than consumers desire, but more than they collectively can afford. It means that the producers have to scramble for markets. How absurd this is in terms of social rationality can be illustrated with one example: in 1980, in a world where famines and food shortages still existed, U.S. wheat producers were angry at their government for the politically motivated ban on grain sales to the USSR. They would not have been angry had alternate markets been easily available. As it was, they felt they were yielding a scarce market for the benefit of Argentina and other producers.

Such overproduction is of course a direct consequence of the steady increase in world production since 1945 in all areas by everyone: first, by the big producing areas (the United States, Western Europe, Japan), second, by the intermediate producing areas (the USSR and Eastern Europe, Brazil, India, South Africa, etc.). Not until the first signs of stagnation in 1967 did the world market begin to buckle; then producers tried to maintain their profit margins by increasing prices amid acute competition with one another. This is, of course, a tricky game and led to wide fluctuations in prices (for example, in the zigzag of airline fares) and unemployment rates (as the major industrialized states sought to export unemployment to each other by financial and fiscal manipulation). Meanwhile, many of the largest firms sought to solve their immediate problems by reducing costs through the most classic of operations in a B-phase—the runaway shop—and in the late 1960s and 1970s a significant proportion of mechanized production shifted out of the core countries to "free-trade zones" in the periphery, to the so-called newly industrializing countries, and even to the socialist bloc (e.g., the Fiat plant in the USSR), in all of which the workforce receives less remuneration.

The end of the period of easy expansion also marked the end of the period of U.S. glory, the short-lived but very striking period of world hegemony. This hegemony was most obvious in the military and political arenas—in the clear superiority of force and the ability of the United States to impose its will—but its root was, as always, in the economy: in the ability of the United States in the postwar period to produce efficiently, cheaply, and with quality and therefore outsell other major industrial producers even in their home markets. By the 1960s, however, the United States could no longer outsell Western European and Japanese producers in their own markets, and by the 1970s it could no longer easily do so in the U.S. market. By the end of the 1970s, Western European and Japanese firms were beginning to establish or buy affiliates in the United States, even in banking.

But we must not exaggerate: the United States is not an economic has-been. It still represents the locus of a significant proportion of world economic activity. It is still stronger than Western Europe or Japan. But it is no longer so strong that it can be called hegemonic, and therefore it can no longer call the tune politically: it must now negotiate and/or compete with its erstwhile client "partners." Furthermore, its cost structure is probably less elastic than that of Western Europe and Japan, not because of the pay level of its skilled workers but because of the size, and therefore indirect cost to enterprises, of its managerial/professional strata. In economic terms there are three giants, not one, in the 1980s, and the primary fact of the world political arena is the struggle among them. But struggle for what? It is a struggle to see which can gain control of the new "leading industries" that will provide the profit base of the next Kondratieff upswing (which will probably begin in about 1990). It is already clear what these new "leading industries" are: microprocessing, biotechnology, and new energy sources. The scientists and engineers have been hard at work. The Schumpeterian innovators will be allowed their space.

The calling into question of U.S. economic hegemony has meant the calling into question of the structure of interstate alliances that was its corollary. In the 1950s, the interstate system functioned in a straightforward manner. The United States dominated the scene militarily, directly, and as the head of a multiple alliance system (NATO, Japan, and a series of lesser agreements). The United States was faced with an alternate alliance system, the Soviet bloc, which it was not strong enough to crush, but which it was able to "contain." The major strategic locations and resources were located outside the Soviet bloc. A very few states sought to be "nonaligned."

The first major crack in the stability of this system of alliances came from within the Soviet bloc. The Twentieth Party Congress ended the USSR's relatively unquestioned support from Communist parties elsewhere in the world, and the Sino-Soviet split meant a fundamental shift in the balance of interstate power. The 1960s and 1970s was a period of enormous internal ideological turmoil for China—from the Cultural Revolution to the fall of the Gang of Four—but the one relatively stable element was the slow shift in foreign policy, in which all leadership factions gave primacy to limiting what they called Soviet "hegemonism." While the Chinese initially denounced the Soviet leadership for its détente with the United States, it eventually moved toward de facto cooperation. Even more important geopolitically was that deep anger at the Japanese invasion was overcome and significant economic links were created with this erstwhile rival. Together, China and Japan could become a formidable pair, one that combined economic efficiency and advanced technology with numbers, resources, and political weight, and one that might have strong claims to a prime place in the expansion of the 1990s. The United States might easily find it in its interest to be closely linked to this nexus of rising world economic power, as Great Britain found it in its interest to be linked to the United States in its own post-hegemonic period (the period of U.S. ascension).

In a period of stagnation, the search for markets becomes a prime concern. The acute three-way competition between the United States, Western Europe, and Japan has occurred everywhere—in each other's home markets, in the peripheral countries of the world-economy, and increasingly in the socialist countries. It has been the period of stagnation rather than the period of expansion that has revealed how deeply these countries are still located within the structures of the world-economy. If they could pretend to separate or collective autarky in the 1950s, the veil was lifted in the 1970s. These countries have all evidenced symptoms of the world stagnation, and have increasingly sought to salvage their relative positions by intensifying the flow of the factors of production between them and the core countries, as well as by intensifying their explicit regard for the law of value. Conversely, the core countries, which could afford to ignore the socialist semiperipheral countries as exchange outlets in the 1950s, were by the 1970s scrambling over each other to get access—not only in the form of commodity imports and exports, but in the form of investments. A look at a decade of scramble shows that Western Europe has developed more intense links with the USSR and Eastern Europe than either the United States or Japan.

The counterpart of these slowly developing economic links has been the beginning of a "structure of cooperation" in Europe, one that crosses the ideological lines that were so fundamental in the 1945–67 period. Western Europe's NATO ties are loosening, both in terms of the continuing military input (the intra-NATO quarrel of the 1980s about the MX missiles and the annual increments of defense spending) and in terms of political attitudes toward the USSR (the intra-NATO quarrel over the primacy of continuing détente). Of course, the economic advantage of a Western Europe-USSR structure of cooperation comes up against continuing divisions over ideological issues, particularly over the nature of the regimes of Eastern Europe, and any long-term structure of cooperation would involve some political agreement concerning an internal "liberalization" of Eastern Europe. Up to now, neither the USSR nor the Western European leadership has really wanted this—the USSR because of the threat it poses to its own internal political rigidities, and because of fears of the loss of Eastern European economic partners; Western Europe because of fears of what a "liberalized" Eastern Europe would mean in terms of a subsequent move leftward in Western Europe (among other things, through the incorporation of Eurocommunist parties into the structure of power).

The rise of the Polish workers' movement in 1980 illustrates the uneasy relationship among the various groups. In the diplomacy of détente, Gierek played an important role; but the squeeze of stagnation led to an attempt to raise meat prices (and thus reduce real wages), which set off an explosion with political consequences not merely for Poland but for the possibility of a Bonn-Paris-Moscow axis. Ideologically and emotionally, Western Europe rallied to Solidarity, but prudently. Ideologically and emotionally, the Soviet Union and other Eastern

European regimes reacted negatively but also prudently. And the most prudent of all were the Vatican and the Polish Catholic hierarchy, who were cautious about losing existing advantages in the search for greater ones. Of course, the bounds of prudence may be overcome. But world economic stagnation is as powerful a taskmaster as ideological commitment, and the reluctance on all sides about a new pan-European structure of cooperation may well be overcome in the decade ahead.

6. PROSPECTS FOR THE 1980s

It may therefore be useful to pose the political question of the 1980s in the following fashion: Let us suppose the final result of the long stagnation (1967-90) is the total collapse of the old alliance structure and the emergence of a looser and far less ideologically justified structure which finds Western Europe (perhaps minus Great Britain) and the USSR plus Eastern Europe on one side, and Japan, China, and the United States on the other. Let us suppose that the expansion of the capitalist world-economy in the 1990s brings with it acute economic competition between these two camps. What will be the impact of such a realignment on (1) the role of the countries of southern Asia, the Middle East, Africa, and Latin America; (2) the likelihood of internal stability (as opposed to social unrest) in the industrialized countries, and in the superpowers, the United States and the USSR, in particular; and, consequently, (3) the continuing thrust of world anti-systemic movements to bring about the demise of the capitalist world-economy?

Two facts stand out as one looks at the history of the Third World since World War II. On the one hand, the countries of these regions have gone from political success to political success; successes located individually in the rise of the various independence and nationalist movements and in the achievement of their goals against often fierce resistance by colonial or imperial powers, and located collectively in such expressions as the psychological shock of the Bandung Con-

ference of the 1950s, the flourishing of the nonaligned movement of the 1960s, the power of OPEC in the 1970s. On the
other hand, despite all these political successes, despite all the
revolutions, despite the defeats suffered by the United States,
and Western Europe, the economic situation in these countries taken as a whole is distinctly worse in the 1980s than it
was in the 1950s. The gap has widened. At the very best, the
governments in a few countries, through herculean effort,
have managed to prevent too much deterioration in overall
revenues and internal social differentiation.

This pattern of apparent political success and economic
disaster promises to continue in the 1980s and probably into
the 1990s as well. There is nothing surprising in this; our
whole analysis shows why it should be so. Political success is
the outcome of the steady growth in the strength of the global
network of antisystemic movements. Economic disaster is
continuing peripheralization resulting from the relentless intensification of the capitalist world-economy within which the
Third World countries are firmly ensconced, even (perhaps
especially) the most politically radical of them. Yet we must
wonder whether such a contradictory pattern of political success unmatched (even countered) by economic results can
continue indefinitely. It seems most unlikely. For one thing, it
must lead to some questioning of political strategy by movements in the periphery. We have already referred to the process of shedding the Enlightment heritage that was central to
the antisystemic movements as recently as the 1970s. In this
sense, the Iranian revolution under Khomeini may be a har-
binger of a new style. Profoundly popular, profoundly antisystemic, what distinguishes the Iranian revolutionary movement from its compeers is less its appeal to a religious heritage
as an integrating theme (this, after all, has been done before)
than the enormous resistance it has shown to reinforcing the
Iranian state structure within the constraining framework of
the interstate system. Obviously, the movement pays a price
for such a strategy, and the strategy may fail, but the intense
attention focused upon Iran is in large part precisely because
both the defenders and opponents of the system are interested
in this experiment with a new strategy.

What is probable—whatever the immediate political consequences of the Iranian experiment—is a continuing, seemingly confused, mélange of class-based and cultural-nationalist themes, a series of revolutions within revolutions (not once but several times over), as antisystemic forces seek to destabilize the system, first of all by stirring *themselves* up. Such a process would in fact be considerably furthered by the realignment of the alliance structures of the core powers. The extraordinary ideological confusion (should it come to pass) of a world with Western Europe semialigned with the USSR against the United States and Japan semialigned with China would highlight the incompleteness of previous revolutionary processes, and would facilitate the develoment of an ideological analysis that would take into account the fact that the "crisis" of the system is a worldwide and prolonged process—a single process and not the composite of a hundred separate national processes. Amid a new bipolarization of alliances, one not ideologically based, it would be easier to construct a new form of nonaligned resistance which would not have the internal contradictions of the nonaligned movement of the 1960s (unable to decide if the USSR was a superpower to be shunned or an ideological ally to be cultivated).

The effect of this turmoil will inevitably be felt on the internal structures of the major powers, but unequally. One of the fruits for Western Europe of a structure of cooperation with the USSR will probably be the assurance of a degree of social peace in the 1980s and 1990s, and this for several reasons: an increased ability to weather the economic storm of the 1980s and to take advantage of the economic buoyancy of the 1990s; the incorporation of the remaining major opposition movement, the Eurocommunist parties, into the structure of power; and the defusing of the explosive situation in Eastern Europe (via a limited "liberalization"). For similar reasons, it is unlikely that there will be extensive social conflict inside Japan. China is different, since there there has been, ever since the 1960s, continuing social conflict; however beneficial the emerging interstate economic arangements are, it is not probable that they will tame all the sources of discontent. On the other hand, fuller world recognition of

China's place in the sun will be unifying and may permit China to pass the next twenty years in comparative internal calm.

It is in the United States and the USSR that the most severe internal consequences are to be expected. For both countries, the difficult economic years of the 1980s and even the potentially better ones of the 1990s will be difficult to traverse. In the case of the United States, the problem will be a socio-economic as well as a social-psychological adjustment to the loss of hegemony. It is not that the United States will not continue to be extremely wealthy and powerful—in a real sense it will remain the wealthiest and the most powerful in the world-system. But, no longer hegemonic, it will suffer a decline relative to its past status, and it will perceive it as such. Indeed, this was already the case in the 1970s. The biggest problems will be in the economic sphere. With an outdated and inefficient industrial plant, the United States will face painful collective choices, the response to which will probably be indecisive. Acute surgery (allowing the weaker industries to flounder and fail) would be very costly in terms of political unrest, yet salvaging such industries (through subsidies and/or protectionism) can only defer the day of decision, and will be costly in terms of foregoing alternative expenditures of social capital. The same might be said of increasing defense expenditures, a likely mode of fighting economic stagnation in the 1980s but one which will not enable the United States to be more competitive in the 1990s. Some money, private and public, will therefore concentrate on the new leading industries, but probably not enough to match (except perhaps in selected fields) the growing investment in Western Europe and Japan.

Meanwhile, some U.S. plants will be reconditioned for a lesser semiperipheral role in production chains that may be controlled by either Western Europe or Japan. This will require the employment of less costly labor, and hence will further enhance the role of the United States as a recipient of immigrant Hispanic and Asian populations. In a situation in which there will continue to be a stratification that highly correlates class and ethnicity, in which the percentage of socially defined "minorities" (especially Blacks and Hispanics) will begin to approach one-third or more of the population, and these concentrated in the large urban centers, in which there will be considerable unemployment over a long period and the upturn of the 1990s will not be as advantageous as elsewhere, and in which the collective *Zeitgeist* will be one of "decline," there cannot fail to be acute social conflict, which could verge on civil war. The "minorities" will raise high the banners which will be flying in Latin America and Africa, also in turmoil. They will find themselves facing right-wing, xenophobic, populist movements.

Although the social situation in the USSR is markedly unlike that in the United States, the outcome of the 1980s and 1990s may not be too different. If the USSR enters into a structure of cooperation with Western Europe, it will be precisely in order to avoid internal social conflict. And although such an association will no doubt reduce tensions at first, there are reasons to suspect that its economic benefits may not be great enough to overcome the unusual political rigidities of the state structure. While the industrialization of the USSR since the Russian Revolution has been an extraordinary achievement (without which the Soviet Union might have looked somewhat like India in terms of its economic structure), its industrial production is highly distorted by the military priorities of its successive governments. The impact of a still freer flow of the factors of production across its borders could be a further diminution of real income for the direct producers, combined with a greater consciousness of the economic gap and of the political possibilities of syndical organization. Since the USSR is a multinational state, with considerable uneven development, the internal social quarrels, if allowed freer expression, could begin to take on ethnonational clothing. To a resurgence of nationalism by the nationalities (those of the western USSR and the Caucasus looking to a model of Eastern European "liberalization" and those of Central Asia to a model of Asian "civilizational" reassertion), the response might be one of exacerbated Russian/Soviet nationalism, both inside and outside the party structure. This nationalism might even blend traditional pre-Soviet symbolism with a Stalinist ideological orthodoxy that would find itself unable to cope with the regenerated antisystemic ideology of the evolving network of world antisystemic movements, to which at least some of the non-Russian "nationalist" movements might attach themselves. The USSR would then find itself faced with its own version of hegemonic decline. The United States was the hegemonic power in the world-system; the USSR was hegemonic in the network of antisystemic movements. Despite the fall from grace resulting from the Twentieth Party Congress and the Chinese opposition, the role of the Soviet government as heir to the Russian Revolution has not yet been undermined. This kind of internal strife might, however, have this effect.

But it is on the antisystemic movements themselves that the greatest impact of an interstate realignment will be felt. In their past mobilizing phases, such movements have been at one and the same time politically radical and ideologically ambivalent, the latter the inevitable outcome of constructing the "fronts" necessary for successful struggle. (The recent history of the Nicaraguan struggle is a case study in this tactic). The restructuring of the interstate system cannot but be a blessing to those who, under cover of this ideological ambivalence, seek to transform the antisystemic struggle into a struggle for a reallocation of the appropriated surplus. Much of the language of the "new international (economic) order" pushes in this direction. This effort of some elements located inside the movements to move in the direction of economistic demands for reallocation may in fact have a countereffect, stirring up acute conflict within the antisystemic mobilizing movements and pushing them in the other direction. What can probably be anticipated is an increasing skepticism about the efficacy of seizing state power—which was, after all, virtually the be-all and end-all of such movements at the beginning of the twentieth century. Increasingly, these movements may call into question not only the formal structures of the world-economy but the formal structures of the interstate system.

To do this effectively, such movements would have to move in the direction of organizing other than within state boundaries. It is not a question of internationalism (almost always a vain slogan, where it is not a cynical ploy) but of trans-state organizing—not a new idea, although the trend since the early nineteenth century has been away from it. One effect of the present stage of the crisis (and in particular of the cumulative history of the network of antisystemic movements in the context of an interstate realignment) may be to reverse this trend.

I am not talking about new pan-movements, which have tended to be nationalist movements that defined in more extensive terms the proto-state boundaries within which they wished to organize. Pan-movements were an early phase of nationalist protest, easily contained by the core powers through the divisive tactic of according separate independences to entities that were the would-be constituents of such pan-states. I am talking of the construction of actual organizational structures that cut across the basic political ghettos of the contemporary world: the "Western" core countries, the "Third World," and the "socialist" countries. These labels may be unhappy or deceptive, but the reality and efficacy of such political ghettos is great. One of the most effective continuing supports of the present world-system has been the inability of the world network of antisystemic movements to create structures that cut across these political boundaries. The most delicate question for such trans-state structures to resolve, and one on which all previous efforts have foundered, is how such movements will relate to governments that are themselves heir to previous mobilizations. Up to now, movements out of power have tended either to support (for the most part without public qualification) some or all of the movements in power in other countries or to reject them as "treasonous" or "revisionist." What may occur is a major change in stance. Instead of thinking of such governments as incarnating, or failing to incarnate, revolutionary virtue, they may come to be viewed as the locus of continuing political struggle, or even as the locus of the key political struggle in the transformation of the world-system. One state after another within the world-system is coming to be "socialist" in at least three senses: self-proclamation, state ownership of key production or marketing units, and the ideological heritage of a previous antisystemic movement. In the 1980s, and even more in the 1990s, the survival of the capitalist world-economy may depend less on the nature of the diminishing number of old-style state structures and more on the realities of these new structures.

7. THE OUTCOME OF TRANSITION

We come here to the heart of the crisis. There is a crisis, we have said, in the capitalist world-economy. A crisis means a situation in which the contradictions of a system, because of its internal development, have become accentuated to the point where it cannot continue to maintain the same basic structure. The structure must be transformed, but transformed into what? There is no certainty here. There are in fact three major tendencies in the transition process. We are moving from the stage of the crisis where the struggle was between those who wished to destroy the system and its defenders to the stage where the struggle concerns the nature of the structure that will replace the existing historical system.

The dominant logic seems to be that of socialism. But what is socialism? There are two kinds of answer to such a question. One is definitional, the second empirical. In definitional terms, there are a certain number of characteristics of socialism inherent in the critique of the present system. I believe they are essentially three. Capitalism is a system in which production decisions are made in terms of optimal profitability for the producer; this leads to social irrationality. Socialism, by contrast, must therefore be a system in which production decisions are made in terms of social utility. Capitalism is a system in which there is an inequality in distribution, one which grows over time. This is unjust. Socialism, by contrast, must therefore be a system in which real inequalities are diminished and will diminish still further over time. Capitalism is a system in which formal liberties are tolerated only up to the point where they begin to undermine the stability of the political structures. Socialism, by contrast, must therefore be a system in which these formal liberties are so substantively rooted that they cannot be revoked or distorted at the will of political authorities, even when the political structures themselves are being effectively challenged.

According to this definition, none of the so-called socialist states are socialist. Nor could they be, for they are not autonomous systems, but remain part of the capitalist world-economy, subject to its law of value and bound by the constraints of its interstate system. These "socialist states" are in fact states within the capitalist world-economy controlled by governments that have emerged out of antisystemic movements. These governments are in turn the expression of these movements in power, suffering all the contradictions described before. The fact that such governments exist has made a considerable difference in the political functioning of the world-system; it is in fact one of the elements that constitutes the unfolding of the crisis. But these governments are not the incarnation of a future socialist mode of production, and it is even doubtful that they prefigure it in any significant way. Such a socialist mode of production can only be created by a transformation of the entire world-economy, the end point of a process that has been launched and somewhere in the middle of which we find ourselves now. Exactly what institutional expression such a socialist world order would take is difficult to know. The interstate system would undoubtedly be replaced by a unified political structure (else, how could social decisions on production in the world-economy as a whole be mediated?), but what this would look like in formal terms is unknown. It would be as futile, and as dangerous, to extrapolate the political forms of the socialist world order from the forms we now know as it would have been to extrapolate those of the capitalist world-economy from those of feudal Europe. As for the cultural expressions of a socialist world order, I believe history reserves its surprises.

Socialism is not the only possible outcome, however. There is another logic, that of domination. Those who hold power in a dying system seek to take the lead in the transformation so as to preserve their power. This has, after all, been tried before. The world bourgeoisie will not commit suicide; it may rather increasingly use the language of socialism to try to create a system that is neither capitalist nor socialist in any of the three

senses adduced above. The continuing process of bourgeoisifi-
cation of the upper strata may render totally archaic the traditional model of an independent, capital-investing entrepreneur.
Indeed, one could say that the essential difference between
the contemporary multinational corporation and the huge
capital conglomerates of earlier moments in the history of the
capitalist world-economy lies precisely in the degree to which
those who run it are quintessentially bourgeois, required to
live off *current* appropriation of surplus and therefore unable
to operate on other than profit-optimizing principles. Such
bourgeois no longer need legal guarantees of property rights
(which largely concern controlling the savings of *past* ap-
propriations of suplus). All they need is a structure that guarantees privileged access to the continued appropriation of
surplus. This means they can be very flexible as to forms and
status, concerned only with the realities of unequal power.
The whole meritocratic thrust of the period of crisis reflects
this logic of domination, all the more insidious in that it seeks
to preempt the language of social transformation.

There is, however, a third logic, which is in some sense
the great unknown variable and which may be the arbiter
between the forces of socialism and the forces of domination.
This is the logic of the civilizational project. One of the most
important peculiarities of the capitalist world-economy has
been that its mode of operation has permitted one historical
system to expand to cover the entire globe and thereby eliminate other historical systems. This was accompanied, as we
suggested, by a generic racism which, in its less virulent but
more efficacious form, was expressed as the universalization
of Western civilization. It follows therefore that the rise of
antisystemic movements involved a challenge to this cultural
premise of the capitalist world-economy, an insistence on the
"renaissance" of other "civilizations." It would be politically
meaningless to try to analyze the thrust of antisystemic movements today in, say, China or Egypt without taking this factor
into account. And not marginally: it is central to the blending
(and the confusion?) of social and national movements in the
twentieth century.

Once having said that these civilizational renaissances are a principal sociopolitical phenomenon in the present situation, we are not much enlightened as to what this implies for the process of transformation. It could theoretically push in opposite directions. On the one hand, these renaissances may contribute to the institutional inventions that would inevitably be a part of the creation of a socialist world order. Since we need to rethink all of our basic premises, what better way than to dip into the multiple wisdoms to which the world has given birth? On the other hand, civilizational renaissances may also provide the outer clothing for the logic of domination. Since what the world bourgeoisie needs is to continue the reality of inequality under new forms of more equal statuses, what better way than to dress in new exotica, renewing the world bourgeoisie with fresh elements? Indeed, just as I suggested that the key political battleground for the transformation process may be inside the antisystemic movements and the transitional and transitory state structures to which they are giving birth, so the key ideological debate may be the content to give these civilizational renaissances. The question may not be, is "nationalism" truly compatible with "socialism," but what kind of "nationalism" is compatible with the creation of a socialist world order, one which will have a unified political structure?

The most agonizing aspect of a crisis of a historical system is that, full of turmoil, it is nonetheless slow moving. Amid our individual and collective anxieties, the crisis works itself out both logically (in terms of the contradictions of the system) and unpredictably (in terms of the range of solutions). Such a situation calls for neither patience nor prudence, but for a long perspective on the present and some imagination about the future. The forces of domination have in many ways been more inventive in recent years than the forces of socialism. The dilemmas we face are within the antisystemic movements themselves. They need to restate their theories in more long-range terms and to evaluate soberly their history in the first stage of the crisis. The present period of stagnation may serve as a helpful shock, but not if we mistake cyclical downturn for the crisis itself. I repeat: there will doubtless be a cyclical upturn in about 1990. Yet the crisis will be no less real. For the objective fact that most fundamentally accounts for it is the ongoing development of the capitalist world-economy itself. The crisis is objective and ongoing. But its resolution will be the outcome of our collective human intervention and is not preordained.

A CRISIS OF HEGEMONY

Giovanni Arrighi

1. THE CRISIS DEFINED

My definition of the current crisis will differ from that given by Wallerstein in the previous chapter. I shall take for granted that we are living in a period of transition from a capitalist world-economy to a new world order that future generations, when they see it, may or may not want to call "socialist." In taking this long crisis for granted, however, I do not rule out the possibility of shorter crises (within the long crisis), defined as periods of "discontinuous change." On the contrary, I am inclined to think that a crisis of transition can be said to exist only if such periods become longer or more frequent.

"Discontinuous change" is not a simple downturn in the rate of growth of world production under given institutional arrangements. It is rather a period in which the institutional arrangements themselves are transformed or destroyed and new ones created. In this century we can recognize a first such period in the thirty years stretching from 1914–17 to 1945–47. It is a thesis of this chapter that in 1968 the world-economy entered a second period of discontinuous change, whose unfolding can be divided into two stages. In the first, from 1968 to 1973, though the expansion of world production seemed to continue unabated, some key institutional arrangements in which the long and steep postwar boom was embedded were radically upset. In the second, from 1973 up through the present, the destruction of previous institutional arrangements has manifested itself in the anomalous behavior of the world-economy (persistent stagflation) and in generalized institutional instability.

In the first part of this chapter I will outline the ensemble of institutional arrangements whose transformation defines the current crisis, and the main aspects of its transformation. In the second part, I will try to relate this transformation to what I consider the main structural characteristics of postwar economic expansion. In the third part, I will explore the relative likelihood of three alternative scenarios for the 1980s.

To make my task easier I have restricted my scope not only in time but also in space. Though my aim is to throw some light on current tendencies in the world-economy at large, my focus is on core areas, and developments elsewhere are analyzed only when they are crucial to an understanding of the dynamic of these areas.

The Pax Americana: Formal and Substantive Aspects

The most dramatic and spectacular change of the last twelve years has been the crisis of the world political-economic order established after World War II under U.S. hegemony—the Pax Americana as it is sometimes called. The main feature of this order was an imperial dualism, i.e., a peaceful duopoly of world power, in which a "free enterprise system" established under U.S. hegemony in the "capitalist world" was matched by a "state enterprise system" established under Soviet hegemony in the "communist world."[1] The institutional arrangements typical of the latter are not of immediate relevance to our analysis and will only be considered tangentially at a later stage. As for the former, it is important to distinguish between the formal and substantive aspects of U.S. hegemony.

The formal aspects relate to the transformation of the economic and military supremacy that the United States enjoyed at the end of World War II into a hierarchical interstate system that empowered the U.S. government to act within the capitalist world as a state above other states. In this sense we can speak of a U.S. imperial order—an order particularly evident in the military and financial spheres, with U.S. military power strategically placed throughout the world through a system of military alliances (NATO, SEATO, etc.), the CIA acting as an imperial secret police, and the dollar performing the function of universal money. To be sure, the institutional arrangements for the exercise of U.S. power were rather loose.

Yet this looseness did not prevent the U.S. state from performing overall political and economic regulatory functions throughout the 1950s and a good part of the 1960s, including a significant redistribution of resources through military and economic aid to subordinate states tied to the formation and consolidation of the free enterprise system.

U.S. power, and the institutions that were created to make it operational, were not ends in themselves. They were instruments for the transformation of the capitalist world in the U.S. image, the scaffolding for the substantive elements of hegemony. These elements were three: the reconstruction of the world market, the transnational expansion of capital, and the spread of Taylorism and Fordism.

The restoration of the unity of the world market, largely destroyed by the resurgence of state protectionist and mercantilist policies in the first half of the century, was promoted by the U.S. imperial order in a number of ways. It provided a cohesive political and ideological framework within which (1) relations among capitalist states could be enduringly pacified; (2) a process of decolonization could be initiated and, by 1965, largely completed; and (3) quantitative restrictions on trade among advanced capitalist countries could be eliminated and tariffs reduced. At the same time, the convertiblity of the most important currencies at a fixed exchange rate with the dollar, and therefore among themselves, was reestablished, thus reducing the risks to capital of, and so favoring, the expansion of international trade and investment.

It was not in the least, however, a self-regulating world market economy that was being established but an economy regulated and sustained by systematic state action. The U.S. state, in its imperial capacity, redistributed and expanded the supply of liquidity to maintain the growth of world production, trade, and investment. Satellite states, on the other hand, being constrained to apply the monetary and budgetary policies necessary for the establishment and maintenance of the convertibility of their currencies with the dollar at a fixed parity, tended to enforce market discipline over their own national economies and to counteract major overproduction tendencies that might develop within them. A hierarchically structured system of capitalist states thus sustained and regulated the reactivization of market-like forces, succeeding where an anarchic interstate system had failed in the 1920s.

The world system established under U.S. hegemony was not even free-tradist, as was that established under British hegemony in the nineteenth century. Though the United States actively promoted the liberalization of trade, it did so through bilateral and multilateral negotiations rather than through *unilateral* measures, as Britain did in the 1840s when it repealed the Corn Laws and Navigation Acts. Moreover, it is significant that immediately after the war the United States gave priority to the liberalization of intra-European trade rather than to the liberalization of its own trade with European countries. As a matter of fact, the main objective of U.S. imperial domination seems to have been to guarantee an "open door"—not primarily to trade but to capitalist enterprise, particularly against threats of nationalization. Throughout the 1950s and 1960s, this was indeed the major dividing line between the communist and the capitalist worlds and the rationale of U.S. political rule over the latter. It is in this sense that I speak of a free enterprise system rather than a free trade system.

One of the main reasons for this different emphasis was probably that, as we shall see, direct investment rather than trade had become the main weapon of U.S. core capital in international competition and, from this point of view, some measure of protectionism could enhance its competitive edge. Be that as it may, the Pax Americana, once firmly established, unleashed a spectacular increase in U.S. direct investment abroad which led to the rapid transnationalization of the industrial, commercial, and financial operations of U.S. core capital.[2]

U.S. hegemony did not merely imply a different historical relation between the interstate system and the world-economy, or between world-scale trade and investment. It also implied the spread of the revolution in industrial and social relations that had developed on a limited scale and with limited success in the United States during the first half of the century. I am talking about the practices usually referred to as Taylorism and Fordism. In a sense, these two phenomena were not new, since they simply represented the extension to new leading sectors (mechanical and engineering industries) of tendencies that had traditionally characterized capitalist production in general: the expropriation by capital, through the division of labor and mechanization, of the direct producers' control over the labor process.

In other respects, however, the phenomena were new. For one thing, as managerial and corporate *policies,* they consciously and systematically pursued what had previously been the unplanned outcome of struggles between labor and capital or of competition within capital. As such, they tended to institutionalize the former and forestall the destructive aspects of the latter, while extending and intensifying the traditional effects of the capitalist division of labor and mechanization. Partly related to this was a second new aspect, particularly significant in Fordism: a policy of relatively high wages aimed at transforming labor's attitudes toward, and motivations to, work, i.e., shifting them from the realm of production to that of consumption. As a side effect and to the extent that it tended to spread to other enterprises and industries, this policy also contributed to the transformation of consumption patterns and the creation of a mass market for the new lines of production with which Fordism was or came to be associated (mechanical consumer durables).

The U.S. imperial order contributed directly and indirectly to the spread of Fordism outside of the United States. Much of the U.S. government's aid to industrial countries was tied to the purchase of, or consisted in-kind of, capital goods that embodied technologies requiring or favoring Taylorization and Fordization of production. Moreover, the pacification of inter-state relations, combined with the centralization of armament production in the United States, freed/forced capital in other industrial countries to seek out new ways in which to employ the Taylorized techniques already adopted in war production. The tendency toward the spread of Taylorism and Fordism was then progressively strengthened by the reconstruction of the unity of the world-economy, the subsequent reactivation of competition, and its intensification through direct investment.

The Demise of the U.S. Imperial Order

Formal U.S. hegemony lasted for about twenty years. In the first ten, from about 1947 to about 1957, it was established; in the following ten, it produced its effects in the form of a rapid expansion of U.S. direct investment abroad and a boom in production and investment in most Western European countries, in Japan, and to a lesser extent in some less developed countries (Mexico, Brazil, South Africa, South Korea, etc.). Even in the United States and the United Kingdom, growth in output and trade, while relatively sluggish by comparison, was still exceptional by previous standards.

By the mid-1960s, the success of the U.S. imperial order in reestablishing the unity of the world market, in unleashing the transnational expansion of U.S. capital, and in transforming industrial and social relations in the core and semiperipheral regions of the capitalist world was unquestionable. This very success, however, undermined some of the main foundations of that order and eventually brought about its downfall. Between 1968 and 1973, the world monetary crisis and the U.S. military's defeat in Vietnam created the conditions for the destruction or radical transformation of some of the institutional arrangements on which *formal* U.S. hegemony depended.

Even by the early-to-middle 1960s, however, at the height of U.S. hegemony, the Bretton Woods agreements (which had attributed to the dollar the role of universal money) began to be challenged by some Western European states. These challenges led, at the end of 1967, to an agreement on the creation of a new and truly international monetary instrument to supersede both the dollar and gold: the Special Drawing Rights (SDRs). By that time, a second, far more powerful, challenge to the gold-dollar exchange standard had gathered momentum. It came not from states but from "impersonal" market forces in the form of speculation against the dollar. In an attempt to forestall such forces, the states of the gold pool, except France, agreed in March 1968 to discontinue buying and selling gold on the open market. This agreement made central bankers reluctant even to exchange gold among themselves at the official parity, and the dollar became de facto unconvertible. Speculative pressures, far from being discouraged, were emboldened by this reluctance, and in August 1971 the U.S. government was forced to declare the dollar officially unconvertible into gold and, two years later, the abandonment of fixed exchange rates.

It is important to emphasize that the downfall of U.S. *political* control over world finance was not associated with the emergence of an alternative state authority capable of regulating world liquidity—a development that would have spelled continuous rather than discontinuous change. On the contrary, what the monetary crisis revealed was the emergence of supranational market-like forces that had become autonomous from, and indeed dominated, the policies of all states alike, if not equally. States attempted to regain control over liquidity either by imposing restrictions on international trade, by limiting the convertibility of their own currencies, or by making competitive devaluations and raising interest rates. These efforts merely fed speculation and further expanded the margin of national and international liquidity that escaped their control. The World Bank, formerly an instrument of the U.S. government's sovereignty over world finance, turned more and more into an agency of supranational market forces.

The crisis of the U.S. imperial order in world finance was matched by a crisis in the sphere of world military and political relations. In this case as well, forebodings of a crisis began to appear in the early-to-middle 1960s, as evidenced by the Gaullist claim to an independent *force de frappe* that accompanied the claim of a return to the gold standard. But again the crisis was not precipitated by states that aimed at replacing the United States in the role of hegemonic power; it was precipitated instead by the inability of the United States to enforce imperial rule in a key region of the periphery.

After the Tet offensive in the spring of 1968, it became increasingly clear that national liberation movements could, by shifting the confrontation with conventional armies onto nonconventional terrains (as in a guerrilla war), erode and eventually disintegrate the social, political, and military position of cumbersome imperial forces. This strategy was so effectively applied by the Vietnamese that within five years the United States had to acknowledge defeat and begin a withdrawal that drastically reduced its *active* military presence throughout the world. At the end of 1973, the uncertain outcome of the Yom Kippur war shattered the myth of Israeli invincibility, providing further evidence of the ungovernability of the periphery through external military force.

As already mentioned, the downfall of U.S. military supremacy in the periphery was not precipitated by the rise of competing imperial powers. No other core capitalist state provided a serious challenge. As for the USSR, the 1960s were years of thaw in the Cold War, and ideological and military competition was giving way to collusion in enforcing the duopoly of world power along the lines established at Yalta. True, Soviet military aid was essential to the Vietnamese in waging and ultimately winning the war, but that aid was to a large extent prompted by the Chinese challenge to Soviet hegemony in the communist world, and by the competition for the support of national liberation movements unleashed by that challenge. To put it crudely, the "independent variable" in the military crisis of the U.S. imperial order was not the competition of rival imperial or would-be imperial states, but the development of nationalist forces within the United States and the Soviet empires that challenged that legitimacy of the U.S.-Soviet duopoly of world power.

That the financial and military crises of the U.S. imperial order occurred and developed together is no mere coincidence. Though partly determined, as we shall see later on, by different factors, the two crises were strongly interdependent. Particularly after 1965, the U.S. escalation of the war in Vietnam in an attempt to win a clear-cut victory became a major factor in the weakening of U.S. financial power. At the same time, the more U.S. financial power was undermined, the greater were the constraints imposed upon the escalation of the war, because the negative effects of the U.S. balance of payments tended to stiffen the opposition of other states to the gold-dollar standard and to embolden speculation against the dollar. When the two crises came to a head at the beginning of 1968, their interdependence was further strengthened and led within five years to the total collapse of U.S. *imperial* rule.

The most dramatic and immediate result of this collapse has been the energy crisis, i.e., the sudden and sustained increase in the price of what had become the main source of energy in the industrial econmies, oil. The high inelasticity of demand for oil that had been engendered by the pattern of world capitalist accumulation in the 1950s and 1960s, and the growing inelasticity of supply due to the progressive exhaustion of known reserves, were undoubtedly necessary conditions for the outbreak of the crisis. There can be little doubt, however, that the timing and the particularly acute form that the crisis has taken can be traced to the simultaneous downfall of the gold-dollar standard and of U.S. military domination in the periphery.

The former event exploded the contradiction between the scarcity of oil resources and the unlinking of the monetary unit (the U.S. dollar), against which such resources were exchanged, from any "objective" standard of value, which in a way gold was. The second event was even more significant, however, because the downfall of U.S. military domination in the periphery created the world political conditions that allowed for the transformation of the ineffectual cartel formed by some oil-exporting countries in the early 1960s into a powerful means to charge a rent for the use of energy resources. The new balance of forces between core and peripheral political formations, cause and effect of the U.S. defeat in Vietnam, was first tested by the Arab countries through the oil embargo enforced during the Yom Kippur war. Having become conscious of their new bargaining power, these countries subsequently were not only able to impose the payment of a mineral rent but were able to protect themselves from subsequent devaluations of the dollar.

The energy crisis has had an effect on its causes, deepening the crisis of the U.S. imperial order. On the one hand, it has disclosed the vulnerability of the core capitalist countries to restrictions on the flow of energy resources from the periphery, further weakening U.S. imperial authority over the latter. On the other hand, it has deepened the monetary crisis both by contributing (through the increase in oil prices) to world inflationary pressures and by inflating (through the investment of rent) the mass of money capital engaged in speculation in supranational financial markets.

The feedback of the energy crisis on the monetary crisis has not, however, been the only—and possibly not even the main—factor explaining the monetary disorder that has characterized the world-economy since 1973. Far more important have been the dysfunctions of market mechanisms to be discussed in the next section and the reaction of the U.S. state to the downfall of its own imperial rule. For the abandonment of imperial responsibilities has not led the U.S. government to greater restraint in monetary and budgetary policies; on the contrary, with the exception of a shortlived deflationary experiment under Nixon in 1973, which precipitated the most serious recession of the U.S. economy since the 1930s, U.S. governments, freed from the constraint of the gold-dollar standard, have pursued up to very recently highly expansionary monetary and budgetary policies.

To be sure, the resurrected rule of market forces over world finance "punished" this lack of restraint through a steady devaluation of the dollar, not only relative to gold but also relative to the currencies of states that followed more "orthodox" monetary and budgetary policies (Switzerland, Germany and its monetary satellites, Japan, and, recently, even the United Kingdom). Yet this very devaluation, and the expansionary policies that have occasioned it, while engendering world monetary instability and feeding world inflationary pressures, have contributed to partial reversal of some negative trends that characterized the U.S. *national* economy in the 1950s and 1960s: the massive "emigration" of capital and a more sluggish rate of growth than that of Western Europe or Japan.

It would seem, therefore, that the U.S. government has been able to elude, at least in part, the disciplining powers of the market. More precisely, the downfall of the U.S. imperial order, has not restrained but has emboldened U.S. governments in the pursuit of national economic interests, in partial disregard of world capitalist interests. This pursuit of a national interest has not been limited to monetary and budgetary policies. Particularly significant has been the two-tier pricing of crude oil, which has led to the hoarding of U.S. energy resources and to lower oil prices in the U.S.—at the cost of higher oil prices elsewhere in the capitalist world.

In general, the U.S. government has simply exploited, in the pursuance of national interests, the core position that the U.S. national economy still retains in the world-economy. Its internal reserves of energy and other natural resources, the sheer size of its internal market, and the density and complexity of its linkages with the rest of the capitalist world imply a basic asymmetry in the relation of the U.S. economy to other national economies: conditions within the U.S. state's boundaries influence, much more than they are influenced by, conditions within the boundaries of any other national economy. This asymmetrical relation, though independently eroded by other factors, has not yet been significantly affected by the undoing of the U.S. imperial order. What has been affected is the *use* made by the U.S. state of its world economic power: while in the 1950s and 1960s the national interest was often subordinated to the establishment and reproduction of a world capitalist order, in the middle and late 1970s the reproduction of such an order has been subordinated to the pursuit of the national interest as expressed in efforts to increase domestic economic growth.

In a sense, this redeployment of U.S. world political-economic power in the pursuit of national interests has been a major symptom of, and factor explaining, the state of anarchy that has characterized international economic relations since 1973. It is important to realize, however, that, at least insofar as the advanced capitalist countries are concerned, this state of anarchy in interstate relations has been strictly limited to monetary and budgetary policies and that it has yet to undermine the two main "products" of formal U.S. hegemony: the unity of the world market and the transnational expansion of capital. These substantive aspects of U.S. hegemony have survived the downfall of the U.S. imperial order; and their operating reach throughout the world capitalist economy has, if anything, been continually extended in the course of, and as an integral part of, the crisis.

As a matter of fact, one of the most striking features of the

1970s has been the intensification and extension of capitalist competition through trade and direct investment, on the one hand, and the absence of major protectionist drives on the other. Even more significant is the fact that, while before 1968 the transnational expansion of capital was predominantly, if not exclusively, a U.S. and British phenomenon, in the 1970s it has become a general characteristic of core capital. As for protectionist measures, what is significant about the 1970s is not that an increasing pressure to adopt them has been brought to bear upon states (which is only natural under conditions of intensifying competition) but that so few of such pressures have materialized in terms of actual protectionist measures. From this point of view, if advanced capitalist states have moved at all in the course of the crisis, they have moved in the direction of further liberalization (Tokyo Round, Lome and Yaounde, etc.).

The Crisis of the Substantive Aspects of U.S. Hegemony

From what has been said so far, it would seem that the downfall of the U.S. imperial order has not led to the end of U.S. hegemony but simply to its transformation from formal, state-organized hegemony to an informal, market-enforced/ corporately organized hegemony. Quite apart from the continuing dependence of all capitalist states on the U.S. nuclear deterrent in dealing with the other duopolist of global military power (the USSR), the substantive elements of U.S. hegemony have not been challenged but have rather been increasingly adhered to by these states, and particularly by those that have been most successful in moving to core status (Germany and Japan).[3] Moreover, the U.S. national economy, though less dynamic than other national economies by the usual measures, still represents the center of gravity of an increasingly integrated world-economy.

Yet the transition from formal to informal rule has not been completed and is not proceeding smoothly. As we have seen, the U.S. government has been pursuing monetary and budgetary policies that are intended to sustain domestic growth in output and investment but that also feed world monetary disorder—a result of a lack of institutional arrangements at the international level—or, at the least, of conventionally accepted rules of state behavior in monetary and budgetary policies—and a certain "dualism of power" between the U.S. state and market forces in regulating the world market economy. In this sense, the crisis of the world capitalist system, which began with the downfall of the U.S. imperial order, is far from being overcome. We are still in a period of "discontinuous change." There is, however, another more fundamental sense in which the world capitalist system has been and still is in a crisis: in the sense that throughout the 1970s the "rule of the market" has been characterized by dysfunctions for which no solution seems to be in sight.

I shall characterize these dysfunctions as the unruliness of the periphery—the unruliness of capital and the unruliness of labor. Let us examine each briefly. Peripheral countries have been affected even more than semiperipheral and core countries by the entrenchment of two of the substantive aspects of U.S. hegemony, the growing sway of market rule and the transnational expansion of capital. Only a relatively small number of such countries has been able to take advantage of the demise of the U.S. imperial order by charging or increasing the rent for the appropriation of their natural resources. As stagnation set in in core regions in the middle and late 1970s, the price of most primary commodities actually failed to keep up with the galloping inflation in the price of industrial products and energy resources. This tendency, combined with a tightening of "aid" (intergovernmental transfer payments and credits) from core states, has forced a growing number of peripheral countries to accept market discipline in order to obtain finance in the "open" market. At the same time, the intensification of competition within core capital has taken the form of a major decentralization of industrial production through direct investment and subcontracting in peripheral regions in order to take advantage of their abundant reserves of relatively cheap labor. As a result of these two converging tendencies (the growing dependence of peripheral countries on private finance and the growing dependence of core capital on the labor resources of peripheral countries), the 1970s have witnessed the rapid growth of export-oriented industrial production in a *few* peripheral countries (the so-called newly industrializing countries) and a growing competition among *most* of them to "capture" the demand for cheap labor by established and in-the-making transnational corporations (TNCs).

Yet informal market rule has fared no better than U.S. imperial rule in disciplining the peripheral countries. For one thing, peripheral countries in the capitalist world have enjoyed and taken advantage of considerable formal freedom in generating and installing avowedly anticapitalist regimes aiming (how successfully it does not really matter) at some form of "delinking" from the world capitalist system. The different but equally significant efforts by regimes in Mozambique, Angola, Ethiopia, Afghanistan (before the Soviet invasion), Nicaragua, and Iran illustrate the point. At the same time, peripheral countries in general have shown throughout the 1970s an increasing promptness and independence in resorting to war as a means of regulating their mutual relations and of consolidating or protecting their own fragile national unity or undermining that of their neighbors. The almost uninterrupted series of open wars that have broken out in the vast region stretching from East Africa through the Middle East and the Indian subcontinent to Indochina vividly illustrates this tendency, most recently expressed in the Iraqi-Iranian war. In the periphery, in other words, the anarchy in interstate relations that has accompanied the transition from U.S. imperial rule to informal market rule has not been confined to, and indeed has not manifested itself mainly in, state economic policies, but has tended to take the form of political and military confrontations among states.

As already mentioned, this unruliness of the periphery has been matched by a growing unruliness of capital. By the latter I designate two distinct but closely related phenomena: a relative lack of responsiveness on the part of capital to market incentives and the "perverse" behavior of prices. Though the expansion of global effective demand does not seem to have significantly slowed down in the 1970s as compared to the 1960s, world capitalist production after 1973 has tended to stagnate, and expansion of demand has thus overwhelmingly been manifested in inflation rather than real growth. It would seem that the propensity of profits to remain in liquid form and to be channelled into speculative activities, particularly in supranational money markets, rather than into productive investment has increased notwithstanding an accelerating inflation. Moreover, this tendency has persisted even when stagnation has led to high and growing rates of unemployment. Expanding effective demand and idle labor resources no longer seem adequate incentives to stimulate capitalist accumulation.

At the same time, slowdowns or even decreases in aggregate demand, spontaneously produced by market mechanisms or induced by state action aimed at restraining inflationary pressures, have generally failed to slow down inflation, which accelerated throughout the 1970s. This perverse behavior of prices, whereby they tend to increase irrespective of market conditions and to increase faster the more sluggish the rate of growth, together with the lack of responsiveness on the part of capital to increasing effective demand and unemployment, is what has come to be known as "stagflation"—a phenomenon generally held to be one of the most significant of the market-mechanism dysfunctions that characterize the current crisis.

This phenomenon must be clearly distinguished from another, closely related dysfunction, which I shall refer to as the unruliness of labor, a phenomenon that has also manifested itself in two distinct ways. The first, predominant in the 1968–73 period, consisted in an outbreak of industrial and social conflict of a noninstitutional character that swept core areas, particularly Western Europe. In the area of industrial conflict, its noninstitutional character surfaced in different ways. For one thing, it was not normally initiated, and often not even sustained, by the action of established labor organizations (unions and parties). Such organizations did attempt to direct, control, and even generalize strike activity once it had broken out, but conflict was generally initiated and sustained by spontaneous movements. Moreover, it tended to assume forms that made its institutionalization difficult: small numbers striking often and for short periods rather than large numbers striking occasionally and for long periods. As a matter of fact, the dividing line between open conflict and resistance to discipline in the workplace through absenteeism, slowdowns and poor performance, sudden and undeclared stoppages, petty sabotage, etc. was often blurred and, even where conflict did not break out openly, on-the-line resistance adversely affected productivity. The noninstitutional character of conflict was also evident in the objectives of the struggles—in the nature of the wage claims and the pursuance of nonwage claims. Refusals both to limit wage claims to increases in costs of living and productivity and resistance to speed-ups, the fragmentation of work roles, overtime and night shifts, pay differentials, and a hierarchical organization of the labor process spread to a hitherto unknown extent.

After 1973, as unemployment increased and inflation accelerated in core areas, the form and objectives of industrial conflict changed significantly. Wage demands became more "defensive," in the sense that they now aimed at counteracting the negative effects of inflation on real wages, while nonwage claims focussed on the defense of existing jobs against the threat of lay-offs rather than on the quality of jobs. Moreover unions came to play a more prominent, though by no means exclusive, role in initiating and sustaining strike activity. Notwithstanding the high and increasing rates of unemployment, however, industrial conflict did not subside and labor in core areas has on the whole shown a remarkable capacity to counteract the encroachments of inflation upon its standard of living and to resist managerial attempts to raise productivity through dismissals and a corresponding intensification of work for the employed.

This unprecedented relative imperviousness of industrial relations to conditions in the labor market is the other side of the stagflation coin. Just as stagnation and depression no longer seem able to force corporations into price competition, so unemployment no longer seems able to force labor into wage competition. In both instances, effective market forces, with their alleged disciplinary powers, are notable for their absence.

2. THE ROOTS OF THE CRISIS

To sum up: the current global crisis consists of two quite distinct phenomena. First, it is a crisis of formal U.S. hegemony, i.e., of the institutional arrangements, coordinated and enforced by the state, in which U.S. military and financial supremacy became crystallized after World War II, and in which postwar capitalist accumulation was embedded. This crisis has gone through two phases. Between 1968 and 1973, while the monetary crisis destroyed the gold-dollar exchange standard, which had given the U.S. state regulatory powers over world liquidity, the defeat in Vietnam destroyed, at home and abroad, the legitimacy that the U.S. state and associated agencies had previously enjoyed in enforcing, politically and militarily, the free enterprise system throughout the capitalist world. After 1973, U.S. formal rule over financial and military relations in the capitalist world was largely replaced by the informal rule of market forces. If we still speak of a crisis, then, it is because the transition is far from complete, the "dualism of power" between the U.S. state and the world market is a source of considerable institutional instability in world, and international economic relations and the arrangements that will in time become institutionalized, and through which capitalist accumulation will resume, remain uncertain.

We can, however, also look at the crisis as a crisis in the substantive aspects of U.S. hegemony. This is altogether different from the crisis of formal hegemony. The reestablishment of market-like rule over the capitalist world-economy was, after all, one of the main objectives of formal U.S. hegemony, and the United States is probably better equipped than any other state to take part in, and to benefit from, the exercise of an informally organized, corporately mediated world hegemony. If we speak of a crisis in the substantive aspects of U.S. hegemony, it is because market rule has been showing dysfunctions that undermine its stability. These dysfunctions are what I have called the unruliness of the periphery, of capital, and of labor. In this section, then, I shall relate both aspects of the crisis, formal and substantive, to the pattern of capitalist development that has characterized the capitalist world since the establishment of the Pax Americana in the late 1940s. In doing this, I am trying to show that the current crisis is not simply a crisis in U.S. hegemony but, more fundamentally, a crisis in world capitalism.

Uneven Development

As already mentioned, the reestablishment of some kind of market competition under U.S. hegemony after World War II resulted in an upward expansion in world capitalist accumulation of unprecedented length and steepness. The reconstruction of the unity of the world-economy created a favorable environment for innovations in commodities produced and in techniques of production; these in turn increased productivity and sustained global effective demand. The process of expansion was only in part the outcome of market-like forces, since the redistributive policies of the U.S. state, in its imperial capacity, were crucial in reconstructing world market unity, sustaining demand, and spreading innovations.

Growth was not evenly distributed over the various regions of the capitalist world. By and large, most of it came to be concentrated neither in the U.S. core nor in the periphery proper, but in a number of countries and regions which, in the immediate postwar years, were occupying positions that we may broadly designate as semiperipheral: Japan and Western Europe (except Britain), which moved rapidly to core position, and some of the larger Latin American countries (Brazil and Mexico), the southern tip of Africa (South Africa and what was then Rhodesia), and some Southeast Asian industrial enclaves (South Korea, Formosa, Hong Kong, etc.), which moved to or consolidated their semiperipheral position.

A variety of factors seems to have contributed to the location of growth in these areas, and in Japan and continental Western Europe in particular: the availability of large and competitive internal reserves of labor; the existence of an indigenous entrepreneurial stratum strongly motivated to take advantage of the economic opportunities afforded by the reconstruction of the world market and by the spread of Taylorism and

Fordism; the availability of financial resources directly or indirectly created by U.S. military and economic "aid"; and, with the notable exception of Japan, the "immigration" of U.S. industrial capital in the form of direct investment, subcontracting, and joint ventures. The particular combination of factors that prompted the concentration of growth in these countries, as well as the social, economic, or political effects of such concentration, varied, but if we look at the overall development with reference to the effect it had on the economic positions of these countries in relation to, and relative to, the position of the United States, a few general remarks are possible.

Those countries that because of past historical development were endowed at the beginning of the period with a competitive and strongly motivated entrepreneurial stratum had two fundamental competitive advantages vis-à-vis the United States: they had a much larger backlog of productive innovations to exploit within their own borders, and they were largely unencumbered by an expensive technologically sophisticated defensive and offensive military apparatus. In some instances these advantages were increased by the existence of larger or more competitive internal reserves of labor (continental Western Europe and Japan); in other instances they were lessened by the cost of performing residual and subordinate imperial functions (Britain and to a lesser extent France); in most cases they were compounded by the enhanced international mobility of U.S. productive capital, which tended to expand abroad precisely to exploit the greater competitiveness of other national economies as sites of production. This mobility tended to dampen further growth within the boundaries of the U.S. national economy and to sustain it elsewhere, particularly in Western Europe.

The concentration of growth in selected semiperipheral countries had a contradictory effect on their allegiance to U.S. hegemony: while allegiance to its substantive aspects was naturally strengthened, its formal aspects were increasingly challenged. The greater competitiveness of these countries as sites of production led to a progressive worsening of the U.S. balance of payments, which was further burdened by the increasing cost of performing imperial functions in the periphery. With the weakening of U.S. financial capacity, the gold-dollar exchange standard tended to become a de facto dollar exchange standard, a situation which Western European governments and capitalists saw as favoring the penetration of their national economies by direct U.S. investment. This became the main rationale for the challenges by Western European governments to the role of the dollar as universal money that, as we know, set the stage for the world monetary crisis of 1968–73.

For quite different reasons, uneven development undermined U.S. hegemony in the periphery as well. Here the free enterprise system generally produced more social and economic dislocation than real growth. Local entrepreneurship, often deprived of the only instrument that could protect it from an intensifying world market competition (e.g., state capitalism), was frustrated in its development and either further subordinated to world capitalist interests or diverted into defensive political pursuits. Foreign capital, on the other hand, was overwhelmingly channeled into activities (services, final-stage manufacturing oriented to the internal market, extractive industries) whose expansion, by deepending dependent development, entrenched relationships of unequal exhange with core and semiperipheral regions. These tendencies created the conditions for a widespread nationalist reaction against the U.S. imperial order, and this induced the United States to rely increasingly on direct military intervention or indirect military rule to compensate for the fading legitimacy of the free enterprise system.

As we know, military means ultimately failed to reproduce the U.S. imperial order in the periphery. Deprived of the capacity to enforce formal hegemony, the U.S. government also lost the capacity to constrain the growing dysfunctions of market rule from producing an orderly and peaceful deepening of the periphery's integration into the world capitalist economy. As a matter of fact, the crisis itself has further exacerbated the dislocating effects of market rule in such regions. The increasing price of energy resources has become a major factor in curtailing the financial resources that peripheral states can mobilize for long-term development projects and short-term relief programs. At the same time, the widely differing circumstances faced by peripheral countries—with respect to opportunities for charging rents for the use of their natural resources, and to possibilities for capturing the demand of core capital for sites of production endowed with competitive labor resources—have heightened uneven development and competition among them.

Formally unregulated market rule, in other words, has proved highly subversive of the ability of peripheral states to form national societies and of their sovereignty vis-à-vis other peripheral states. It is not surprising, therefore, that the demise of the U.S. imperial order should have led in peripheral regions to a greater political instability of internal regimes and to a displacement of competition among states from the economic to the military terrain, both of which we have identified as major symptoms of the crisis in the substantive aspects of U.S. hegemony.

At this point it should be noted that uneven development undermined the legitimacy of the U.S. imperial order not only in the periphery and semiperiphery of the capitalist world, but also within the U.S. core itself. As we have seen, the U.S. national economy was not one of the main beneficiaries of postwar economic expansion, though that substantial fraction of U.S. capital that could develop transnationally and/or through the defense industry certainly was. Throughout the 1960s, the growth of wages and employment was sluggish, while the dislocating effects of market rule, traditionally strong in U.S. society, increased further, thereby contributing to the development of mass protest movements, particularly among blacks and youth. Attempts by the U.S. state to deal simultaneously with such movements at home—by increasing welfare expenditures—and with nationalist movements in the periphery—by increasing expenditure in warfare—became major sources of weakness in its financial position. And when the U.S. government was induced, among other things by the tightening of international financial constraints, to use relatively more repression than welfare at home (at a time when the toll of U.S. lives in Vietnam was escalating), the various protest movements gathered momentum and merged into widespread opposition to the war.

It follows that U.S. hegemony was characterized by a major contradiction between its formal and substantive aspects. While formal hegemony required the reproduction of the military and financial supremacy that had brought it about, the substantive aspects of such hegemony (reestablishment of world market competition and the transnational expansion of U.S. capital) tended to weaken supremacy because they concentrated growth in semiperipheral regions and undermined the legitimacy of imperial rule in both the periphery and the core. Uneven development was not, however, the only—or indeed the main—cause of the demise of formal U.S. hegemony, and even less of the subsequent crisis.

The Transnational Expansion of Capital and the Perverse Behavior of Prices

The pattern of world market competition that developed under U.S. hegemony after World War II has three main characteristics: (1) competition is oligopolistic, i.e., "among the few" rather than "among the many"; (2) its main weapon is product innovation and differentiation rather than the systematic price cutting of relatively homogeneous products; and (3) its main vehicle is direct investment rather than trade. Let us deal with the last characteristic first.

The fact that direct investment rather than trade has become the main vehicle of world oligopolistic competition does not mean that the latter has been superseded by the former. As a matter of fact, world trade—as measured in movements between national frontiers—has never grown faster than in the last thirty years. It simply means that the most advanced capitalist enterprises operating in the dynamic sectors of the world-economy tend to strengthen, and take advantage of, their competitive position not by expanding the scale of production in their original locations, but by developing a complex *organizational* network of productive and service activities *across* national borders.

As a rule, this development requires and enhances the international mobility of entrepreneurship, money capital, and commodities, which is recorded as an expansion of international trade. Much of what appears statistically as international trade, however, is not *trade* at all but transactions internal to, and determined by, the organizational networks of established or in-the-making TNCs. Had the same movements occurred within a national jurisdiction, they would have been recorded, if at all, as parts of freightcar loadings.

This transnational expansion of capital may have different orientations. For our present purposes it will be enough to distinguish between primary transnational expansion, oriented to the appropriation, processing, and distribution of natural resources, and secondary transnational expansion, oriented to the exploitation of the cost advantages of different national locations due to their proximity to actual or potential markets or to reserves of labor. Both types were fostered by the establishment of the Pax Americana: the pacification of capitalist interstate relations and the imperial guarantee against nationalization created a reliable world legal framework which reduced the risks of transnational expansion; decolonization opened up the entire periphery to primary transnational expansion based on competitive advantage rather than on the monopolistic privileges and restrictions with which rival metropolitan states had increasingly enmeshed their colonial possessions; the gold-dollar standard restored the possibility of carrying out capitalist accounting on a world scale, thus enhancing secondary transnational expansion, which depends decisively upon reliable calculations of the cost advantages of alternative national locations of production; and, to the extent that national currencies *actually* became convertible into dollars, the gold-dollar standard ensured the possibility of realizing the profits of the various subsidiaries in a universally accepted means of payment—and therefore of repatriating or transferring them from one country to another—without incurring excessive risks on the exchange or excessive transfer costs across currency zones. Moreover, the redistributive and expansionary world monetary policies pursued by the U.S. state in the heyday of its imperial rule further enhanced secondary transnational expansion in two ways: by easing the restoration of the convertibility into dollars of other national currencies, and by promoting the formation in Western Europe of a continental market large enough to allow the employment of the techniques of production and distribution that had become typical of large-scale nonfinancial capital in the United States.

The transnational expansion of U.S. core capital, however, tended to undermine the imperial framework that had provided the scaffolding for its growth. As we already noted, it was a major factor in weakening U.S. financial supremacy, particularly vis-à-vis some Western European countries. Even more significant, in the mid-1960s a growing proportion of profits produced abroad by U.S. TNCs were not repatriated but began to be hoarded as Eurodollars and used in short-term speculation, giving rise to those supranational money-market forces that precipitated the monetary crisis of 1968–73.

This tendency of U.S. TNCs to hoard profits in a supranational money market and to invest them in speculative activities against the dollar can be traced in part to tendencies analyzed in previous sections. The weakening of the U.S. financial position occurred precisely at a time when the main source of financing for the transnational expansion of U.S. capital was no longer domestic but lay in profits accumulated abroad in currencies other than the dollar. As a consequence of this shift, U.S. TNCs were losing interest in an overvalued dollar which increased the risk of net losses on the exchange, i.e., a foregone gain in the case of the permanent repatriation of profits, and an actual loss in the case of temporary repatriation in view of future re-exports to finance transnational expansion. Hence the tendency toward speculation aimed at the devaluation of the dollar, which was obviously enhanced both by the uncertainty in monetary markets engendered by the challenge of the Western European states to the gold-dollar standard and by the attempts of the U.S. government to resist devaluation by regulating transnational expansion. When, at the end of 1967, President Johnson tried to run for cover in a sharply deteriorating financial situation—when, that is, he limited capital investment abroad, effectively prohibiting any such movement to continental Europe and the industrialized countries for 1968, and demanding repatriation of U.S. profits—speculative pressures gathered momentum, precipitating the final crisis of the gold-dollar standard. Unleashed by the U.S. imperial order, and indeed emerging from within it, supranational economic forces had won a degree of autonomy that would subsequently stand firm against any attempt to tamper with them.

As we shall see in the next sections, more powerful factors than a change in the source of financing for U.S. TNCs and the government's tampering with their expansion abroad were involved in heightening the propensity of core capital to hoard profits in supranational money markets and to invest in speculative activities. For the time being, it is necessary only to point out that the actual outbreak of the crisis, and the related downfall of the U.S. imperial order, strengthened such a propensity—indeed, made it a rational necessity—thereby dampening real growth and fostering monetary instability.

To be sure, the progressive devaluation of the dollar lessened the resistance of U.S. TNCs to repatriating profits. In addition, it created an incentive for those sectors of non-U.S. capital (particularly German and Japanese) that had attained core position, and whose national currencies had increased in relative value, to follow the lead of U.S. capital and to expand transnationally by investing not only in peripheral and semi-peripheral areas but within the very domain of the U.S. national economy. Yet monetary instability, on the one hand, and anarchy in peripheral interstate relations on the other, have simultaneously increased both the risk of primary and secondary transnational expansion and the opportunities of reaping speculative profits. Hence a strengthening during the 1970s of the tendency toward global stagnation and speculative pressures on world money and commodity markets.

A special case—but one of universal significance for its repercussions on the crisis—is that of primary TNCs operating in the field of oil extraction and distribution. When it became clear in 1973 that the balance of forces between peripheral and core states had shifted dramatically in favor of the former, and that core economies were entering a period of stagnation, these TNCs were quick to move from a policy of real expansion based on low and falling oil prices to one of speculating on, and sustaining, the steep increase in prices claimed by the oil-exporting countries. In this way they contributed to the strengthening of world inflationary pressures and to the enlargement of the mass of money-capital (rent of oil-exporting countries and profits of the oil TNCs) available for, and engaged in, speculative activities.

More generally, as soon as stagnation became pronounced during and after 1973, inflationary and speculative tendencies became more widespread and intense, deepening and spreading stagnation. In order to understand both these tendencies and the relative stability of stagflation we must, however, bring into the picture the other two characteristics of the new pattern of world market competition mentioned at the beginning of this section: competition "among the few" and competition through product innovation and differentiation.

According to the theory of oligopoly, the former characteristic implies the "perverse" behavior of prices, in the sense that they tend to be sticky downward, and, other things being equal, price reductions are more likely to occur in periods of expansion than in periods of contraction and stagnation. In the latter, prices tend to increase in order to lessen the effect on total profits of rising unit costs and declining output. We should not therefore be surprised if, under conditions of oligopoly, stagnation is accompanied by inflation.

The experience of the first half of this century, when oligopoly had already become dominant in most of the then leading sectors of the world-economy, might seem to suggest that the perverse behavior of prices is always a historically short-term phenomenon: by strengthening overproduction tendencies, it ultimately results in "price wars" among oligopolists, reflected in sudden and precipitous falls in prices. But the fact that no such "wars" have occurred so far in the current crisis, and do not appear likely in the foreseeable future, suggests that there may be an important difference between the leading sectors early in the century and the leading sectors today. And indeed there is: today, product innovation and differentiation have become the main competitive weapons of core capital, whereas before the leading sector of the world-economy (heavy industry) were ill-suited to product differentiation, and reductions in the costs and prices of relatively homogeneous products remained an essential, and ultimate, weapon in competition among oligopolists. Market competition could of course be restrained through restrictive practices, and indeed it was restricted through the transformation of oligopolies into monopolies and the transfer of competition from the market to the arena of interstate relations. Yet to the extent that market competition was allowed to reemerge, these restrictive practices merely postponed, and thereby radicalized, the eventual confrontation over the cost of production and prices.

The industries that emerged after World War II as leading sectors of the world-economy (a variety of mechanical and engineering industries producing consumer durables and complex means of production) opened up unlimited opportunities for product innovation and differentiation, and these therefore became the main weapon of oligopolistic competition. In other words, it became more profitable for oligopolists to reduce, through real or imaginary differentiation, the price elasticity of the demand for their individual products than to engage in "price wars." The intensification of competition in periods of stagnation has thus tended to take the form of higher expenditures on product differentiation and innovation (including sales promotion and advertising), which sustains both the push of unit costs on prices and the demand necessary to absorb a stagnant output at higher prices.

If this reasoning is correct, and we are in a historical period of relatively stable perverse price behavior, then we reach a paradoxical policy implication: in the present-day oligopoly situation, the only way in which a state authority can have a long-term restraining influence on inflationary pressures is through an expansionary policy, one that by keeping up the rate of accumulation reduces unit costs and the otherwise quite rational reluctance of oligopolists to cut prices. This, in capsule form, is what seems to have happened in the 1950s and 1960s when the U.S. government, in its imperial capacity, pursued a deficit-financing policy on a world scale and in this way helped sustain a long boom during which unemployment declined in core and semiperipheral countries and relatively stable prices prevailed overall.

Toward the end of the 1960s, however, this policy began to have contradictory effects, generating more inflation than growth in output and employment in the world-economy at large, and so feeding speculative pressures in international money markets. These effects do not contradict the hypothesis that the persistence of inflation under conditions of stagnation can be traced to the perverse behavior of prices under oligopoly. They simply bear witness to the fact that today expansionary policies are unable to promote and sustain capitalist accumulation, and that this inability persists even when stagnation begins to generate unemployment. What we need, therefore, is an additional hypothesis to explain stagnation itself, with reference to factors other than demand deficiency or the achievement of full employment.

The Development of Labor's Workplace Bargaining Power

One such factor has undoubtedly been the unruliness of labor, which has tended to squeeze the rate of profit without itself being greatly affected by the consequent increase in unemployment. In order to understand the nature of this factor, let us draw a distinction between labor's marketplace bargaining power and its workplace bargaining power. The first refers to the bargaining power of workers when they are selling their labor power individually or collectively—a concept with which we are all familiar, perhaps overly so; the second refers to the "bargaining power" of workers when they are expending their labor power within the course of the capitalist labor process, a concept we need to develop and become more familiar with.

Marxist theory has traditionally focussed its attention on marketplace bargaining power, emphasizing its cyclical fluctuations, connected with alternating periods of expansion and contraction, as well as a long secular or historical downward trend, connected with the growing subjection of labor to capital inherent in capitalist accumulation. With respect to this historical trend, this line of thought maintains that at first the subjection of labor to capital is only a *formal* result of the fact that laborers, instead of working for themselves, work for, and consequently under, capitalists, because they have lost to the latter the ownership of the means of production. However, as soon as the cooperation of numerous wage workers is developed by capital through its increasing concentration, the sway of capital becomes a *real* requisite of production—and so of livelihood.

Simple cooperation of course leaves the ways in which each person works for the most part unchanged, so that the subjection to capital is largely external to the work process, rather than internal to it. As the division of labor develops, however, it thoroughly revolutionizes the capital-labor relation, forcing the laborer's detail dexterity at the expense of a world of productive capabilities and instincts. This dexterity has neither use nor value outside its employment within the prevailing division of labor of a capitalistically organized labor process. Here, then, the workers have to sell their labor power, not merely because they do not own the means of production, but because their labor power has neither productive nor remunerative use unless and until sold to capital. The labor power latent in workers can perform its function only when activated within a capitalist organization after its sale, a circumstance that deepens and extends the command of capital over labor.

The process is completed in machinofacture, which further subordinates labor to capital by inverting the relationship between workers and material means of production, the latter now determining the actions of the workers instead of the reverse. The expansion of capital is thus freed from its previous dependence on the personal strength and skill with which the detail workers in manufactures, and the manual laborers in handicrafts, wielded their implements. This appropriation of skill from people and its incorporation into material means of production undermines the workers' marketplace bargaining power, since the trained and "natural" abilities required for production are fewer and fewer. Traditionally, this appropriation was the unintended result of the continual struggle between labor and capital over the control of work and work procedures that has historically accompanied capitalist accumulation. With Taylorism, a systematic and conscious element has been added to the process, which has greatly quickened its pace and widened its scope.

Under these circumstances, wage labor can counteract the steady undermining of its bargaining power only through some form of organization (unions) capable of restraining competition within its own ranks. It can do this in two main ways: through "monopolistic" restrictions upon the supply of certain skills, and through collective attempts to resist entirely or at least to slow down transformations in the labor process that would reduce the demand for those skills. This organization at the economic level can be, and normally is, supplemented by political organizations (labor, social-democratic, socialist, and communist parties), often the outgrowth of trade unions, that endeavor to strengthen marketplace bargaining power through action in the political arena.

There remains, however, within this conventional account of the transformations and directions of the capital-labor relation an unanswered elemental query: how is this combined action at the "economic" (trade union) and "political" (party) levels, however sustained by consciousness and organization, to carry out successfully the sisyphean task of rolling labor's marketplace bargaining power up the growing hill of the capitalist accumulation process when this in turn only, or largely, grows by continually rolling labor's marketplace bargaining power back downhill? It is not a question that is often posed—let alone answered—in analyses and debates on working-class history and strategies and so remains a mystery of the Marxist creed. The mystery, however, is solved as soon as we look at the *same* process from another angle, that of the workplace bargaining power of the wage worker, i.e., as producer and member of the industrial army. The same factors that steadily undermine labor's marketplace bargaining power can be seen to strengthen its workplace bargaining power. For one thing, the concentration of workers in ever larger productive units creates the conditions for their growing cooperation for the benefit of capital and for their association in a struggle against their common exploitation. And the larger the productive unit, *ceteris paribus,* the greater the damage that can be inflicted upon capital by such common struggle.

More important are the effects of the division of labor. A first effect is the formation of a stratum of "wage" workers that can no longer be analytically distinguished from capital. Even in the latter nineteenth century, Marx could point out that an "industrial army of workmen, under the command of a capitalist, requires, like a real army, officers (managers), and sergeants (foremen, overlookers), who, while the work is being done, command in the name of the capitalist."[4] Directing authority was merely the first function appropriated by capital. The knowledge, judgment, and will previously required of, and practiced by, every individual worker in greater or lesser degree became progressively a requirement and practice of the workshop as a whole.

As Marx pointed out:

> Intelligence in production expands in one direction, because it vanishes in many others. What is lost by the detail labourers, is concentrated in the capital that employs them. It is a result of the division of labour in manufactures, that the labourer is brought face to face with the intellectual potencies of the material process of production, as the property of another, and as a ruling power. This separation begins in simple cooperation, where the capitalist represents to the single workman the oneness and the will of the associated labour. It is developed in manufacture which cuts down the labourer into a detail labourer. It is completed in modern industry, which makes science a productive force distinct from labour and presses it into the service of capital.[5]

Knowledge, judgment, and will are thus progressively concentrated in capital, and, like directing authority, are "delegated" to a stratum of wage workers whose labor may retain, or even acquire, a complex or skilled character.

These higher echelons of "wage labor," far from being increasingly subordinated to capital, actually embody to a growing degree the command of capital over labor and so in effect progressively replace the legal owners of the means of production in the role of capital in the active capital-labor relation. Not surprisingly, they tend to form a relatively stable component of the "industrial" army, largely free from the short-run pushes and pulls of the labor market. As for the wage workers who remain in the role of labor in the labor-capital relation, the increasing division of labor, as the result of the deskilling of work roles in *direct* production, deprives them of any interest in such roles and heightens solidarity among them. At the same time, by increasing the connectedness of work roles and the weight of *indirect* labor costs, it makes capital more vulnerable to work stoppages or passive resistance by any and every disgruntled group of workers. This vulnerability is further enhanced where the damages inflicted by any interruption or slowdown in the labor process is compounded by the high organic composition of capital.

Fordism has tried, through the policy of competitively high wages and stable employment, to block the maturation of the growing contradiction between the alienation of labor from productive work roles and the vulnerability of capital to this alienation. By granting in advance what would have to be conceded anyway if conflict broke out, and by shifting motivations to work from the realm of production to that of consumption, Fordism attempts to weaken tendencies to convert alienation from work into an antagonism in the workplace.

Its success in this has varied considerably in time and space. All we can say, is that in general it has been a double-edged weapon: as new commodities have been incorporated into customary subsistence, wage claims have increased correspondingly, generating—when they go unmet—the increased likelihood that antagonism to capital will be expressed in the workplace. At most Fordism is an attempt on the part of core capital to divert the growing workplace bargaining power of labor, not to fight it head-on, which it cannot do without jeopardizing capitalist organization itself.

The downward tendency of labor's marketplace bargaining power, emphasized by Marxist theory, is thus historically accompanied by, and in principle corresponds to, an upward tendency of labor's workplace bargaining power. The sequenced outcomes of these two opposing tendencies depends on the actual social structure of the settings in which capitalist development is taking place. From this point of view, the most important determinant and locus of the effect of the trend in the actual bargaining power of labor is the cultural homogeneity of the workforce, particularly with regard to the social arrangements through which labor power is daily, annually, and generationally reproduced. Generally speaking, the greater the cultural heterogeneity of labor—so that socially distinctive groups have quite different and structurally distinct arrangements for reproducing labor power—the greater the competitive pressures within the workers' ranks, and the stronger the influence of marketplace on workplace bargaining power. More specifically, the intensity of the competitive pressure within the ranks of labor depends on the existence of workers (often part-time and part-life-time wage workers) who, because of their positions in households in the social structure, have to sell their labor power but at a price that does not cover the costs of its reproduction at the prevailing customary subsistence level. This may be possible because they are "dependents," or the households they belong to derive substantial parts of their subsistence from other, nonwage sources (normally nonwage employment), or the culturally customary subsistence of such households is lower than that of the households whose traditional supply of wage labor has set the national standard for customary subsistence levels. Whatever the reason, the effect is an enhanced competitiveness within the ranks of the industrial army—that is to say, a stronger influence of marketplace on workplace bargaining power.

Capitalist accumulation, however, while aided by differences in the conditions of reproduction of labor power that find reflection in wage-level demands, tends over time, within a region, to reduce or even eliminate such differences—and precisely insofar as they are due to, or reproduced by, differences in the degree of involvement in wage employment. By extending and deepening the workers' dependence on wage employment, it dampens the competition generated by part-time and part-life-time wage workers, and therefore the influence of marketplace on workplace bargaining power.

Insofar, then, as there has been an increase in labor's actual bargaining power in the core areas of the capitalist world-economy, this has been due to technological and cultural transformations—to structural changes and processes—and not primarily to such "superstructural" aspects of class formation as consciousness and organization. As noted above, the organization of labor in unions and parties performs a key function in making effective the structurally possible bargaining power of labor in the face of the secular downward trend of its marketplace bargaining power. But as the influence of marketplace bargaining power on workplace bargaining power decreases, this function of economic and political organization becomes increasingly obsolete. Not surprisingly, the more this is so the more labor unions and parties play increasingly different roles, reflecting more closely the changed structural position of labor in capitalist production. In general, unions tend to bargain away their original functions of limiting the supply of labor within given trades/crafts and transformations in the labor process for a stronger mediational role within labor/capital relations themselves. The mediation they take on typically consists in inducing greater restraint in the use of workplace bargaining power on the part of labor and greater restraint in the use of the right to hire and fire on the part of capital.

This mediational role on the part of unions is usually paralleled by an analogous role on the part of labor parties in the political sphere. We shall return to this point when discussing the development of "liberal corporatism" in core capitalist countries. For the time being, we need only point to two ways in which the influence of a weak marketplace bargaining power can be, and historically has been, brought to bear on a strong workplace bargaining power.

The first is labor immigration, to which core regions have generally resorted, not merely to expand labor supplies on the market but also and especially to reproduce the command of capital in production. In the long run, however, the advantages to capital of labor migration tend to peter out: as competition from immigrants grows, "native" labor protests, and the value of existing immigrants' labor power, thereupon rise somewhat; moreover, the social tensions between "natives" and "immigrants" tend to impinge directly or indirectly on industrial relations and work processes, thus in effect weakening capital's command of labor in production; finally, in time immigrants become settlers. As these effects begin to materialize, the immigration of labor tends to be partly or wholly

superceded by the emigration of capital, i.e., by the organization of production on a transnational scale, which presents
capital with a much wider range of opportunities in the re-
cruitment of competitive labor, and at the same time breaks up
local concentrations of labor forces.

If this line of argument is correct, we may interpret the
development of capital on a transnational scale as a means of
restoring the profitability of capitalist production jeopardized
by the growth of labor's workplace bargaining power. That
this development first occurred in the United States can accordingly be interpreted as a result of two factors: the greater
concentration and more developed technical division of labor
that have characterized U.S. capital ever since the beginning
of the century, and the relatively small reserves of competitive
labor available within the United States.

The emigration of U.S. capital to Western Europe appears
to be a key factor in the reproduction of the command of core
capital over labor and, therefore, in generating and sustaining
the postwar boom in capitalist accumulation on a world scale.
By the mid-1960s, however, capitalist accumulation had induced changes in the labor processes and social structures of
Western European societies that, by raising labor's bargaining
power, undermined the viability of further accumulation in
the region. The attainment of this situation, evinced by the
wave of industrial conflict that ran through Western Europe
between 1968 and 1973, meant that capitalist accumulation
could take off again only through an *enlarged* decentralization
drive toward other regions of the world-economy.

As we have seen, some decentralization of industrial production did indeed take place in the period 1968–73, as witnessed by the sharp increase in secondary transnational expansion toward countries and regions still endowed with reserves of competitive labor. Yet the increase in financial and
speculative investment by core capital has been even more
marked, particularly since the mid-1970s, when direct investment tended to give way to less risky forms of transnational
expansion such as subcontracting and licensing. But the decentralization of core capital toward peripheral regions has not
proceeded smoothly and swiftly enough to recreate conditions

for sustained accumulation on a world scale, and the reasons for this are not difficult to find.

In part, they are due to the resistance of core-region labor, which has naturally endeavored to use its strong workplace bargaining power to prevent the emigration of capital. This resistance, however, has either been weak (as in Germany and Japan) or self-defeating (as in the United Kingdom and, to a lesser extent, in Italy). The main reason, in my opinion, lies elsewhere, in the anarchy in interstate relations that has followed from the demise of the U.S. imperial order. The risks of organizing production on a transnational scale were greatly enhanced by the replacement of the gold-dollar standard by floating exchange rates and by the greater national sovereignty and international anarchy obtaining in the periphery; and while the latter has increased the uncertainty involved in making transnational cost calculations and in converting profits produced in different national currencies into a universally accepted means of payment, the former has increased the political uncertainty of secondary, and reduced the scope of primary, transnational expansion. Moreover, any conscious and coordinated effort aimed at redistributing world economic resources to facilitate industrial relocation, as happened with the Marshall Plan (on a smaller scale than would now be necessary) has become impossible with the disappearance, rather than the widening and strengthening, of a world political authority capable of pursuing the general capitalist interest.

In sum, at the end of the 1960s the long postwar boom of capitalist accumulation on a world scale produced two contradictory results. On the one hand, it produced in Western Europe—and, to a lesser extent, in Japan—conditions of rigidity of labor supply in the workplace analogous to those that had prompted the emigration of U.S. capital in the 1950s and 1960s. Hence an enlarged and stronger tendency toward the relocation of industrial production from core to peripheral regions has emerged, which in turn requires some measure of world monetary and political stability as well as some systematic redistribution of financial resources to ease this relocation. On the other hand, the long postwar boom produced the downfall of the U.S. imperial order, thereby enhancing world monetary and political instability and the concentration of financial resources in the hands of the TNCs and the rentier (oil-exporting) states. Given the perverse behavior of prices typical of oligopolistic competition, this contradiction has manifested itself throughout the 1970s in the phenomenon of stagflation, which has in turn reacted on its causes, reproducing and deepening institutional instability in the world-economy at large.

3. SCENARIOS FOR THE 1980s

I shall now try to project into the 1980s the main tendencies analyzed in the first two parts of this chapter. To simplify the discussion, I shall limit myself to speculating about the likelihood of one of three alternative scenarios materializing. The first is what we might call the "resurgence of interimperialist rivalry" or, more simply, "mercantilism,"[6] with its characteristic tendency toward another break-up of the world "market" economy and its resulting tendency toward another "universal war" as the polarization of core capitalist countries into two antagonistic blocs takes place. This would be a repetition of what happened as a result of previous crises of world hegemony, not only in the first half of this century, with the crisis of British hegemony, but also in the century (from the 1650s to the 1760s) that followed the crisis of Dutch hegemony. The second scenario is what we may call the "peaceful solution of the crisis," that is, the simultaneous overcoming of the institutional instability and economic stagnation of the world-economy through the emergence of a new world *political* hegemony that is not the product of war among core capitalist countries. The third scenario is one in which the 1980s will witness neither the precipitation of the current crisis into a new mercantilist/imperialist phase nor its peaceful solution, but a continuation of the tendencies of the 1970s. In this connection, we shall discuss whether such a continuation is likely to bring the world-economy in the 1990s closer to, or farther away from, a solution to the crisis.

A Resurgence of Interimperialist Rivalry?

(1) The prelude to the outbreak of interimperialist rivalry at the end of the nineteenth century was the development, during the great depression of 1873–96, of strong protectionist/ expansionist tendencies, aggressively or defensively motivated, that began to break up the unity of the world market and to shift the focus of capitalist competition from the economic (market) arena to the arena of political (interstate) relations. Such tendencies are always a possibility in the capitalist world-economy because of the inherently contradictory directions of the dominant relational structures through which accumulation processes operate, the structure of interstate relations and the structure of division/integration of labor. But no tendency of this sort is at all apparent in the current great depression. On the contrary, we have seen that, notwithstanding predictably strong pressures to adopt protectionist measures, old and new core countries alike—and many semi-peripheral ones as well—have moved in the direction of further liberalization of trade. As for state expansionism, leaving aside the Soviet Union (to be discussed presently), the United States has largely relinquished its imperial responsibilities and no other core capitalist country, with the possible partial exception of France, has shown the least propensity to take them over through a more active political/military presence in the Third World.

Our previous analysis suggests three main reasons for this weakness of state protectionism/expansionism among the core capitalist countries. One is the form of competition that has come to characterize core capital since World War II. For one thing, protectionism and mercantilism were closely connected with price competition, and to the extent that the latter has been superceded by product innovation and differentiation as the main weapon of competitive struggle, to that extent the capacity of protectionism to strengthen the position of competing national capitals has been undermined. More important still, direct investment rather than trade has become the main vehicle of the competitive thrust of core capital. Under these conditions, protectionist measures undertaken by any given state can neither protect the weaker sectors of domestic capital from the competition of stronger foreign capital nor sustain the expansionist tendencies of the stronger sectors of domestic capital. Protection of the national economy will not restrict, and may actually encourage, its penetration by foreign capital through direct investment; and it will discourage the transnational expansion of domestic capital aimed at producing abroad at a lower cost, commodities destined for the home market.

Analogous considerations apply to state expansionism aimed at creating areas of exclusive or privileged exploitation for domestic capital. The development of secondary TNCs and the strengthening of the competitiveness of primary TNCs has radically changed the situation obtaining at the beginning of the century, when the export of capital from core countries (largely limited to speculative and interest-bearing investment and to the appropriation of natural resources) directly depended for its profitability on monopolistic positions backed by state power. The profitability of modern TNCs does not normally depend on the establishment of such positions but rather on superior organization which can fully develop, and be fully deployed, only under conditions of universal freedom of entry. To be sure, as I emphasized earlier, TNCs require state support and protection to secure property and other appropriated rights, contractual obligations, and monetary stability on a world scale. It is, however, a very different kind of support and protection from that afforded by core states in their mercantilist and imperialist phases, since it is not oriented to the creation of political zones of *monopolistic* exploitation, but the reproduction on an enlarged scale of the economic space of oligopolistic *competition*.

Even if we accept this line of argument, we may still question one of its premises: the supposition that the current tendency toward the transnational expansion of the core capital, and the structural solidarity among core capitalist states that ensues, is a stable tendency. As a matter of fact, if demand deficiency, rather than inelastic supplies of labor and energy in core regions, were to become the dominant aspect of economic stagnation, the tendency in question would in all likelihood be reversed. Each individual state would then be tempted to pursue mercantilist policies of the "beggar-thy-neighbor" type in order to concentrate demand, and the production to meet it, within its own borders. Overproduction tendencies in the world-economy at large would then worsen, other states would be forced to follow suit, and a new break up of the world market would be precipitated.

If I consider this development unlikely to occur, at least in the foreseeable future, it is because of my supposition that the inelasticity of labor supplies in core regions is not simply a conjunctural phenomenon due to conditions of full employment (conditions that have long ceased to exist anyway) but a structural phenomenon connected with a high workplace bargaining power and exhausted reserves of competitive labor. This is indeed the second reason suggested by the previous analysis for the weakness of mercantilist tendencies among core capitalist countries. Generally speaking, if the main obstacle to expanding capitalist accumulation is the strong workplace bargaining power of labor, mercantilist policies will be self-defeating: the concentration of demand within a core national economy will accentuate inflationary pressures, weaken its industries' world competitive position, and result in a greater increase in the value of imports over exports. Under these circumstances, therefore, core states are much more likely to pursue (as many did in the 1970s) policies that directly or indirectly favor the transnational expansion of "their" national capital (including tariff policies that do not block the "importing" of the products of the TNCs branch operations) to take advantage of lower costs of production in semiperipheral and peripheral regions.

The third reason for the weakness of mercantilist tendencies among core capitalist countries is to be found in the changed relationship of forces between core and peripheral countries. As we have seen, the strong nationalist movements that have developed in the periphery have become an "independent variable" in world politics that makes territorial expansion by core states extremely costly, if not altogether impossible, particularly if such expansion is to take place in competition with rival powers. A new "re-division" of the world, even if it suited the interests of core capital (which it does not) would no longer be an uncontested option at the present historical juncture.

This argument may seem to be invalidated by the apparently growing expansionist tendencies manifested by the USSR. Cuban intervention in Angola, Soviet and Cuban intervention in the Horn of Africa, Vietnamese expansionism in Indochina, and the Soviet invasion of Afghanistan all undoubtedly testify to an escalation in the form and scope of Soviet intervention in the Third World that represent a clear departure from the earlier cautiousness of Soviet policy outside the boundaries set for the communist world at Yalta. The USSR, in other words, has shown a marked propensity to exploit the void of power and the consequent situation of anarchy in interstate relations that have emerged in the periphery with the demise of the U.S. imperial order. The question is whether this propensity will drag the United States and other core capitalist states into competitive expansionist drives that will resurrect the ghost of the interimperialist rivalries of the first half of the century.

In this connection, it must first of all be remarked that it is the USSR, rather than established or emerging core capitalist countries, that shows the most pronounced state expansionist tendencies—tendencies that in historical perspective are weak indeed. This indirectly supports the claim made above that such tendencies are not positively correlated with the transnational expansion of core capital. If anything, there seems to be a negative correlation. For whatever assumption we may want to make concerning the class nature of the Soviet state and society, one thing is certain: Soviet capital, either from a strictly technological point of view or from the point of view of its propensity/capacity to develop a transnational organization of production, has not attained core position. As a matter of fact, Soviet capital has shown little tendency to expand abroad, and what has ocurred has been politically determined and taken the form of noncompetitive commercial and financial operations.

As far as I can see, this competitive backwardness of Soviet capital is the legacy of the state enterprise system, still strongly entrenched in the Soviet economy. The causes of this back-wardness are of no immediate relevance to our analysis; what matters is that the USSR is deprived of "economic" mechanisms of external domination and is therefore overdependent on ideological and political (ultimately military) means of enforcing its hegemony. The strictly political nature of Soviet domination has probably helped shelter it from the kind of unruliness of capital and labor that has undermined and resulted from U.S. *formal* hegemony over the capitalist world. At the same time, however, it has represented a serious obstacle to the extension of hegemony outside of Eastern Europe (as witnessed in different ways by the Chinese and Egyptian experiences of the 1960s), and even there could only be reproduced through the continuous and open use of force. Moreover, recent events in Poland seem to indicate that the unruliness of labor may very well become a destabilizing factor in Eastern Europe, as it has been in Western Europe.

To put it differently, the establishment and reproduction of the U.S. imperial order was always a means to the creation of world political-economic conditions in which the United States could exercise, and even share with other core capitalist countries, an informal hegemony based on economic mechanisms of domination. This "internationalism" was and is based on the attainment of a transnational dimension by capital from the core, irrespective of its original nationality, and has in turn put core states in a position where they can minimize *formal* domination over states in the periphery and semiperiphery. The Soviet imperial order, on the other hand, had and still has no such economic base. And whatever ideological base it might have had at its inception ("proletarian internationalism") has been progressively undermined by the continuous attempt to reproduce domination through purely political/military means—an endeavor that has enhanced nationalist sentiments and resentment in most communist countries.

It follows that, whatever its social origins, Soviet hegemonism is characterized by a fundamental contradiction: on the one hand, it has little or no *substantive* ground to fall back on if it sheds its formal aspects; on the other hand, its continuing reliance on formal hegemony enhances nationalism in the countries over which it is exercised and puts serious limits on its capacity to expand elsewhere. As the Afghanistan experience is demonstrating, the USSR is no better equipped than the core capitalist states to subject peripheral countries to formal domination, and prolonged attempts to do so may well help destabilize Soviet hegemony over Eastern Europe.

These considerations lead to the proposition that the *tactical* (short-term) advantage that has accrued to the USSR with the demise of the U.S. imperial order conceals a fundamental *strategic* (long-term) disadvantage in the struggle for world hegemony. If this is correct, the recent expansionist tendencies of the USSR can be interpreted as an attempt to exploit a tactical advantage to compensate for a basic strategic weakness. As such, they are not likely to escalate beyond rather narrow limits, because the resistance against the establishment of formal rule in peripheral areas will not only impede such escalation but will enhance the precariousness of established formal hegemony elsewhere. Neither are such expansionist tendencies likely to call forth competitive drives on the part of the core capitalist countries, because of the weakness of state expansionist tendencies autonomously generated within them; and, above all, because these countries can be expected to exploit their strategic advantage in the struggle for world hegemony by opposing Soviet expansionism indirectly, that is, by supporting the resistance that spontaneously develops in the Third World against external *formal* domination.

In sum, the forms of capitalist competition, and the relationships of forces between core and peripheral countries and between capital and labor in core areas that have developed since World War II, all seem to justify the supposition that the crisis of U.S. hegemony will not be followed in the foreseeable future by a new mercantilist/imperialist phase. It is important to realize that this conclusion in no way rules out the possibility that a nuclear war may break out as a result of what Edward Thompson has recently defined as "exterminism"[7]—a possibility that deserves careful consideration but cannot be explored here because it falls beyond the scope of the political-economic analysis undertaken and because I am not competent to do so. All I can do to take this possibility into account is to qualify the above conclusion by saying that the current crisis of the world-economy has no *inherent* tendency to develop into a new mercantilist/imperialist phase. Yet it may very well end in a nuclear holocaust determined by tendencies such as "exterminism" that are beyond the horizon of political economy.

A Political Solution of the Crisis?

Assuming that no such holocaust will actually occur in the 1980s, can we expect the current crisis to be solved within the next decade or so through the peaceful emergence of a new world political hegemony? In this case, too, the answer has to be negative, largely because the same factors that are preventing the current crisis from developing into a new mercantilist/imperialist phase are also preventing its peaceful political solution.

Let us first see what would be involved in a solution of this kind. According to the previous analysis, what would be required is a political action that reestablishes the conditions of sustained world capitalist accumulation by overcoming/neutralizing the unruliness of labor in core regions, thereby making superfluous a major decentralization of industrial production toward the periphery, or by overcoming/neutralizing the unruliness of the periphery, thereby creating conditions favorable to such decentralization. As for the unruliness of capital, to some extent we may assume that, if the conditions of sustained world capitalist accumulation are reestablished in either of the above two ways, the high precautionary and speculative demand for liquidity by core capital will tend to fall, and its propensity to invest in productive activities will rise. And as stagnation gives way to expansion, the perverse behavior of prices will result in a slowdown of inflation, further enhancing monetary stability and productive investment. Yet the strong interdependence among the three types of unruliness, emphasized throughout this chapter, means that neither the unruliness of labor nor that of the periphery can be successfully tackled without at the same time impinging upon the unruliness of capital.

Turning now to an examination of the way in which core capitalist states may attempt to overcome/neutralize the unruliness of labor, we can conceive of at least three possible courses of action. The first is what we may call "corporatist-repressive." This course of action, typical of totalitarian regimes, would involve some combination of the following: the smashing of labor organizations or their subordinate incorporation into the state apparatus, legal restrictions on the right to strike, and the creation of political/administrative bodies entrusted with the enforcement of labor discipline in the workplace. No core capitalist state has shown any propensity to move in this direction during the current crisis. Indeed, even some semiperipheral countries (such as Spain, Greece, and Brazil in the capitalist world, and now apparently Poland in the communist world) that experienced fast industrial growth in the 1960s by relying on corporatist-repressive practices have shown a distinct propensity to abandon them.

This decline of repressive corporatism can be traced to the strengthening of labor's workplace bargaining power. Repressive corporatism can be an effective weapon in the reestablishment of the command of capital over labor only when the unruliness of the latter is the product of favorable market conditions or of the organization of labor (in parties and unions) aimed at neutralizing unfavorable market conditions. In both instances, the substitution of state rule for market rule in regulating labor/capital relations and the disruption of labor organizations may actually succeed in breaking or weakening the capacity of labor to resist the command of capital. On the other hand, when the source of such power is neither market conditions nor organization but is the joint product of technological transformations in production and of cultural transformations in reproduction, repressive corporatism, far from being effective in disciplining labor, may actually lead to the opposite. As argued earlier, under these circumstances labor organizations tend to play more of a mediational than a conflictual role in industrial relations, so that their disruption may result in an enhancement rather than in a dampening of the unruliness of labor. Moreover, such disruption is much less feasible than it was because of the power positions acquired by labor organizations within core states and societies either through past struggles or, more often, in exchange for the mediational role they play in industrial relations.

We shall return to this last point in our discussion of liberal corporatism. Before that, however, let us deal briefly with a second course of action that states in core areas may pursue in the attempt to curb the unruliness of labor: wildly deflationary policies of the Thatcher type. From the point of view under examination here, the logic of this course is that, however "impervious" labor may have become to "market discipline," there must still be a point beyond which unemployment will reestablish the command of capital over labor. We can safely assume that such a point does in fact exist. However, quite apart from the fact that as soon as the recovery of accumulation reduces unemployment below this point it would bring back in manifest forms the problem of the unruliness of labor, there are two other problems involved in this course of action.

The first is that, in the short run, it tends to heighten social and industrial conflict, the more so the more the deflationary policies are aimed at weakening the power of labor organizations, so that they abandon mediational stances in favor of conflict. Assuming that a government pursuing such policies can outlast these short-term effects, there is a second, more fundamental, problem involved in this course of action: the high cost and risk involved for capital itself. The dislocating effects of strongly deflationary policies on capitalist enterprises may in fact be such that the long-term advantages of a disciplined labor force are outweighed by the cost of bringing it about. Moreover, if all core countries were simultaneously and systematically to pursue this course of action, they might precipitate a global overproduction crisis whose cost to core capital would be much greater than that of the current stagflation crisis.

True, if world political-economic conditions were favorable to the transnational expansion of core capital into peripheral regions, the cost and risk of such deflationary measures would be greatly reduced: core capital would benefit from external expansion, and this expansion would in turn sustain global demand. Under these circumstances, deflation in core countries might even represent a healthy stimulus to industrial decentralization. But until such conditions are created, attempts to reestablish the command of capital over labor through strong deflationary measures alone can be expected to be short-lived and ineffective.

As a matter of fact, the most successful course of action core area states can pursue (and to some extent have been pursuing) is neither to disrupt labor organizations through "extra-economic" force or to antagonize them through wildly deflationary policies. It is instead to involve them in governmental responsibilities, thereby strengthening their mediational role in labor/capital relations. The mediation typically consists of a political-economic exchange whereby core labor is granted security of employment and relative price stability, while core capital is granted industrial peace and freedom to expand transnationally. The instruments typically used to enforce the mediation are (1) reliance on nonmarket mechanisms in regulating direct labor/capital relations, and (2) reliance on monetary orthodoxy in regulating indirect labor/capital relations and relations with the world-economy.

This course of action, pursued by West German social democracy in the 1970s but recognizable, in an authoritarian variant, in some aspects of Japanese economic and industrial policies, can be called "liberal-corporatist." Stretching and distorting the usual definition a bit, I shall use this designation to emphasize the difference of such a policy from the two courses of action examined above and from traditional social democracy. It is liberal because of its reliance on monetary orthodoxy and because it does not aim at restricting the mobility of capital. Yet it differs from wild "deflationarism" because it attempts to overcome the unruliness of labor through political bargaining rather than through market mechanisms. It is corporatist because it presupposes, and endeavors to enhance, a common interest between labor and capital, but it differs from repressive corporatism because it relies on the active involvement of labor organizations in governmental responsibilities rather than on their disruption.

As compared with traditional social democracy, liberal corporatism recognizes the impossibility, under present circumstances, of attaining and reproducing full employment in core capitalist countries through deficit spending and deficit financing. This was an adequate course of action under conditions of elastic labor supply in both workplace and marketplace and of relatively closed national economies. However, when unemployment is primarily due not to demand deficiency but to rigidities of labor supply in the workplace, and when national economies are densely and closely connected to the world-economy, deficit financing can only enhance inflationary pressures without improving (and possibly even worsening) employment situations. Under these conditions, deficit financing tends to benefit capital more than labor, since it creates the monetary conditions for passing increases in costs on to consumers (overwhelmingly wage workers) while forcing labor into a continuous defensive struggle just to keep real wages constant. However, under conditions of intensifying world market competition through trade and direct investment, it is not altogether advantageous for core capital either: quite apart from the world monetary disorder it helps reproduce, if domestic inflation is not reflected in a devaluation of the national currency, domestic capital's ability to compete through trade (at home and abroad) is undermined; and if a devaluation occurs, the ability to compete through direct investment is impaired.

It follows that monetary orthodoxy is a necessary condition for the successful mediation of the interests of core labor and core capital because, by containing domestic inflationary pressures, it sustains both real wages and the ability of core capital to expand transnationally. But whether or not this tendency will actually succeed in simultaneously reproducing conditions of relative full employment and industrial peace depends on three further conditions.

First, it depends on the existence of political and cultural forces capable of restraining the unruliness of labor and capital independently (at least within certain limits) of market conditions. That is to say, labor must be restrained from exploiting its strong bargaining power to press for increases in wages over and above increases in productivity, and capital must be restrained from exploiting its freedom of movement to press for lower levels of employment and higher prices. More important still, the success of liberal-corporatism depends on the competitive strength of domestic capital in the world-economy. If domestic capital has little competitive strength, which in the contemporary world-economy means little capacity to innovate and differentiate products as well as to expand transnationally, monetary orthodoxy will simply enhance capital's liquidity preference, ultimately leading to higher rates of unemployment and inflation. It is only if domestic capital is competitively strong that monetary orthodoxy will sustain its transnational expansion, and that this will generate new demand for complex goods and services back in the domestic economy.

What this second condition implies is that, quite apart from the existence of suitable political and cultural conditions (which are not reproducible at will), liberal-corporatism can be pursued with some success only by a limited number of countries, i.e., those core countries whose capital is endowed with great competitive power (actual or potential) in the world-economy at large. How limited that number will be at any given time, and how successful the countries that will actually pursue the course in question will be, will depend on a third condition: the world political-economic condition of the transnational expansion of core capital. The possibility of exploiting the reserves of competitive labor in peripheral regions is even more crucial to liberal-corporatism than it is to plain deflationarism. For liberal-corporatism can ultimately succeed only if the decentralization of deskilled work roles toward peripheral regions can be "wide" enough to allow the upgrading (in skills and status) of a substantial proportion of the labor force in core countries.

Two effects are involved. One is merely quantitative and consists of the *increase* in employment in core regions connected with the recovery and expansion of world capitalist accumulation once deskilled roles are competitively performed in peripheral regions. The other is qualitative in the sense that the increase takes place mainly in occupations that embody the productive and unproductive functions expropriated from the lower echelon of labor, while the segments of the labor process that engender the unruliness of labor are transplanted and expanded in regions still endowed with reserves of competitive labor. The quantitative effect implies the profitable reproduction of high levels of employment in core regions. It realizes an important element of the political-economic exchange between core labor and capital that is the aim of liberal-corporatism. The qualitative effect does much more: it strengthens the structural solidarity between core labor and capital, thereby establishing a still firmer social basis for liberal-corporatism.

It follows that an enduring neutralization of the unruliness of labor in core regions largely depends on the possibility of creating world political-economic conditions favorable to the transnational expansion of capital, particularly toward peripheral regions. Let us therefore turn to an examination of the second possibility envisaged at the beginning of this section, namely that some kind of political action will in the foreseeable future overcome/neutralize the unruliness of the periphery.

In this connection we can also conceive of three courses of action. However, whereas in discussing the unruliness of labor we could take for granted the *subject* of political action (the nation state), here the question of who will undertake it is very much open and has to be solved in each instance.

The first conceivable course of action is, again, a purely repressive one whereby core capitalist states, individually or jointly, reimpose with force of arms some kind of imperial order over the periphery. This possibility has in fact already been discussed when dealing with the chance of a resurgence of interimperialist rivalries. The strength of nationalist sentiments and movements, and the vulnerability of conventional to guerrilla warfare in peripheral regions, are the main conditions that make any attempt to reestablish formal hegemony over such regions extremely costly and risky. These costs and risks are increased by the fact that such an attempt would strengthen the tactical advantage of Soviet hegemonism and weaken the strategic advantage enjoyed by core capitalist countries in the struggle for informal hegemony. In the previous section I argued that, given the weakness of mercantilist tendencies among core capitalist countries, it is highly un-likely that any individual core state will undertake such an enterprise. We may now add that, precisely because of the high costs and risks involved *and* of their different evaluation by core states with different geographical and social locations in the world-economy, a combined repressive action is even less likely.

This does not of course exclude localized actions done to make an "example," such as those envisaged by France against Libya or the United States in Central America. Even less does it exclude support by core states for military regimes in peripheral and semiperipheral countries aimed at creating favorable conditions for the transnational expansion of core capital. From the point of view under consideration, however, these are double-edged weapons because, even if they were to succeed in their immediate purpose, they would tend in the longer run to heighten the unruliness of the periphery by enhancing nationalist sentiments/resentments and military interstate competition among peripheral countries.

As a matter of fact, the only way core capitalist states can hope to overcome/neutralize the unruliness of the periphery is through some kind of informal hegemony. To this end they can pursue two very different courses of action. One is to strengthen the "discipline of the market" through such moves as cutting state financial and technical aid to peripheral countries, thereby forcing them to compete with each other in making concessions to core capital in exchange for finance and technology. This type of policy would simply strengthen a tendency that has been at work since the downfall of the U.S. imperial order. It would, therefore, face the problem that market rule is no better equipped than imperial rule to dis-cipline peripheral countries—that the unruliness of the periphery reflected the failure of the market mechanism as much as the demise of imperial rule.

Moreover, financial and technical assistance is the main (low-cost, low-risk) "mercantilist" weapon left in the hands of core states to strengthen and protect (vis-à-vis both the core capital of other nationalities and states and capital in the host countries) transnational expansion of "their" core capital. It is therefore highly unlikely that they will severally embark upon major cuts in economic and technical assistance, giving up dependable short-term advantages for uncertain long-term ones. It is even less likely that they will do so jointly, not only because growing competition in the economic sphere prevents collusion in the political sphere, but also because they would thereby weaken their joint strategic advantages in the struggle with the USSR for informal world hegemony.

The other, more promising, course of action that core states could pursue to enhance informal hegemony is that of strengthening their *mediational* role in core capital/peripheral state relations. The most obvious step in this direction would be an "enlarged" Marshall Plan of the type envisaged, though weakly rationalized, in the Brandt report. What this implies is nothing less than a reduplication for the periphery as a whole (or large regions thereof) of the coordinated action, backed by a major redistribution of financial and real resources, whereby in the immediate postwar years the United States managed to create in Western Europe conditions of political stability and economic cooperation that in due course favored a major decentralization of industrial production from the U.S. core. Were it feasible, an enlarged plan of this kind would undoubtedly contribute to an early and simultaneous solution of the crises in core/periphery and labor/capital relations. But its feasiblity in the present historical conjuncture is, to say the least, doubtful.

For one thing, a united political will capable of pursuing the general capitalist interest with this kind of coordinated action does not exist, and cannot be expected to emerge in the near future. This is not so much a question of the lack of political awareness of core *capital*'s interest, as of the diversity of trajectories along which core *states* are moving. States are subject to pushes and pulls that originate in different historical configurations of class struggle, nation-building, and position in interstate relations. Though the structural solidarity among core capitalist countries brought about by the transnationalization of core capital is, as argued in the previous section, strong enough to prevent these differences from escalating into a new mercantilist/imperialist phase, it is not strong enough to bring about a united political will of the kind required by an enlarged Marshall Plan.

Moreover, even if such united a political will were to come into existence, it would not have the command over world financial resources necessary to implement the plan. As we noted in the first section, the current crisis is, among other things, a crisis of political rule in general—not just of U.S. state rule—over world liquidity. A hypothetical united political will would, therefore, have to be strong enough to wrest from the invisible hand of supranational markets some measure of control over the financial resources of the TNCs and rentier states, a requirement that makes its emergence even less likely.

Finally, world power relations cannot be expected to make any easier the implementation of an enlarged Marshall Plan. The Western European recipients of the original Marshall Plan had exhausted themselves in a mutually destructive war that left them all relatively powerless vis-à-vis U.S. political and economic might. In addition, they were ruled by classes strongly motivated by a capitalist recovery that promised to buttress their tottering internal hegemony and to reestablish their power and status in the world-economy. In the present historical conjuncture, on the other hand, a hypothetical core state authority would face as recipients of its redistributive measures a multiplicity of sovereign states jealous of their political independence, still in competition with each other at economic and political (and often military) levels, and ruled by classes and elites weakly motivated by a capitalist recovery that promises, at best, to deepen their structural subordination to core capital. This is to say, our already overburdened core political authority would have to engage in a complex (indeed impossible) task of mediation, bargaining, and administration to secure the acceptance, and then the effective implementation, of the redistributive plan.

The 1980s and Beyond

It follows from what has been argued in the previous two sections that the current crisis is as unlikely to be solved *politically* in the foreseeable future as it is to degenerate into a new phase of mercantilist/imperialist rivalry. More positively stated, this means that the tendencies characteristic of the mid- to late 1970s (war and political instability in peripheral regions, industrial conflict in semiperipheral and core regions, stagflation in the world-economy at large) will most probably continue through the 1980s.

There is no guarantee, however, that the continuation of these tendencies in the 1980s will bring the world-economy closer to a solution of the crisis in the 1990s or, as Wallerstein seems to assume, to a new upturn in world accumulation. To some extent, it may work in this direction. The inability to curb the unruliness of labor and periphery through political-economic mechanisms will progressively enhance the profitability of new lines of production (most probably robotry and new sources of energy) capable of relaxing the dependence of core capital on elastic supplies of labor and on energy from existing resources. To the extent that these lines of production are actually developed, an upturn in accumulation (and a downturn in the rate of inflation) may ensue.

These, however, are long-run tendencies that operate not in a vacuum but in a political-economic space continuously structured by the interstate system, which is itself changing in response to these tendencies. As a matter of fact, if I were to take a view longer than I have taken in this chapter, I would probably consider the possibility of a political solution or of a political exacerbation of the crisis even more likely. If the continuation of current trends through the 1980s strengthens liberal-corporatist and informal-hegemonist tendencies in states in the core, then an upturn in the 1990s is likely. But if the continuation of the crisis leads those states to resort simultaneously and persistently to strong deflationary measures, rather than to political mediation, then we may very well witness, not an upturn, but a transformation of the current stagflation into a cumulating crisis of increasing overproduction, with a collapse of output, investment, prices, and possibly even a new breakup of the world market. Whether all this will ultimately result in a new capitalist world order, in a revolutionary reconstitution of world society, or in the common ruin of the contending classes and nations, we can only guess at this point. What is certain is that no viable political alternative to the economic "internationalism" of core capital has emerged as a force in world politics so far.

CRISIS OF IDEOLOGY AND IDEOLOGY OF CRISIS[1]

Andre Gunder Frank

Crisis does not mean the end. On the contrary, "crisis" refers to the critical time during which the end will be avoided through new adaptations if possible; only failing these, the end becomes unavoidable. The Concise Oxford English Dictionary defines crisis as: "Turning point, especially of disease. Moment of danger or suspense in politics, etc. as cabinet, financial. From Greek KRISIS, decision." The crisis is a period in which a diseased social, economic, and political body or system cannot live on as before and is obliged, on pain of death, to undergo transformations that will give it a new lease on life. Therefore, this period of crisis is a historical moment of danger and suspense during which the crucial decisions and transformations are made, which will determine the future development of the system if any and its new social, economic, and political basis.

INTRODUCTION TO CRISIS

Public awareness and concern about crises (plural) and crisis (singular) in the West has been growing in view of persistent inflation and the 1973–75 recession, the weakness of the 1975–79 recovery, and the renewed 1979–80–82 recession on top of the unresolved problems from the previous one; the increasingly severe economic plan failures and recent or impending domestic political upheavals in, and wars between, socialist states in the East; and the endemic failures of economic development programs resulting in resurgent nationalist and religious movements in, as well as increasing warfare between, the countries of the Third World South. These and other developments have led to growing public realization that the world faces new crises (or indeed perhaps, as Wallerstein and I suggest, a single world crisis) that are (or is) not locally or temporally restricted and that will not soon pass. The fear is spreading that things will, or indeed must, get worse before they get better.

In the West, political leaders and the press have drawn increasing parallels with the crisis of the 1930s, though perhaps still insufficient ones with the development of fascism and war that were part and parcel of that crisis. Economic historians can draw additional analogies between the development of the present crisis and the interwar crisis of a half century ago (which centered on the depression of the 1930s but included the two world wars), as well as the crisis of a century ago, which was associated with the so-called great depression of 1873 to 1895 and whose repercussions included the rise of monopoly capitalism and imperialism but also the end of the Pax Britannica, as Britain began its decline from world leadership in the face of challenges from Germany and the United States. As Arrighi argues, the present world crisis seems to be spelling the beginnings of the end of the Pax Americana and may hold untold other major readjustments in the international division of labor and world power in store for the future.

From the perspective of the West, the present crisis increasingly appears as a capitalist crisis of (over)accumulation of capital analogous to those of half a century and a century ago and thus as another capitalist "B" phase of stagnation in the "long waves" of economic ups and downs in capitalist world development (sometimes in part associated with the name of Kondratieff), which Wallerstein and I believe reach back for several centuries. It is uncertain whether this long wave and its present crisis phase are also part of still larger, more than a century long, economic fluctuations, sometimes called logistics.[2] I question the thesis that the present crisis, at least for the foreseeable future, represents an acceleration and deepening of the final crisis of capitalism that, according to Wallerstein and Amin, began with the October Revolution in the Soviet Union (where this thesis is particularly popular). I find most unrealistic the sub-thesis, defended by some but not by Wallerstein, that this crisis is supposedly carrying capitalism to its speedy end, soon to be replaced by world socialism.

More probably, the present crisis and the profound economic, social, cultural, and political transformations that this crisis (like all previous ones) is bringing in its train will result in the regeneration of the capitalist system and its renewed expansion. Both of these processes will, no doubt, also contribute to the long-term metamorphosis of the system and the ultimate transition beyond capitalism, as discussed by Wallerstein, though it still seems premature to foretell when and how this transition will occur. In the coming decades, the participation of both the underdeveloped Third World South and of the supposedly socialist West in the world capitalist crisis and in these transformations of the world system are likely to contribute to the resolution of the crisis and to the recovery of the system in favor of capital and world capitalism by the end of the century—if we do not blow ourselves up before then.

Since their successive incorporations into the emerging worldwide capitalist system between the sixteenth and the nineteenth or twentieth centuries, the various parts of the miscalled Third World have been integral parts of a capitalist world economy dominated from and by the metropolitan and imperialist center, first of Western Europe and more recently the United States. From a Western or Southern perspective, the present crisis was generated in the Western center and, like all previous ones, has immediately been transmitted to the Southern periphery, first through changes in international trade and prices, which result in balance of payments crises and forced financial, economic, and political adjustments in the Third World, and then through productive and social reorganization in most of the Third World countries and indeed in the international division of labor in the capitalist world as a whole. Some of the details of this reorganization, to be examined below, suggest that the participation and the burden of the Third World South in this crisis and its resolution is likely to contribute significantly to world capitalist recovery. Moreover, the renewed increasing participation of the "socialist" economies in the capitalist international division of labor also seems to contribute similarly to a probable future capitalist recovery.

However, from a global perspective, the development of this world economic crisis should perhaps be interpreted not simply as spreading outward from the Western center, but rather as developing out of the imbalances in changing productive capacities, supply and demand, and international trade flows in the world economic systems as a whole. The necessary analysis of *world* economic developments, including the development and foreseeable resolution of the present economic crisis, have to our knowledge never yet been undertaken from such a global perspective, which is now proposed by Wallerstein. With adequate historical and futuristic scope, such analysis would facilitate appreciation of the changing roles of the world's productive, trading, and consuming units of the West, South, and East in the capitalist international division of labor. Moreover, such global analysis might eliminate the surprise element from the apparent pragmatic adaptations to circumstance of the "socialist" economies, which otherwise seems to violate the (socialist and bourgeois) ideologies of their supposed noncapitalist takeoff and of their supposed development of a socialist alternative to world capitalism. Indeed, such a global analysis, much of which unfortunately is still beyond our capacity, could provide the political-economic basis for the interpretation of the resulting ideological crises, as well as the many seemingly separate social (including class), cultural (including nationalist and religious), and other crises and movements in various parts of the world as part of a single crisis in a single world economic, social, and political system.

If such a global world system analysis of the present crisis were available—and as necessity is the mother of invention, one of the consequences of this crisis is likely to be the emergence of such analysis, which is incipiently exemplified by Wallerstein—it might suggest that this crisis (or these crises) involve social convulsion(s) of perhaps three decades duration, whose outcome can be another equally long period of world economic expansion on the basis of the resulting reorganization of the world productive structure and social organization. Though widespread ravages through nuclear war and/or famine and disease can by no means be ruled out in this crisis, Washington, Moscow, and Peking, each in its own way, are already telling us that even such disasters could provide an adequate basis for a brave new world expansion.

In the meantime, even the most separatist nationalist movements, the most seemingly other worldly religious movements, and the most irrational individual reactions to an unsatisfactory rational world order need not necessarily spell the breakup or downfall of the world system. Indeed, all teleology but perhaps not all functionalism aside, it may be noted that many social movements have often quite despite themselves ultimately proven useful to the capitalist development of a single world system. For instance, the spread of Islam by traders and of Christianity by conquerors, as well as the age-old clash between them since the Crusades, contributed to the spread of capitalism and the development of a worldwide capitalist system. Nationalism and religion could promote capitalist development again today and tomorrow. At the very least, nationalism, religion, and irrationality can and probably will more than neutralize, if not divide and destroy, the force of class-based movements through which capitalism was long since supposed to end as rational "workers of the world unite: you have nothing to loose but your chains." Evidently, many workers and others think they have their nationalism, their religion, and their irrational personal stake in a capitalist future to loose and for the foreseeable future only utopian socialism to gain.

In the absence so far of an adequate global *analysis* with which to study the present crisis and its seemingly disparate ideological manifestations, we will begin with a simple review of some current developments from a global *perspective*. Then we will rely on this global perspective to examine the development of real and ideological crises in each of the West, the South, and the East, but with due regard for the implications of each in the other and with special reference to the apparently increasing conflict between waning socialism and resurging nationalism. Finally, we will draw on the global world system perspective to pose some futher analytical questions or at least some questions for further analysis of the crisis and nationalism.

CRISIS IN THE WORLD SYSTEM

In the capitalist world-economy of the modern world system, accumulation on a world scale can no longer proceed as it did in the postwar era of expansion until and unless unequal development and dependent accumulation are put on a new footing. Among the most important elements of the therefore emerging new international division of labor are the reincorporation of the socialist economies in the world market and the transfer of certain world market industries both to them and to selected parts of the Third World, where wages are lower and labor discipline is higher; and the "rationalization" of industrial production in the West itself through investment in labor-saving technology, such as microchips and robots, and the use of the resultant unemployment to depress wages in the industrial capitalist countries themselves. It was not an incidental accident that when trade among the industrial capitalist countries declined by nearly 15 percent in 1975, industrial exports to the socialist countries and the Third World increased sufficiently so that total world trade only declined by 5 percent. Indeed, while between 1962 and 1973 only 15 percent of the growth of exports from the West went to the South, between 1973 and 1977, 30 percent of the increase in the Western industrial economies' exports was absorbed by the underdeveloped countries. In 1978, the South absorbed one-fifth of the manufacturing exports of the Western European countries, most of whose exports are to each other (or twice as much as the one-tenth taken by North America and Japan put together), one-third of the manufacturing exports of North America (compared with the one-fourth taken by Western Europe and Japan combined), and 46 percent or nearly half (and more than the combined purchases of Western Europe and North America) of Japanese industrial exports. This importance of the Third World as a market for the exports of Western (including Japanese) industry has continued to rise and accelerate, particularly during recessions when Western demand slackens even more than Third World imports. Thus, profits from exports to and work in the East and the South provide a significant safety net for business and safety valve for governments in the West, while stagnating investment has shifted from expanding and new production facilities to the rationalization of existing ones with excess capacity.

The concomitant social and political transformations that apparently accompany this new international division of labor include militarism, war, and the East-West competition in the South, some Soviet-American detente and a Washington-Peking-Tokyo axis between West and East, and technological rationalization with economic austerity policies and renewed militarism in the "national interest" in the West. These policies lack the erstwhile legitimation of a red scare, but they conjure up a new East-West defense gap, which is reminiscent of the phony missile gap of the 1960s, and apparently they forget the subsequent credibility gap.

It is to be expected that all this economic, social, and political transformation poses serious challenges to existing policy, theory, and ideology. The political-economic crisis (or crises) is (are) also producing a crisis (or crises) of ideology, theory, and of course political praxis. In the West, the deepest economic crisis in over a generation has produced "a crisis of confidence" in the United States, in the words of President Carter on July 15, 1979, and a "moral crisis," according to the motto of the "Moral Majority" in its campaign to defeat him in the 1980 election. The crisis has also led to an abandonment everywhere of the Keynesian theory and welfare state policies that were supposed to guarantee that a crisis of the interwar type could never recur again. The bankruptcy of Keynesianism and the recourse to austerity policies to combat the crisis are shaking the very foundations of social democracy in the West. A whole new generation now looks forward to a foreseeable future of youth unemployment rates of 20, 30, and 40 percent, and local pockets of up to 80 percent unemployment. There can be little wonder that this generation is also looking for an ideological alternative to the "ever bigger and better" of their postwar parents. Even in the socialist East, unemployment (now estimated at 20 million in China) now violates a cardinal tenet of planned economies that are unable to meet even half their planned growth rates or to "catch up and bury the West," while domestic social and political tensions become increasingly dangerous and the danger and even reality of war among socialist states now exceed those between them and capitalist ones. The *People's Daily* complains of a "crisis of faith in Marxism" in China, while students in Poland strike to demand that obligatory courses be removed from the curriculum in Poland. No wonder that the East faces and poses a severe crisis of socialist ideology, which is losing one battle after another to the nationalism and religion that socialism was supposed to make outmoded. In the South, 300 million unemployed is perhaps not so new; but the repeated failures of development policy through aid and trade, or trade not aid, and successively through specialization in raw materials exports, and then the promotion of import-substituting industry, and most recently of manufacturing export-led growth (as in South Korea and Brazil, whose miracles suddenly turned to nightmares) have made a tragic farce of the first (1960s) and a second (1970s) United Nations development decades, and promise to make a cruel joke of the third one just launched for the 1980s. Instead, hundreds of millions of people in the Third World are suffering growing economic poverty, social oppression, moral anxiety (if only from conflicting values, corruption, etc.), and political repression at home and more frequent war or the threat of war between their country or region and their neighbors in the context of shifting global political alliances and changing ideological policies (as in East Africa, the Near East or West Asia, and Southeast Asia). No wonder that a mixed bag of confusing ideologies and half-baked theories are competing for the leadership and allegiance of massive social movements, which challenge authority within states and threaten international relations among them. Not the least among these movements are virulent nationalism and resurgent religion.

Resurgent nationalism manifests itself through previously

unthinkable wars between socialist states and the resurgence of ethnic, regionalist, and nationalist movements within them. Increasingly virulent nationalist stances by several of the major capitalist powers also threaten the Atlantic Alliance, NATO, and the European Common Market, and pose serious challenges to trilateral trade among North America, Western Europe, and Japan. Each of these simultaneously seeks greater penetration of, and protection from, the economies of the other—while regionalist and nationalist movements gain increasing strength within many of the Western states as well. In the Third World, nationalism, ethnicity, and sometimes racism fuel international and civil wars, increasingly at the expense of social progress and socialist pretenses (as when Somalia and Ethiopia change sides in the international system of alliances, revolutionary Ethiopia steps up its imperial repression of Eritrean nationalism and socialism, and revolutionary Iran increases its oppression of several minority nationalities). Globally, the threat of war, including nuclear devastation, looms greater as detente is weakened and great power rivalry strengthened with appeals to nationalism; and new waves of racism appear on the resurgence as well. At the same time, widespread disillusion with previously accepted worldly promises and expectations of material benefits and social progress, as well as exasperation with rational means to pursue or attain them, seem to have led to increasing popular rejection of the Western rationalism (including "goulash communism" in the East and Third World "modernization") that has been so influential around the world during the postwar decades. Instead, growing masses of people in the West, East, and South are turning to religion, "spiritual" values, and nonsecular leadership and organization, which guide them in the political pursuit of largely reactionary ends. This religious trend, or even shift, is visibly manifested in the massive popular response to the visits of Pope John Paul II to Poland (5 million people cheered him), Ireland (a third of the island's population appeared at one time), the United States (receptions surpassing those of the astronauts), Mexico (3 million people lined the streets), Brazil (a major national political event), and various countries of Africa. The Pope is parlaying this enthusiasm into support for his usually very conservative political stance and some very reactionary social programs. The religious revivalism is also manifested by the rapid growth of evangelism, fundamentalist religions, cults, such as the "Moonies," and the growing appeal of spiritualism in various Western countries; and by the revival of religion in various socialist countries of the East, including the Soviet Union and China, while in Poland the Catholic Church exerted widespread influence on strikers during their 1980 protests, which brought down the government of Edward Gierek. In the Third World, Islamic revivalism has not only taken political power under the leadership of the Ayatollah Khomeini in Iran, but new Islamic currents have also swept through other parts of the Middle East (and rendered Saudi Arabia far less stable since the occupation of the sacred mosque in Mecca by Islamic fundamentalists), Pakistan (where General Zia has sought to harness Islamic fundamentalism to his reactionary war chariot), Afghanistan (where Islam is used to oppose both social progress and Soviet intervention), India (where communalism is dangerously on the rise), Malaysia, the Philippines, Indonesia, and elsewhere. Significantly, the new Islamic movement is everywhere carried by the younger generation. In Latin America, the Catholic Church offers political leadership in loyal opposition to various military regimes, and Christian-Democratic parties, movements, and ideologies (in competition with social-democratic ones) offer themselves as realistic alternatives as never before in recent memory. Even the most revolutionary movements, as in Nicaragua, have a strong component of "liberation theology" and radicalized priests.

The manifestly increasing—and increasingly manifest—inadequacy of partial theories to analyze this reality in crisis and of the related crises of ideology to guide political practice in different parts of the world, to say nothing of the world as a whole, cry out for an alternative theory and ideology. The recent publication—and indeed the very titles—of *The Crisis of Democracy: Report on the Governability of Democracies* to the Trilateral Commission, *The Alternative* by the East German Communist Rudolph Bahro, *The Limits to Growth* and

Reshaping the International Order by the Club of Rome, as well as the call for a New International Economic Order by the United Nations incited by the Third World governments and the Brandt Commission Report, *North : South—A Programme for Survival,* are some of the visible manifestations of crises or crisis. Excepting Bahro, they seek for alternatives on the theoretical and ideological levels on behalf of the already ruling classes or dominant groups in the West and the South.

CRISIS IN THE WEST

Turning to a review of the development of the crisis in the West, the postwar industrial expansion, like previous major expansions, produced more capital relative to the labor used (in Marxist terminology, an increase in the organic composition of capital), particularly in industry. Associated with relative overinvestment in capital equipment in industry there was relative underinvestment in productive capacity in the mining and agricultural sectors in most of the capitalist world. At the same time, there was a substantial expansion of the "tertiary" service sector, but without any concomitant increase of labor productivity in the same, which raised this sector's share in total employment. The primary-sector underinvestment is substantially responsible for the oil and agricultural crises of the 1970s and perhaps the 1980s. The increase in the organic composition of capital (that is, an increase in the capital/labor ratio) and productivity, and the in part associated increase in worker bargaining power and militancy in the industrial economies have, since the mid-1960s, led to a decline in the rate of profit and a reduction in the rate of growth, and in some instances to an absolute reduction in the demand for industrial commodities and most particularly for capital or investment goods. The decline in the rate of profit is frequently also attributed to the growth of the service sector in general, and of the public sector and the welfare state in particular. However, it could equally well be argued that their supposed negative influence on the rate of profit is due not so much to their large size (say, as a proportion of GNP) as to the low productivity (and therefore the high employment and labor cost) in the service and public sectors. The previous imbalance may now perhaps lead to a relative increase in the provision of raw materials from mineral (including seabed and perhaps Antarctic) and agricultural (especially agribusiness) sources and to the improvement in labor productivity (but with a threat to employment) in the service sectors through the microchip and data processing revolutions.

Additionally, productivity and production have grown at different rates in the major industrial capitalist economies. Productivity in Western Europe has grown at twice the U.S. rate, and Japan's productivity grew at twice the European, and nearly four times the U.S. rate. During the 1970s, the growth of productivity dropped sharply almost everywhere in the West. In the United States, the rate of productivity growth fell from 3 percent annually in the 1950s and 1960s to 1 percent through most of the 1970s and to nil and even a decline at the end of the decade. The decline in productivity growth common to all Western economies has now reduced the differentials among them. These differential changes in productivity seem to be at the root of the relative (but not yet absolute) decline of U.S. economic and political power and the rise of Western Europe (especially West Germany) and Japan. This development is reminiscent of the relative decline of Great Britain in the crisis of a century ago, followed by Britain's absolute decline during the crisis of a half century ago. The U.S. decline, examined by Arrighi, may be expected to follow a similar course. Historically, the most acute political-economic struggles among rival economic centers and political states for hegemony typically take place during crisis "B" phases, and the strongest rivalry typically is less between the declining hegemonic power and the pretenders for its throne than among the pretenders themselves, with the old hegemonic power tactically allied to one of the latter. Wallerstein is probably right in the importance he assigns to the conflict during the crisis for dominance during the next expansion among the United States, Europe, and Japan, though the rivalry between the latter two may exceed that between (either of) them and the former. The further prospect of a European bloc including the USSR and (part of) Eastern Europe—dimly visible already in the emergence of a Paris-Bonn-Moscow axis—confronting Japan and the United States—already represented by a Washington-Peking-Tokyo axis—is less clear.

The development of economic crisis has also led to the following major consequences and manifestations. One has been the attempt to postpone or restrain, or indeed in some monopolized sectors to prevent, the decline in the rate of profit and the restriction in the market through mass programs of printing money and credit creation. This effort took its most spectacular form in the United States through the deficit financing of the war against Vietnam, which flooded the world with dollars. Secondly, competition increased particularly among national sectors of capital from one country to another for the remaining market. This competition manifested itself most particularly in the repeated devaluations of the dollar, which have been an attempt to maintain or increase the overseas market for U.S. exports and to protect them and the U.S. home market against the incursions particularly of Germany and Japan. Their currencies have been revalued and have risen very markedly against the dollar, without however so far turning the balance in favor of the United States on the world market. The decline of the dollar has, however, cheapened U.S. wage and property costs relative to those in Europe and Japan, and has therefore reversed the flow of foreign investment, which is now going from these areas into the United States. Slack demand and increased competition have also accelerated bankruptcies and monopolization nationally and aggressive export drives and renewed protectionism internationally.

Another major manifestation of overproduction and inadequate demand has been an increase in unutilized excess productive capacity in industry, especially in steel, ship building, automobiles, and petrochemicals. The steel industry has been in a worldwide slump for some years and, after shutting down a number of steel mills, is still only working at 60 or 70 percent capacity in various parts of the industrialized world. In consequence there has also been a marked slump in industrial investment. With excess but unused capacity and low profits, business sees no good reason to engage in mammouth new investment. The 1973 level of investment in the industrialized economies was not re-attained until 1978, and in Britain still not until today. Thus, there is a gaping investment hole from 1973 to 1978. Investment has declined again, because of a new recession, since then. Moreover, the nature of investment has changed. Expansive investment to provide new productive capacity for more and new goods has increasingly been replaced by rationalizing investment designed to produce at lower costs, and most particularly with lower labor costs. There has been a lot of talk about new technology in the energy supply and in a number of other fields. Despite the fact that, as we all know, the price of energy shot up rapidly after 1973, and did so again in 1979, there have not been any major new investments in the energy field except for prospecting and drilling for petroleum, which has increased markedly since 1973. But there has not been any major new investment in petroleum refining, which is a major reason for the bottlenecks of the 1970s. There also has not been any major new investment in alternative sources of energy from shale oil, coal, or nuclear fuel. The nuclear industry is economically in virtually complete shambles, which explains much of the adamant drive to sell nuclear reactors at home and abroad and has led to the strong competitive reactions and squabbles (e.g., between the United States and West Germany over Brazil and between the United States and France over Pakistan) internationally and the strong NO NUKES reactions in many parts of the world. All these alternative sources of energy, including solar energy and synthetic fuels, have been the subject of much talk, but so far it is all talk and no action. The main reason is that the general rate of profit and prospective markets do not yet justify any major investment either in the energy or in any other field. The apparent exception in the computer industry, particularly the use of microchips, is so far primarily a rationalizing investment designed to reduce labor costs of production and so far is not a major new innovation that puts production on an entirely new footing, though it may soon revolutionize the service sector by reducing labor costs and employment. The other technological revolution on the horizon is in the new genetics and biotechnology areas, which may revolutionize parts of the biochemical, medical, agricultural, food, and other industries. But before a major new investment program can be undertaken and such major new technology can be put into place, the profit rate has to be elevated again, and in order to do that vast economic, social, political, and ideological transformation on a world scale will be necessary.

Instrumental in both the decline in profits and their possible future recovery are another set of consequences and manifestations of the development of this crisis through recurrent and deepening recessions. Since the mid-1960s, recessions have become increasingly frequent, increasingly long, increasingly deep, and increasingly coordinated from one major industrial country to another. An index of the growth of these recessions is their impact on unemployment in the industrial countries of the OECD. In North America, Europe, Japan, Australia, and New Zealand, registered unemployment rose to 5 million during the recession of 1967, in which the United States barely participated because, so to say, it kept the recession wolf from the door through the war against Vietnam. By the recession of 1969–70–71, which also hit the United States, registered unemployment rose to 10 million in the industrialized countries. Unemployment then fell back to 8 million in the subsequent recovery from 1972 to 1973. In the next recession, which hit almost the whole capitalist world simultaneously from 1973 to 1975, and which was the deepest one since the 1930s, registered unemployment rose to 15 million in the industrialized countries, 9 million or about 60 percent of which was in the United States. Then unemployment again declined to less than 6 million in the United States but continued to rise in the industrial capitalist countries of Europe and Japan (as well as Canada and Australia). Indeed, the number of unemployed in these countries rose so much during the so-called recovery from 1975 to mid-1979 that total OECD registered unemployment increased from 15 million at the bottom of the last recession to 17 or 18 million in 1979. The new recession raised official unemployment to 23 million by the end of 1980 and was expected by the OECD itself to exceed 27 million by

1982. This massive increase in unemployment has of course reduced the total wage payments by capital and the earnings of labor, and it has also exerted considerable downward pressure on the wage rate by weakening labor's bargaining power. Existing unemployment and the threat of its increase has prompted labor to capitulate to capital in one major strike after another, as at British Leyland and British Steel, Fiat in Italy, and in the steel strike in Germany. The average real wage rate has declined in several Western countries, as was confirmed in 1981 for the last three years in the United States by President Reagan himself. In the un- or less-organized labor markets, the degree of exploitation, forced overtime work, sweatshop conditions, and health hazards has increased significantly again.

There are very substantial reasons to anticipate that the 1979–82 recession may turn out to be even more severe than the one of 1973–75. One reason is that this recession is much more welcome (on which more below) and "needed" than the previous one, which did not drive enough capital into bankruptcy to clean up the capitalist house sufficiently and did not successfully break the back of labor organization and militancy. Therefore, the capitalist states will do even less to combat this recession domestically than they did in the last one. The "debt economy," as *Business Week* aptly calls it, has grown so spectacularly in an attempt to keep the wolf from the door that another further acceleration in the growth of debt threatens to aggravate any possibly impending crash of the already excessively unstable financial house of cards; this has made worried bankers even more prudent and has reinforced economic conservatism. A major world financial crash is a real possibility. It may be sparked by bankruptcy (of a company like Chrysler), debt default (of a country like Brazil or Poland), currency flight (by Arab states trying to get out of the dollar), or a political event (revolution or war in the Middle East, etc.), or some combination of these. Technically, it is possible to ward off such a crash by rescheduling debts by mutual agreement, but it may be politically impossible to come to a quick enough agreement on who is to bear the economic cost of such an emergency bailing-out operation to prevent a crash that could spread through the entire world financial and economic system like a chain reaction.

The previously available financial and institutional resources for use against the spread of recession, such as the development of speculative Euro- and Asian currency markets, and to counteract them the introduction of flexible exchange rates and international economic coordination through economic summit conferences and the like, have already been substantially exhausted or have failed outright. Internationally, moreover, the safety valve or net that the socialist and OPEC countries offered capital through increased demand for Western exports is already significantly exhausted and much less likely to be available during this new recession. After their last expansion, and because of their limited capacity to pay, these economies have already had to restrict imports and are not likely to come to the rescue of Western capital again as they did after 1973. Thus, there would seem to be significant limits to consumer, investment, and export demand during this new recession. Thus increased military spending (and possibly other state-financed capital expenditures to develop new sources of energy, for instance) are the only other sources of additional demand. The Iran and Afghan crises should be regarded more as justifications of than causes for such expenditures.

Another manifestation and consequence—indeed, an essential part—of this process of deepening crisis through successive recessions has been the attempt to reduce costs of production through austerity policies and cuts in welfare, which have resulted in increased unemployment. Moreover, it can be demonstrated that in most industrial capitalist countries there has been a deliberate unemployment policy. Past recessions or the present one are not due to government policy "made in Washington," as Paul Samuelson said about the recession that started in 1979. The recessions are an essential part of the crisis of accumulation, which is an integral aspect of uneven capitalist dvelopment. But these recessions are demonstrably further promoted by the policies made not only in Washington, but also in London and Bonn, Paris and Tokyo, and elsewhere. World capitalist political leaders, such as U.S. President Carter (who was elected on a "fight unemployment" platform but predictably soon switched to making "inflation the public enemy number one"), Prime Minister Raymond Barre (France's best-known economist!), Labour ministers Callaghan and Healey, followed by their Conservative successors Thatcher and Howe in Britain, and many others like them elsewhere have repeatedly declared that they would prefer to pursue conservative deflationary monetary, fiscal, and other economic policies to combat inflation, even at the cost of growing industrial shutdowns (as in the French steel mills, whose workers reacted vociferously) and rising unemployment.

The same argument is advanced everywhere: we need to combat and hold down inflation because it hurts all of us at home equally (although inflation characteristically reduces real income from work and raises the real values of property) and particularly because inflation at home would price us out of the world market, cut our export capacity, and therefore create unemployment. The principal cause of inflation supposedly is high public spending and high wage demands (although wage costs are a small and declining component of selling prices, and the evidence shows that prices are pushed up by the attempt to protect profits in monopolized industry). These same arguments are used everywhere to defend the imposition of austerity policies and to demand political restraint in public spending (except for defense and other business expenditures, of course) and in "responsible" union wage demands, which are to be kept below the rate of inflation (both of which result in a decline of real wages and income, especially at the lowest end of the income scale). In addition, however, to resting on very doubtful scientific grounds domestically (as suggested in the parentheses above), these arguments suffer from the logical fallacy of composition: when everybody pursues the same policy (as when everybody gets up on their toes to improve or maintain their view of a passing parade), then nobody finds their relative cost and export position (or vantage point) improved by their efforts; but everybody ends up with lower wages (or comfort). The analogy, however, only goes so far: diminished comfort may be an entirely unintended consequence of crowd behavior, but lower wages definitely are not unintended consequences of herding people against "public enemy number one: inflation." Indeed, there is reason to believe that this lower wage objective and consequence is the principal economic purpose of the political slogan to fight inflation (which is felt by everybody) at the cost of unemployment (which only hits some people directly but indirectly immediately weakens labor's power everywhere to defend its wage level and working conditions). In view of these official pronouncements, theories, and policies, it should come as no surprise that the world capitalist press has blithely summarized them in plain English by saying "the world needs a recession" (*New York Times,* May 3, 1979).

Austerity policies have been imposed in each and every one of the major and minor capitalist economies in an attempt to get workers to tighten their belts. This attempt has been more successful in some places and less successful in others. Certainly in the United States and in Britain real wages have gone down. In other industrial economies there is some evidence that wage rates have gone down and some that they have not. But if we refer not to wage rates, but to the mass of real wages paid out after we consider the increase in unemployment of those who receive no wages at all, then real wage receipts have fallen since 1973. At the same time, there has been a concerted capitalist worldwide cut in welfare. The motto in the capitalist world today is to shift from "unproductive" to "productive" expenditures, of course including armaments, and welfare: farewell. Another major attempt to cut costs of production is to change the way people work by reorganizing the work processes on the shop floor and in the office. In general, the new work processes involve the speed-up of work and the deskilling of the worker.

All of these policies have so far been implemented wherever possible, and certainly in most parts of the Western world, through social-democratic governments and often with the support of Labour and Communist parties, as in Britain, Italy, and Spain. Austerity and incomes policies are also implemented in many places with the direct collaboration of labor unions, including even Communist unions as in Italy, who call on their members to tighten their belts. The argument is to pursue a sort of lesser evil policy, according to which it is better to tighten belts voluntarily than to be obliged to do so by some alternative right wing or, as the Communists in Italy would say, fascist government. In some, indeed many, places this union and Communist policy has led to some considerable militancy on the shop floor and revolt of the mass base. This revolt has been visible most particularly in Italy and in Britain, where workers have rejected the social contract and collaboration with the government austerity policy, which the union leadership had so far implemented. (The Spanish Communist Party and its unions suddenly decided to oppose the austerity policy there as well, but to what extent?) In Britain this very considerable militancy on and off the shop floor has led the newly elected Conservative government to the very explicit determination to try to put a tight rein on labor mobilization, the unions, and their power through all kinds of legal action against picketing and other union organization and through explicit policies to increase and use unemployment—2 million in 1980 and 3 million in 1982—to discipline labor.

A significant increase in unemployment makes militant union action for higher wages, or even to maintain real wages, increasingly difficult. Indeed, before—and if—capital is to recover "adequate" levels of profit and to launch a renewed investment drive that could bring capitalism out of its present crisis of accumulation and into a new period of expansion, not only will capitalism have to have a new technological base, but both the profitable introduction of new technology and such investment will have to be based on another major political defeat of labor as between the 1920s and 1940s.

These circumstances have led to very marked shifts to the right of the political center of gravity in most industrialized countries. In the United States, Carter shifted to the right after his election in 1976 and defeated the bid for the Democratic nomination in 1980 by Kennedy and his Keynesian program before he himself was defeated in the 1980 election by the far-right Republican Ronald Reagan. Partly as a result of the growing influence of the religious ultra-right, most of the liberal Democratic senators were also defeated in the same election and replaced by right-wing Republicans with whose help their party gained control of the Senate and its crucial committee chairmanships. In Britain the election of Margaret Thatcher—as she rightly pointed out—with significant support from labor voters who were disillusioned by the Labour Party's antilabor program launched the most concerted implementation of dogmatic monetarist and supply-side economic policies, which decimated social welfare programs and even undermined British industry. Conservative prime ministers Fraser in Australia and Muldoon in New Zealand are pursuing similar policies, while in Canada the Liberal Pierre Trudeau reversed the Conservative challenge only to invoke increasingly conservative measures himself. In West Germany similarly, the Social Democratic government of Helmut Schmidt turned back the conservative challenge of Franz Josef Strauss but itself promotes increasingly conservative economic and political policies with its liberal coalition partners. In France, President Giscard d'Estaing and his Prime Minister Raymond Barre pursued antilabor and especially anti-immigrant labor measures at home and outright colonialist policies abroad. The Socialist Party President Mitterand, elected in 1981, encountered one domestic and international obstacle after another to implementing his more progressive Keynesian economic program. In Scandinavia, the two generational rule of social-democratic parties has ended or is threatened by the right. In Japan, there has been a marked shift to the right and accelerating preparations for rearmament at the national level while Socialists and Communists have been all but eliminated from municipal and regional governments. The marked shifts to the right are not only manifest on this political level but in a whole variety of other fields, such as education (as a counteroffensive against the progressive measures of the 1960s), health, immigration, and race and sexual relations (against women's lib.), and on the ideological level in general, where the "new right" is advancing by leaps and bounds in most industrial capitalist countries.

The American dream of bigger and better and continuous prosperity is finished in the United States and elsewhere in the West. In his July 15, 1979, speech on the crisis of confidence, President Carter said that the vast majority of Americans think the next five years will be worse than the last five.

Carter's appraisal is quite realistic, but he might have added that the last five years had already been worse than the previous twenty-five. This crisis of confidence confronts the political right, left, and center with a growing ideology crisis of what to offer. The same Carter speech is itself a manifestation of complete ideological bankruptcy. The only universal agreement in the commentary on Carter's speech was that he offered absolutely no solution to the crisis of confidence (which reflects the decline of U.S. economic and political—in a word, imperialist—power), or even to the energy crisis which he said is a subproduct of this crisis of confidence. This lack of confidence also had the result of getting Carter voted out of office.

The economic crisis has also brought on a crisis in economics, which in the words of *Business Week* has been brought to complete "bankruptcy" as a source of economic forecasting, analysis, or policy. On the one hand, this bankruptcy of economics manifests itself most visibly in the face of simultaneous unemployment or stagnation and inflation—dubbed "stagflation," or in 1975 even "slumpflation"—in every Western capitalist country. On the other hand, growth, inflation, and exchange rates, etc. differ and fluctuate from one country to the next and repeatedly checkmate all attempts to analyze, let alone to regulate, the international monetary and economic system. The periodic "economic summits" held in France, Puerto Rico, London, Bonn, Tokyo, Venice, and Ottawa among the leaders of the principal Western industrial powers are no more than the open admission of this failure of international economic coordination—and even analysis—which is reminiscent of the complete failure of the World Economic Conference held in London in 1931 during the last Great Depression.

The "theoretical" problem is that Keynesian economic theory and policy only offers deflationary remedies for inflation or reflationary ones for unemployment. Keynesianism only offers the same two contradictory answers, in effect no remedy at all, to simultaneous unemployment and inflation. The essential reason for this theoretical and political failure of Keynesianism is that it is based on the assumption of competition while the increasingly monopolized structure of the economy generates simultaneous inflation and unemployment. Moreover,

Keynesian theory and policy are essentially limited to the national economies in which states can wield substantial regulatory influence, or to an international one in which one state, such as the United States after World War II, can have overriding influence. But the problem is that the world capitalist crisis is international and that no single national state (since the relative decline of U.S. power), nor any supranational institutions (which are useless in the face of the speculative private banking Eurocurrency market and nationalist state economic policies), can stabilize the world economy. Thus, as Arrighi argues, the "anarchy" of the market becomes dominant again. It is ironic that Keynesianism was born during the Depression to combat depression, but that it became universally accepted and "successful" only during—and because of—the postwar expansion, when the United States reigned supreme. At the first sign of renewed world recession, Keynesianism has proved itself to be a snare and a delusion that has gone into bankruptcy.

The underlying problem seems to be that Keynesian demand theory and demand management may be appropriate for the period of expansion at the end of and after a contraction, when adequate effective demand is needed to fuel that expansion. But in the early phases of a major economic contraction, such as that of the interwar period and the present, the primary exigencies of capital are not increasing effective demand but reducing supply costs of production in order to protect and revive profits and to stimulate new investment in and through more cost-effective production processes. Therefore, not Keynesian demand management but "supply-side" economics, which stresses the cost and productivity of labor especially, becomes the order of the day. The concomitant bankruptcy of Keynesianism and of "post-Keynesian synthesis" (with neoclassical economics) is also the theoretical reason for the literally reactionary exhumation of the simplistic neoclassical and monetarist economic theory of the 1920s. This revival of old theory is highlighted by the award of Nobel prizes in economics to Friedrich von Hayek, whose theoretical work was done before the Great Depression, and Milton Friedman, whose lone voice echoed in the desert until the new world economic crisis put his unpopular and antipopulist theories on the agenda of business board rooms and government cabinet rooms in one capitalist country after another. The real reason for the recent recourse to fifty-year-old theories is that capital now wants them to legitimize its attack on the welfare state and on "unproductive" expenditures on social services, which capital claims to need for "productive" investment in industry, including armaments.

Keynesian theory and its successful application through expansionary government fiscal and welfare policies in the West have provided the economic basis of the historically exceptional spread of social democracy in the West since World War II. The bankruptcy of Keynesianism therefore threatens to pull the economic rug out from under the viability of social-democratic policies and thus poses a serious threat to political democracy itself. Social-democratic, as well as Communist and other left, political parties and regimes can no longer offer viable social-economic programs or credible political-economic promises. Thus the onset of economic crisis with low and sometimes negative growth rates, permanent inflation, and structural unemployment, and the reinstatement of the outworn economic theories and policies of the 1920s (and indeed 1890s) as emergency measures in the face of the bankruptcy of Keynesianism, as well as the drive to bid welfare farewell, have generated a serious ideological crisis in the West. Moreover, right-wing and middle-of-the-road political parties can no longer plausibly offer a fundamental challenge to the former, lest the political center of gravity shift even further to the right or toward fascism in response. Thus, throughout the political spectrum in the West everybody's best offer is the lesser evil. In other words, a game of musical chairs develops in which every political party and faction rushes to sit in the just vacated chair to the right (in the United States, under the leadership of the populist President Carter, the Democratic administration pursued an orthodox conservative Republican economic program, which obliged the Republican Party to scramble around in search of other economic policies to differentiate itself from the Democrats). A few parties violate the rules of the game by moving two or three seats to the right at one jump, sowing confusion and making those who shift right more slowly appear to be almost radically left by comparison. But offering and choosing the lesser evil by moving to the next political chair on the right can only be a stopgap measure in the face of deepening crisis until some political force(s) find some new "positive"-sounding ideology with which to legitimate their so far retrograde and increasingly reactionary crisis policies. So far, the new-right ideology sounds libertarian and supports "monetarist" and "supply-side" economic policies in a "free market." But what will happen when these policies fail to deliver their promised economic and political fruits? The probabilities are growing that the next economic remedies to be proposed for the crisis will include wage and price and possibly income controls and state investment planning. Then 1984 may become not only an important election year but also a significant ideological and political model.[3]

CRISIS IN THE THIRD WORLD

In the Third World, "development" and "modernization" theory have proven inappropriate in a world in which the gap between rich and poor is growing by leaps and bounds and even the number of poor and the depth of their poverty is increasing. The failures of these theories and models have now been publicly recognized by their most authorized spokes-men, like Leontief (1977) for the United Nations, World Bank President McNamara (1977), and former U.S. Secretary of State Henry Kissinger (in his interview on SALT and Iran in *The Economist*, February 3 and 10, 1979).

In his 1977 address to the Board of Governors of the World Bank, President McNamara soberly observed:

Development, despite all the efforts of the past twenty-five years, has failed to close the gap in per capita incomes between developed and developing countries. . . . The proposition is true. But the conclusion to be drawn from it is not that development efforts have failed, but rather that "closing the gap" was never a realistic objective in the first place. . . . It was simply not a feasible goal. Nor is it one today. . . . Even if developing countries manage to double their per capita growth rate, while the industrial world maintains its historical growth, it will take nearly a century to close the absolute income gap between them. Among the fastest growing developing countries, only seven would be able to close the gap within 100 years, and only another nine within 1,000 years.

Since the 1973–75 recession in the developed capitalist countries, their growth rate has declined, however; and the growth rate of the nonoil-exporting (under)developing countries in the Third World has been cut in half.

For the world's poor, the past has been dismal and future prospects are dim. The *World Development Report 1978* of the World Bank observes, beginning on its first page:

The past quarter century has seen great progress in developing countries. . . . But much remains to be accomplished. Most countries have not yet completed the transition to modern economies and societies, and their growth is hindered by a variety of domestic and international factors. Moreover, about 800 million people still live in absolute poverty. These people are living at the very margin of existence—with inadequate shelter, education, and health care. . . . Many of these people have experienced no improvement in their living standards; and in countries where economic growth has been slow, the living standards of the poor may even have deteriorated.

With the deepening world economic crisis, the poorest countries in the Third World, and the poorest third or more of the people in even the richest countries in the Third World, have been getting increasingly poorer and marginalized from the economic and social benefits of the "development" process. Massive famines, caused far more by profit and poverty than by physical shortages of food, are almost certain to stalk many parts of the Third World during the 1980s.

Even in the most "successful" and "model" Third World countries, as recent events in Iran and the end of the miracles in Brazil and South Korea suggest, one economic "miracle" and "take-off" into development after another turns out to be a snare and a delusion really based on ruthless exploitation, cruel oppression, and/or the marginalization of the majority of the population from "development." This experience, which is only sharpened by the present crisis, has now raised the most serious doubts about the very concept of "development" as a progressive, integral, and integrating social process in most of the "Third" World, first called backward, poor, or colonial and then, through successive euphemisms, undeveloped, underdeveloped, developing, new, emerging, and less-developed countries (LDCs). At the same time, though structural impediments to development and dependence certainly are and remain real in the Third World, the usefulness of structuralist, dependence, and new dependence theories of underdevelopment as guides to policy seems to have been undermined by the world crisis of the 1970s. The original sin, inherited from a view of the world divided into parts, or at least the Achilles heel of these conceptions of dependence (or these dependent conceptions), has always been the implicit and sometimes explicit notion of some sort of "independent" alternative for the Third World. This theoretical alternative never existed in fact, certainly not on the "noncapitalist" path—which led nowhere during the 1960s and 1970s in Egypt, Algeria, Ghana, Mali, Tanzania, Iraq, Syria, Somalia, and most importantly in India—and now apparently not even through "socialist" revolutions as we have known them. The new crisis of real world development now renders our partial development and parochial dependence theories, as well as their related apparent policy solutions, invalid and inapplicable.

The recent call for national and/or collective "self-reliance" (but without autarchy) within a capitalist "New International Economic Order" appears to be the consequence of ideological desperation and the desperate appeal to ideology. For instance, Angola's economic support is still largely derived from the payments of foreign exchange that the U.S. Gulf Oil Company makes for petroleum produced in Cabinda under the protection of troops from Cuba. In the meantime, with regard to the model of self-reliance in Africa, *Business Week* (December 25, 1978) reports, "Tanzania: An economy on the brink of collapse," the *International Herald Tribune* (May 7, 1979) headlines, "Amid Economic Difficulties, Tanzania Seen Improving

Ties to U.S. [and] Is Taking a New Look at Western Finance and Expertise," and the Corporate Assessment of Investment Potential in Sub-Saharan Africa by *Business International* (January 1979) places Tanzania in sixth place "in descending order of investment interest [among] countries with the greatest investment potential, 1978–1988." No wonder that Tanzanian President Nyerere commemorated the tenth anniversary of his proclamation of the goal of socialist self-reliance, or *ujamaa,* in the Arusha Declaration by soberly observing that "Tanzania is certainly neither socialist nor self-reliant. . . . Our nation is still economically dependent. . . . [The goal of socialism] is not even in sight" (*International Herald Tribune,* April 21, 1977). The model of delinking without a prior socialist revolution was largely a failure, even before the pressures increased as in recent years for further integration or relinking even of socialist economies. Samir Amin's expressed optimism about delinking and self-reliance appears short on realism.[4]

The Third World has long been, and for the foreseeable future will remain, an important part of the world capitalist system. Indeed, unless working-class resistance in the industrialized West and the Third World South (and in the "socialist" East as well?) can stop the moves of capital toward a new international division of labor, the Third World is destined to play a major role in the attempt of capital in the world capitalist economy to stem and reverse the tide of the growing economic crisis. In the first place, since the Third World is an integral part of the capitalist world, the crisis is immediately transmitted from the center to the Third World through growing balance of payment deficits. As demand in the industrialized countries declined or grew more slowly, prices for exported raw materials other than petroleum did the same. At the same time, the vast world inflation in the industrialized economies increased prices of manufactured commodities imported by the Third World. Therefore, the terms of trade have been shifting again against the underdeveloped countries during this crisis (despite a temporary raw materials price boom in 1973–74, which was completely reversed again after 1974), and the nonpetroleum-exporting underdeveloped Third World countries have faced increasingly serious balance of payments problems and a mushrooming foreign debt. Moreover, it is not accidental or incidental that from 1974 to 1978 the OPEC surplus was more or less equivalent to the increase in the balance of payments deficit of the Third World, suggesting that most of the increases in the prices of petroleum since 1973 have ultimately been borne by the Third World.

A significant portion of the OPEC surplus has been recycled through the banks in the metropolitan imperialist countries to the Third World to cover their balance of payments deficits through private loans with increasingly onerous conditions and costs. Their growing debt, in turn, is then used increasingly as a political instrument to impose austerity and superausterity policies in the Third World. This blackmail through the renegotiation and extension of the debt has received many newspaper headlines in the cases of Turkey, Peru, Zaire, and Jamaica, but it has also become standard International Monetary Fund (IMF) and private banking operating procedure elsewhere throughout the Third World. As these countries' foreign debt increases, they have to get the debt refinanced, both through private banks and through official loans. The IMF then goes and says if the government does not devalue the currency to make exports and foreign investment cheaper, lower wages, cut the government budget, especially for welfare expenditures, and take other antipopular measures, and if it does not throw out Minister A and replace him with Minister B who is more likely to institute the IMF-supported policies, then the country will not get the IMF certificate of good behavior and without it neither official loans nor loans from private banks will be forthcoming. This political-economic club has been used to beat governments into shape to adopt policies of superausterity throughout the Third World. However, the same thing has also happened in Portugal and Great Britain. When the IMF, led by the United States, offered Britain a $3.9 billion loan in 1976, it gave Britain virtually the same treatment as had previously been reserved for Banana Republics and the like—perhaps this is an indication that Britain is underdeveloping into a sort of pseudo-Third World country. Again, however, just as unemployment and recession are not simply or even primarily due to government policy decisions, so are superausterity measures in the Third World not simply the result of pressure from the industrialized capitalist countries through the International Monetary Fund. These external political pressures are simply reinforcing tendencies that have another much broader economic base in the capitalist attempt to maintain or revive the rate of profit by producing at lower costs in the Third World (and also in the socialist countries) with national political support for these repressive measures in the same.

Costs of production are reduced particularly by moving labor-intensive industries, such as textiles and the production of certain kinds of electronic equipment, as well as some very capital-intensive Western crisis industries, such as steel, shipbuilding, automobiles, and petrochemicals, to the Third World. It is perhaps symbolic that the Volkswagen Beetle is no longer produced in Germany and is now made in Mexico for export to other parts of the world. From the point of view of the world capitalist economy, this is a transfer of part of industrial production from high- to low-cost areas. From the point of view of the Third World, this move represents a policy of export promotion, particularly of so-called nontraditional industrial exports. Third World manufacturing export promotion has two seemingly different origins. On the one hand, the economies that had advanced most in the process of import substitution, like India, Brazil, and Mexico, have turned to export some of their manufactures, from textiles to automobiles, some produced by multinational firms, which began as import substitutes. On the other hand, particularly foreign capital went to other Third World countries to set up manufacturing facilities to produce from the very beginning for the export rather than for the domestic market. This movement started in the 1960s with Mexico (which combined both kinds of industry but in different regions) on the border with the United States and in South Korea, Taiwan, Hong Kong, and Singapore. In the 1970s it spread to Malaysia, the Philippines, and increasingly through India, Pakistan, Sri Lanka, Egypt, Tunisia, Morocco, the Ivory Coast, and to virtually every country that borders on the Caribbean. These economies offer cheap labor, and they compete among one another with state subsidies to provide plant facilities, electricity, transportation, tax relief, and every other kind of incentive for foreign capital to come to produce there for the world market. In the case of Chile, the military junta went so far as to offer to pay part of the otherwise starvation wages for foreign capital to keep its cost down.

In order for these countries to provide low wages and indeed competitively to reduce the wages from one country to another as each tries to offer more favorable conditions to international capital, they require political repression, the destruction of labor unions, and/or the prohibition of strikes and other union activity, the systematic imprisonment, torture, and/or assassination of labor and other political leaders, and in general the imposition of emergency rule, martial law, and military government in one Third World country after another. Indeed, the whole state apparatus has to be adapted to this Third World role in the new international division of labor.

This repressive movement has swept systematically through Asia, Africa, and Latin America in the course of the 1970s and demonstrably is not simply due to some kind of autonomous political force to combat Communism (which has become a rather doubtful policy anyway at a time when even the United States is allied with socialist China, which collaborates with these repressive regimes). Demonstrably, this repressive political policy has very clear economic purposes and functions to make these economies more competitive on the world market by lowering wages and to suppress those elements of the local bourgeoisie who are tied to the internal market. This sector of the bourgeoisie pressured for mild restrictions on the operations of multinational corporations in a number of Third World countries during the late 1960s and early 1970s. Since then, however, these restrictions have increasingly been removed again, and one government after another is falling over itself to offer favorable conditions to international capital.

The motto now is to work for the world market rather than for the internal market. Effective demand on the national market is not, and is not intended to be, the source of demand for national production—demand on the world market is, and is intended to be, the source of market demand. Therefore, there is no reason to raise the wages of the direct producers, because they are not destined to purchase the goods that they produce. Instead, the goods are supposed to be purchased on the world market far away. An important exception is the small local market of the high-income receivers, which is supposed to expand. Thus, there is a polarization of income not only between developed and underdevelopd countries on the global level, but also on the national level within the underdeveloped countries, with the poor getting poorer, both relatively and often absolutely, and the rich getting richer. In some cases, such as in Brazil until 1974 but less so since then, the attempt to develop a high-income market for part of local industry has been very successful. However, in Brazil, as elsewhere in the Third World, this "development model" is based on the depression of the wage rate (which as a consequence has been cut by about half in Brazil, Uruguay, Argentina, and Chile, and is increasingly being forced down in Peru and elsewhere), and the forced marginalization and unemployment of labor (which has already increased vastly around the Third World and continues to do so). Both of these processes are rapidly increasing the immiserization of the masses and the polarization of society in the Third World. Moreover, since in general the internal market is being restrained and restricted, the sector of the bourgeoisie that depends on the internal market, as in Chile and Argentina, also has to be repressed. Therefore, big capital must institute a military government that will repress not only labor but even a sector of the bourgeoisie and of the petty bourgeoisie. The governing alliance is between the sector of local capital allied with international capital and their military and other political executors. This arrangement involves a very substantial reorganization of the state in the Third World and often its militarization so that the Third World can more effectively participate in the international division of labor in the interests of capital facing an economic crisis in the imperialist countries and its state monopoly capital allies in the Third World itself. Economic competition for resources and about shares in the changing international division of labor during the crisis, and political conflict about how to participate or not, also generate increasing pressures for military conflicts in, between, and among Third World countries.

Since the late 1970s, there appears to have been a reversal of this tendency toward military coups, emergency rule, martial law, etc. There have been elections in India and Sri Lanka, pseudo-elections in Bangladesh and the Philippines, elections in Ghana and Nigeria, elections or their announcement in various parts of Latin America, and some perhaps significant liberalization in the military regime in Brazil. Some people attribute these developments to President Carter's human rights policy, though it is a bit difficult to sustain the efficacy of his human rights policy when in quite a few crucial cases it either was absent or was restrained in the higher national interests. Other people attribute the liberalization to increasing mass mobilization in many parts of the Third World. Other analysts attribute these apparent changes to a supposed failure of the new policy of export promotion and—certainly according to many Brazilians—to the renewed and prospective importance of a policy of import substitution and the widening of the internal market. However, at this time any such redirection of the Third World economies generally is hardly observable. Such a renewed import substitution in the Third World would be objectively aided and abetted by a far-reaching protectionist drive and/or the substantial breakdown of the system of international trade and finance elsewhere in the world. As the world economic crisis deepens, this eventuality is admittedly a distinct possibility; but so far it has not come to pass. In the Third World, progressive import substitution of consumer goods—though less so of capital goods produced for the export market—would require a relatively more equal distribution of income and a politically more benign regime to permit or reflect a broader coalition or alliance of class sectors. In other words, these people argue that the dark days of the mid-1970s are over and that we are again facing the prospect of a re-democratization, or at least of limited democracy, in many parts of the Third World. Even this measure of democracy would offer better conditions for popular mobilization and for the continuation or acceleration of national liberation movements and of socialist revolutions in one country after another in the Third World.

On the other hand, it may also be argued with considerable
evidence that these recent developments do not represent the
reversal of the emerging new model of economic integration of
the Third World in the international division of labor in response to the development of the world crisis, but that this
apparent re-democratization is simply the institutionalization
of this new model of economic growth based on export promotion. It was necessary to have very severe political repression
as a midwife to institute this new model; but once the model is
in place and more or less working, it is possible to ease off a bit
on the political repression. Then, indeed, it is not only possible, but it becomes politically necessary and desirable to get a
wider social base for the political regime and to institute a kind
of limited political democracy by handing over the government from military to civilian rule. But these political modifications would not be made in order to overturn the present
economic order and again to promote import substitution,
let alone so-called noncapitalist growth or some varieties of
"socialism." Instead, this supposed re-democratization would
be to maintain and to institutionalize the new insertion of the
Third World in the international division of labor as low-wage
producers during the present world economic crisis. If we look
realistically at what is happening in Asia, Africa, and Latin
America, there is very considerable economic and political
evidence for this latter explanation of what is politically going
on today in the Third World.

A political counterpart of this economic alternative is a
renewed populist alliance of labor and other popular forces
and parties with some bourgeois ones. This alliance would
press for the amelioration of politically repressive regimes and
their gradual replacement by formally or superficially more
democratic but essentially technocratic ones to implement the
same fundamentally economically exclusivist and antipopular
economic policy. In the pursuit of such unholy alliances around
the Third World, it now seems opportune(ist) to resurrect all
kinds of bygone politicians or even their ghosts. These politicians did not have left-wing support in their heyday, when
they did not pursue very progressive policies, but they now
receive such support from the left to implement policies that

are far more rightist than their previous ones. Now, however, these rightist policies appear as the lesser evil compared to the recent often military governments and policies. Therefore, for lack of better alternatives the opposition, including the left, is now rallying behind bygone civilian political figures like Frei in Chile, Siles Suarez in Bolivia, Belaunde in Peru, Awolowo and Azikwe in Nigeria, Aquino in the Philippines, Pramaj in Thailand, Indira Ghandi in India, and even the ghost of Bhutto in Pakistan to lead "progressive" movements that are likely to maintain the essentials of the status quo and certainly will not offer any real development alternatives.

To the extent that these policies and politicians are a realistic political alternative around the Third World, orthodox development theory and ideology, as well as progressive dependence or even (not as revolutionary as hoped) new dependence theory—not to mention the Chinese "three worlds" theory and the Soviet supposedly "noncapitalist" third way to national liberation, democracy, and varieties of socialism—are all completely bankrupt. Under these circumstances, today none of these theories and ideologies can offer any realistic policy alternatives and practical political economic guidelines for the pursuit of economic development or national liberation, let alone of socialist construction. Independent national development in the Third World has proved to be a snare and a delusion; and self-reliance, collective or otherwise, is a myth that is supposed to hide this sad fact of life in the world capitalist system. These political compromises of the avowedly revolutionary socialist and particularly the Communist Party left around the Third World are another measure of the ideological crisis of the left in the face of the present world crisis.

Therefore, as the world economic crisis generates further political stress in the Third World, new populist movements increasingly based on nationalism and religion are likely to emerge. However, they are less likely to lead to far-reaching delinking from the world capitalist system and still less to what in the past would have been recognized as socialism or even as the transition thereto. At the same time, previously progressive regimes seem likely to revert increasingly to conservative and even reactionary ones, both by attrition and by coup d'état. Extremely authoritarian regimes like those of the 1970s are likely to persist, even if some give themselves a more democratic appearing makeup or facelift; and they are likely to spread again through the 1980s, especially as economic crisis leads to further political repression. Both local and global political economic conflict will increasingly transcend the borders of states and generate more and more warfare in the Third World, as states compete with each other for resources and markets and some political regimes seek to destabilize, undermine, and overthrow others in neighboring countries and elsewhere. Despite, indeed because of, insistent appeals to ideology in support of these political forces and movements, ideological confusion will spread and open the way to political power by more and more charismatic populist but antipopular ideological charlatans.

CRISIS IN THE EAST AND SOCIALISM

With regard to socialist countries elsewhere, the Stalinist theories of historical progression by inevitable stages through feudalism, capitalism, socialism, and communism; the transitional existence of two world markets, one capitalist and the other socialist; and the post-Stalin Soviet amendment proposing a "noncapitalist path" in the transition to socialism have certainly been relegated to the dustbin of history by experience. Khrushchev's hope of "burying" the West has itself been buried, and the Soviet Union is trying to compensate for its comparative economic and political/ideological weakness (which marks the "popular democracies" of Eastern Europe even more) through increasing military strength (which threatens not only its potential enemies in the West but also its supposed allies in the East). The Maoist theory and praxis of "new democracy," "walking on two legs," "cultural revolution," and "three worlds" (two superpowers, the other industrialized countries, and the Third World including China) has been most seriously challenged by events inside and outside China and has recently been denounced even by the erstwhile most faithful Albanian Workers Party. The world-embracing, albeit not universal, sympathy with the Cuban guerrilla and popular movements, Korean *juche* self-reliance, and Vietnamese national liberation as models have given way to increasingly searching critiques and heartfelt doubts among many of their previously enthusiastic supporters around the world. Trotskyist and new left movements of many varieties have left a trail of disillusioned or disaffected militants to be reintegrated into the establishment, since the latter seemed to tremble in one country after another in 1968 and its aftermath. Now, after the largely self-inflicted electoral defeats of the Communist parties in France, Spain, and Italy (as well as in Japan on the municipal level), observers from left to right and including even *Business International* (beginning with foresight already in 1977) and the U.S. press, announce: "Last Days of Eurocommunism?" (*International Herald Tribune*, April 28, 1979), and "the decline, though perhaps not the demise, of 'Eurocommunism' as a major force threatening or promising (take your choice)" (*Washington Post*, May 12, 1979). They are writing "Eurocommunism" off as a non-starter, which was neither "Euro" nor "communist" while it lasted (and obliging the secretary-general of the French Communist Party, George Marchais, to issue "denials" of Eurocommunism's demise at the May 1979 party congress that celebrated its postmortem of the left alliance with the Socialists and followed Marchais' lead in another about-turn in the direction of Moscow).

In the meantime, Deng Ziaoping's theatrics on his 1979 tour of the United States to get Western technology and credits for the drive to make China a world industrial power by the year 2000, and the resignation of Deng and Chairman Hua at the 1980 Congress to make way for a clean sweep by Deng's modernization team, only highlight Chinese developments over the last decade. Since the defeat of the Cultural Revolution and the downfall of Lin Biao in 1971 (apparently for favoring a rapprochement with the Soviet Union instead of with the United States), the way was cleared for Zhou Enlai's "conciliatory" line of ping-pong diplomacy, the invitation to Nixon to visit China, the launching of the four (industry, agriculture, technology, and defense) modernization programs—no longer so much through self-reliance as with foreign aid and trade (which more than quadrupled in the 1970s and 85 percent of which is with capitalist countries), the rehabilitation of Liu Shaoqi, and reinstatement of the capitalist roader victims of the Cultural Revolution, led by Deng Ziaoping. Now he is taking China on a "great leap backward" to 1957, that is, to the year before the Great Leap Forward, in an attempt to get a better running start to leap to great power status by the twenty-first century.

In the wake of their own economic and related political problems, the "socialist" economies of the Soviet Union and Eastern Europe are implementing a detente with the West (albeit in competition with China) to import Western technology and to pay for it with exports produced by cheap labor through thousands of bilateral production agreements with Western firms and tripartite ones involving Third World states as well. Even so, the East European and Soviet demand for Western technology is growing so rapidly that their cumulative balance of payments deficit and debt with the West has increased from $8 billion in 1972 to over $80 billion in 1981 (of which $27 billion was in Poland alone), despite the Eastern balance of payments surplus with the South, which the East uses in part to offset its deficit with the West. Moreover, as Comrade Brezhnev correctly observes, "Because of the broad economic links between capitalist and socialist countries, the ill effects of the current crisis in the West have also had an impact on the socialist world." And therefore his colleague, President of the Bulgarian State Council Tudor Zhikov, adds, "It may be hoped that the crisis in the West may come to a rapid end." The crisis continues, however, and the European socialist economies grew only half as fast as the last five-year plans called for, and in some of them output has actually declined since 1979. This was especially the case in Poland, where the economic crisis (declines of output of 2 percent in 1979, 4 percent in 1980, and 14 percent in 1981) and its mishandling by the leadership led to the Solidarity movement and martial law.

The economically widespread and politically deepgoing effects of the Western capitalist economic crisis on the socialist countries of the East lays to rest the false claim that there are two separate world markets and political systems, which was propounded by Stalin and is still accepted by some people in the East and the West. Not only is there only one—capitalist—world market, but the repercussions of the Western economic crisis in the East suggest that the same market law of value that underlies the economy of the West also extends into and operates within the socialist East, despite its partial abrogation through "socialist planning." The theoretical plans within—let alone the Comecon plans among—the socialist countries have proven increasingly unrealizable in fact, both because of the apparent survival or resurgence of a law of value within—and between—the socialist economies and because of the intrusion within—and among—them of the law of value operating on the world market, of which the socialist economies remain or increasingly reappear as an integral part.

The prospects for socialism in the West for the foreseeable future have long since receeded, as first the social-democratic parties, and now the Communist parties as well, have become not only integrated in but also defenders of the maintenance of the capitalist status quo. Now, the Eurocommunist parties in the West, for their part, not only hope the crisis will go away; they also do the best they can to help capital overcome the crisis economically by imposing austerity measures on labor, as in Spain and Italy, and to face the crisis politically by strengthening the state and its repressive power, which the Communist Party of Italy is now the first to defend and expand. Any new objective examination of reality must lead one to concur with the author of the classic study of the Soviet revolution, E. H. Carr, when he observes:

> A silent, but very powerful, consensus has been established between employers and workers on the need to maintain profits. The parties still quarrel about the division of the spoils, but are united in the desire to maximise them. . . . Eurocommunism is surely a stillborn movement, a desperate attempt to escape from reality. If you want to return to Kautsky and denounce the renegade Lenin, fair enough. But why muddy the waters by labelling yourselves communist? In hitherto accepted terminology you are right-wing social-democrats. . . . What conclusions can

one draw for our own Left in its present plight? Not very encouraging ones, I fear, since this is a profoundly counter-revolutionary period in the West, and the Left has no solid revolutionary base.[5]

One is left to wonder how and why the official pronouncements of self-styled Communist and revolutionary socialist centers, parties, and movements continue to claim that "the situation is excellent" (Peking), "socialism is advancing stronger than ever" (Moscow), and "revolutionary possibilities are around the corner," at least in Southern Europe (Trotskyists)—in the face of the domestic and foreign policies, now including repression at home and wars abroad, that mark contemporary socialist countries, Communist parties, and revolutionary movements now facing a grave crisis of Marxism that is costing the cause of socialism countless millions of supporters around the world.

The theoretical, ideological, and political dilemma of socialism today derives from, and may be summarized by, the complete abandonment both in theory and in praxis of the famous means and end of the *Communist Manifesto:* "Workers of the world unite." Both the theory and the praxis of proletarian internationalism as a means to the goal of communism have been replaced by "socialism in (my) one country." Moreover, communism itself as the end goal of social development has in practice and apparently even in theory been replaced by "socialism." Though for Marx and Engels, and still for Lenin, socialism meant no more than an unstable transitionary process or stage on the road to communism, "socialism" has been converted into an end station or steady state. Some "socialists" claim to have arrived already, and other more realistic ones (ironically called "idealists" by the former), such as Mao, only claim that their country is or was in the transition to socialism, which requires repeated and successful cultural revolutions (of which the first one in China failed). In "prerevolutionary" Chile, it was customary to talk of the transition to the transition to socialism, before the military coup violently destroyed these illusions and placed only "restricted democracy" on the agenda as the distant goal to be achieved. In a (vain?) attempt to escape a similar fate, the Eurocommunists, with the Italians at their head, therefore proposed a "historic compromise" as their goal. Of course, if "socialism" no longer means the transition to communism through proletarian internationalism, but becomes an established state in one country and a distant goal for others, it becomes endlessly debatable how you recognize such a state if you see one and how you get there if you do not. Thus, socialists become like the person who looks for his lost watch alone under the nearest street light because he claims that there he can see it quicker and better, although the watch for socialism was lost somewhere else down another road and has made the time of communism receed back into infinite darkness.

The more some "Marxist" theory that is supposed to guide and justify this "socialist" praxis is examined under the plain light of day, the more indistinguishable does this "Marxism" become from orthodox everyday bourgeois capitalist theory and praxis of "national development." It is ironic in view of the stated goals of Marxism—but perhaps not surprising in terms of its analysis—that since the state promoted the capitalist ascension of noncolonial Japan into the charmed circle of industrial powers, outside the West only the "socialist" countries have been able to achieve, or as now perhaps in the case of China realistically aspire to, participation in the world capitalist economy on a basis that is even remotely equal to that of the developed capitalist countries. None of the (under)developing capitalist Third World countries have escaped dependent capitalist underdevelopment; nor do any of them show any prospects of doing so in the foreseeable future, despite Brazilian, Korean, Iranian, or Mexican miracles or oil booms. Only some "socialist" economies can now knock on the door of, or challenge, the capitalist inner sanctum, because they were temporarily relatively isolated from the workings of the capitalist international division of labor, and that in turn—oh, double irony—was not because they wanted to be but mainly because the capitalist powers forced this isolation on them during the Cold War in reaction to the socialist transformations of domestic property, productive, and political relations, which are the other reason for their "success" (and which even the most nationalist dependent and state capitalist Third World countries like Nasser's Egypt never attempted).

The irony is, in other words, that the Soviet Union and perhaps parts of Eastern Europe, although much less so China, may be able to join the core of the capitalist world-economy precisely because they underwent or undertook socialist revolution and development. It is too early to tell whether any of these economies will also be able to displace the previous (now U.S.) leadership in the capitalist core and assume it instead, but the possibility should not be excluded for the next periodic crisis, though it seems very premature for the present one. However, the formation of a European political-economic bloc, including West and East, may be a realistic possibility even during this crisis. Thus the further and triple (and quadruple, quintuple,) irony is that—if Deng's China, Phan's Vietnam, Tito's and his successors' Yugoslavia, Kadar's Hungary, Gierek's, Kania's, and Jaruzelski's Poland, etc., and perhaps last but not least Breshnev's and/or his successor's USSR, are any guide—driven on by their own internal economic and political crises these countries do not want to use "socialism" to challenge the West in its time of crisis by beating capitalism, but by joining in as nationalist competitive partners in the capitalist world system on as nearly equal terms as possible and in the process lend the capitalists an economic, political, and thereby also ideological hand in overcoming the world crisis of capitalism.

Someone in the (East) German Democratic Republic suggested that socialists would win the race with the West as soon as they stopped running in the same direction. But can they stop? As long as they play catch as catch can instead, the socialist countries, and with them the cause of socialism in much of the world, will remain caught in a Catch 22 dilemma of being damned if they do and damned if they don't. The regimes, particularly in Eastern Europe, seem to be at a point in their development at which they are damned if they do and damned if they don't persist in their bureaucratic and elitist ways. Their bureaucratic organization was instrumental in promoting extensive economic development by mobilizing the full employment of their resources (and generating absolute surplus value?). But this same bureaucratic organization seems to militate against the passage to intensive development based on technological progress (and relative surplus value?), whose implementation is discouraged by bureaucratic rules. The bureaucracies' attempts to resolve this contradiction bureaucratically are generating political problems of legitimacy, which either erodes in the eyes of the population, as in Poland, or is threatened by wholesale de-legitimation through Soviet military intervention to forestall the possibility of a breakdown.

Significant social sectors and the cause of socialism, if not the regimes themselves, are also damned if they try to defuse their political-economic crisis by substantially increasing external economic, political, and cultural ties with the West and domestic commodification—the "profit motive" and market regulation—at home, as in Poland and Hungary, not to mention Yugoslavia. That increasingly opens the door to the return of the typically capitalist diseases of growing monopoly, inflation, and unemployment, which are already sweeping like a storm through China. Either way, the crisis of socialism at home and of its ideological appeal abroad is churning like a whirlpool that is disappearing into a black hole as the world capitalist system closes in on "socialism in one country."

It may certainly be argued that no existing "socialist" state or major socialist movement really embodies true Marxism and that pure Marxist truth is therefore not besmirched by any such adulteration. On the other hand, these "socialist" states and movements *are* real forces in the world, and if true Marxism is not embodied in these forces, then the potential forcefulness of this Marxism is open to question.

NATIONALISM VS. SOCIALISM

The spread of colonialism in the nineteenth century and then of anticolonialism in the twentieth century united, or at least allied, bourgeois nationalist and proletarian socialist causes and movements, especially in the Third World. Accordingly, both their supporters and their opponents, increasingly since World War I and preponderantly since World War II, came either to identify these movements, or at least to regard them, as natural allies that further each other's causes. Therefore, most observers and participants in the struggle for or against nationalist and socialist causes appear to have forgotten or consider insufficiently that the identity or alliance between them had not always been established in the past and need not remain so in the future. Thus, Marx, Engels, Kautsky, Bauer, Luxemburg, Lenin, and their contemporaries had engaged in an unending debate about the compatibility or conflict between bourgeois nationalism and proletarian socialism and supported the former only where and when it seemed to advance the cause of the latter. The issue under debate was where and when this might be the case and therefore which of the two movements or forces could or would use the other to advance its cause. The "voting of the war credits" by the German social democrats in 1914 and the nationalist support of proletarians for their respective bourgeoisies during World War I effectively cut through this debate, at least for Europe, and demonstrated both the real conflict between bourgeois nationalism and proletarian socialism and the greater strength of nationalism over socialism. Moreover, Lenin's support for a separate peace at Brest Litovsk and Stalin's construction of "socialism in one country" demonstrated the socialist sacrifice as well as proletarian internationalism. It may be observed with Régis Debray[6] that ever since then existing socialism everywhere in Europe, Asia, and Cuba was always born—and borne—with significant nationalist support and that the so-conceived socialist states have defended their sacred national soil with a zeal that is worthy of this (accidental?) religious terminology. In the Soviet Union, World War II is called the "Great Patriotic War," no doubt in homage to the great role that patriotism played in the popular resistance and victory, and socialist Cuba's motto, with which Fidel ends every speech, remains "Patria o Muerte, Venceremos!" The question remains as to whether the socialist or the nationalist force has been or is the more significant in those cases where they built a socialist national state together.

However, the identity or alliance of bourgeois nationalism and proletarian socialism have not been as universal, far-reaching, or deepgoing, even at their twentieth-century best, as many of their supporters and opponents thought or liked to think. Suffice it to recall the passage of Mussolini from the cause of national socialism to fascist nationalism in Italy and the national socialist ("Nazi" for short) movement of Adolf Hitler, which certainly did not further the cause of socialism, at least intentionally. Hitler did, however, make a brief alliance with Stalin's Union of Soviet Socialist Republics and after breaking it again provided the geopolitical reason for the establishment of "socialist" buffer states in Eastern Europe under the aegis of the USSR after the war. Significantly, in Eastern Europe religious nationalism and socialism have always been and remain conflicting alternatives, as the Polish-born Rosa Luxemburg had argued most strongly, and this conflict was only resolved in the uncertain favor of socialism by the Red Army, an alternative that Luxemburg had not considered, perhaps paradoxically because she was so busy combatting the Leninist and nationalist currents that after two world wars made this dubious victory of socialism over nationalism possible. The dubious and tenuous nature of this victory of socialism is now underlined by the Polish workers' strikes for independent union rights under the leadership of Lech Walesa in league with the Catholic Church and the Polish Pope.

In all other cases in which bourgeois nationalism has come into conflict with socialism or internationalism, nationalism has won out like iron against wood, as Debray also correctly observes. This victory of Soviet iron bourgeois nationalism over wooden proletarian socialism was the *leitmotiv* of Stalin's sacrifice of the socialist cause in France, Italy, Greece, Iran, and India after World War II, when as always he made the national Communist parties in these countries put the defense of the Soviet socialist national state (and therefore supposedly socialism) before the fight for socialism at home. Stalin used the Comintern and Cominform as extensions of Soviet diplomacy even to the extent of Browderism—that is, Communist support of U.S. bourgeois interests in the United States and U.S. imperialist interests in Latin America—while the United States and the Soviet Union were allied during the war and Earl Browder was secretary-general of the Communist Party-USA. Stalin only failed to impose the same policy of collaboration with the Koumintang (which led to Chang Kai-shek's suppression of the Communists in Shanghai in 1927) on the Communist Party of China in 1948–49 because under the leadership of Mao Zedong the Chinese Communist Party had become every bit as nationalist as the Chinese National-ists (or the Soviet Russian nationalists, for that matter). Of course, with the Chinese socialist nationalism at heart, Mao Zedong's Communist Party of China did not hesitate to sup-port collaborationist policies by Adit's Communist Party of Indonesia (KPI), which led to the decimation of the nonsocial-ist world's largest Communist Party and the death of an es-timated 1 million people in the 1964 military coup against Sukarno. Indeed, the Communist Party of China has unflinch-ingly continued to sacrifice socialism elsewhere to its own national foreign policy—in Algeria (coup against Ben Bella) in 1965, Pakistan vs. Bangladesh and Ceylon (JVP uprising) in 1971, Chile (support of Pinochet since 1973), Zaire and Angola (support of CIA puppets) through much of the 1970s, opposition to the progress of the revolution in Portugal after 1974, not to mention the occasional support and equally fre-quent abandonment of liberation movements throughout Southeast Asia in accord with the changing circumstances of Chinese interests. Equally significant in each of these cases (excepting Chile but including the Communist Party of Ar-gentina) is that a significant nationalist-socialist movement or Communist Party has voluntarily chosen (with Chinese or Soviet pressure or not) to collaborate with a bourgeois na-tionalist or national bourgeois movement, party, or state in preference to, and at the sacrifice of, more militantly proleta-rian socialist policies.

The most visible and often tragic sacrifice of proletarian socialism—not to mention internationalism—on the altar of nationalism, of course, has been by the states that proclaim themselves to be, or to aspire to become, socialist. Some of the most visible instances are the Sino-Soviet split, which now poses the greatest war threat; the Chinese invasion of Viet-nam and the Vietnamese invasion of Kampuchea, which have made war between "socialist" states a reality; the quick passage

of the Khmer Rouge from supposed socialism to anti-Vietna-
mese Khmer nationalism in alliance with any and all imperialist and reactionary forces in Kampuchea and then the declara-
tion that communism is bankrupt and socialism is no longer
on the agenda in this century; the escalation of the imperial
Ethiopian suppression of the socialist national movement in
Eritrea by the military "socialist" Dergue; the pursuit of
Greater Somali ambitions in league with imperialism and Arab
reaction by the previously socialist-leaning regime of Siad
Barré; the ultimatum by the revolutionary socialist Samora
Machel in Mozambique to the revolutionary socialist Robert
Mugabe of Zimbabwe, obliging the latter to collaborate with
the British and Rhodesian white state apparatuses on pain of
loosing the support which was a heavy charge on the socialist
national development of Mozambique; and the effort to safeguard Mugabe's government in Zimbabwe by greater collaboration with white power and the South African regime at the
sacrifice of land reform in Zimbabwe and support for the
popular struggle in South Africa. All these and many more
instances represent the effective sacrifice of socialist interests
to national and nationalist exigencies—and ultimately bourgeois interests. It is only realistic to suppose that this triumph
of iron nationalist or bourgeois policy over wooden socialist
rhetoric is likely to continue and to increase in the years and
indeed decades to come.[7]

If these conflicts between bourgeois nationalism and proletarian socialism, and these triumphs of the former over the
latter, have seemed exceptional or if their significance has
been underestimated it is because since World War II the
national liberation movements, the indigenous socialist movements, and the socialist states have fought a common colonialist and imperialist enemy. This simultaneous fight of nationalism, indigenous socialism, or socialist nationalism (I am reluctant to use the words "national socialism" because of their
preemption by the Nazis), and socialist national states against
the common imperialist enemy—and not the least the reactionary imperialist policy and propaganda summarized by the
U.S. Secretary of State John Foster Dulles as "those who are
not with us are against us"—produced an apparent identity of

interests, or at least an alliance in a common cause, among these three different political forces. For this reason many progressives, including this writer, found it ideologically unambiguous and politically easy to participate in and/or to support these three causes simultaneously, and often to regard them as a single or at least common cause.

Moreover, there was a degree of realism in the words of Dulles insofar as the strengthening of any of the three forces seemed to weaken imperialism and thereby also to further the fortunes of the other two opposing forces. In many cases two or all three of these political forces also strengthened each other directly through the direct collaboration or even amalgamation of their forces. Even so, this direct mutual aid was usually short-lived—reflecting the underlying conflicts of interest—and led to the renewed falling out, abandonment, "betrayal," and sacrifice of each other's interests in the cases reviewed above and many others. Moreover, this whole period of apparently harmonious honeymoon between nationalism and socialism was itself short-lived and seems to have substantially drawn to a close again already. Consideration of the objective new developments discussed below casts some doubt on the realism of the continued optimism of Wallerstein and Amin with regard to the hoped for cumulative antisystemic consequences of nationalism and socialism, separately or together.

For the foreseeable future, bourgeois capitalist nationalism and proletarian anticapitalist socialism are likely to become immediately conflicting alternatives again for three important objective reasons, each of which corresponds to one of the forces of national liberation, indigenous socialism or socialist nationalism, and socialist national states. These reasons are similar to some of the contemporary changes observed by Eric Hobsbawm.[8] In reverse but temporal order, these reasons and changes are the following: first, the Sino-Soviet dispute and then the growing conflicts among other socialist national states has disrupted the mutuality of interest among the three political forces. Each socialist national state now regards the enemy of my enemy as my friend and the friend of my enemy as my enemy, and applies this distinction to the forces of national liberation and socialism elsewhere. Therefore, alliances among the three forces can no longer be ideologically unambiguous and politically reinforcing. Instead, one socialist camp or country divisively backs some national liberation and indigenous socialist movements against (or at least as against) others as supposed puppets of the rival socialist camp. Moreover, any backing may be, and sometimes is, followed by rapid betrayal, such as in Africa, as positions in the global system of alliances switch back and forth in the service of national interests. Moreover, in the past two decades in the Third World alliances with socialist national states, the advance of indigenous socialism, and often even national liberation, have been far from mutually reinforcing or cumulative. On the contrary, particularly the first two of these have witnessed about as many reversals—in Indonesia, Ghana, Mali, Guinea, Egypt, Somalia, Chile, and elsewhere (including Vietnam for China)—on the state level and far more often at the level of indigenous political movements or parties. These frequent reversals also belie the thesis, on which many imperialists, reactionaries, and socialists strangely agree, that Soviet and/or Chinese influence and socialism have been steadily advancing in the Third World. Far from it: "The overall trend has been down . . . the Soviet Union has *lost* influence during the last two decades," as Paul Sweezy points out.[9] Despite recent successes in Africa, Central America, and the Caribbean, the world economic crisis, including that in the socialist countries, seems to offer little prospect for substantial cumulation of these and further possible successes.

Secondly, as Hobsbawm emphasizes, in contrast to the European nationalism that sought to unify national states a century ago, nationalism has recently become increasingly separatist and divisive. Of course, by definition each nationalist movement is different from the others in the nature of the case of nationalism. Therefore, it will always be argued that for some purposes it is necessary to distinguish between one national movement or one type of nationalism and another. For our analytic purposes, however, it is also important to try to detect any common contemporary influences on, and possible common features or consequences of, nationalism today and tomorrow. A major common influence is that the world

economic crisis is reducing the ability of most national economies and states to satisfy the economic necessities and aspirations of more and more people. Many of these people, therefore, turn to one form or another of nationalism to express
their discontent and to seek relief. In the major national states,
economic nationalism and protectionism are very much on
the rise again, and antiforeign jingoism is again a serious
threat. Within the larger national states of the West, East, and
South, self-styled national minority liberation movements demand ethnic and regional autonomy, if not sovereignty. In the
smaller states their very size and increasing number is producing a plethora of national state forces, each of which conflicts with that of its neighbors. In the struggle over shrinking
or more slowly growing national economic pies, both the national state and the subnational antistate nationalist movements and forces increasingly crosscut and divide the popular
socialist anticapitalist and often even anti-imperialist popular
movements and forces, rather than identifying or fusing with
them as in the heyday of national liberation and socialism
when the opportunities to increase the economic pie were
greater. Moreover, both the increasing number of such separate and separatist nationalist movements and their conflicts
with the socialist movements increase the possibilities and the
likelihood of their use as pawns in the international power
game among (no longer between) imperialist and socialist
national states. Therefore, coincidences of interest are more
apparent than real. Indeed, they are coincidences that soon
pass as alliances shift.

The third reason for increasing conflicts of interest between
national liberation, indigenous socialism, and socialist national
states is the recent change in the significance of national
liberation itself. The end of formal colonialism, which is replaced by neocolonialism, which in turn is itself undergoing
changes, has necessarily altered the tasks and policies of
national liberation. No longer can these movements be anti-
colonial, since they have mostly been successful in this policy
already. However, as Nkrumah argued and Amin insists, national independence (which moreover most countries in Latin
America have enjoyed for over 150 years) does not obviate the

continued need for national liberation, albeit under the perhaps far more difficult and certainly more lasting circumstances of neocolonialism. Moreover, we may be led to suspect
that at least part of the recent success of national liberation
movements against colonialism was due to the opposition to
old-style colonialism by the United States (and the Soviet
Union, supposedly in the service of socialism), and the need of
the colonial powers themselves to adapt to the competition
and the development of neocolonialism itself. Hobsbawm
points out that in a world of multinational corporations, the
dependence of "independent" national states is an advantage
for imperialism and the more the merrier. This advantage also
applies to the socialist national states in their own competition
on the world market.

One might think that national liberation from dependence
in an interdependent neocolonial world-economy would seem
to require socialist revolution, as I have always argued, and
should benefit from the support of the socialist states. In that
case, there would be a coincidence of interests and a common
basis for political action among these three forces. However,
the accelerated reincorporation of the socialist states themselves in the capitalist international division of labor—not the
least as beneficiaries from, if not exploiters of, labor in the
Third World—and the changing export role of the Third World
in this international division of labor occasioned by the crisis
as reviewed above have rapidly undermined the coincidence,
let alone the unity, of interests among the forces of national
liberation, indigenous socialism, and socialist states, and each
of these has accordingly changed its policies if not its nature.
National liberation has been transformed into the quest for a
negotiated settlement of different shares in the increased
exploitation of Third World labor under the guise of the demand for a New International Economic Order. Indigenous
socialist forces are waging a mostly losing battle to preserve a
portion of the social and economic rights of workers, peasants,
and the petty bourgeoisie from erosion in the best of cases and
supporting the domestically repressive and internationally aggressive regimes in the worst of cases, like the Communist
Party of Argentina, as a lesser evil for fear of still worse to

come. The socialist states have sown complete ideological confusion and are themselves fishing in the whirlpool of troubled waters among the increasing conflicts between nationalism and socialism. For all of these reasons and in each of these instances, socialism is the loser, and there seems to be no objective basis on which to offer much hope for any more socialism in the foreseeable future.

The new ideological moving forces instead are virulent nationalism as the new religion around the world and then traditional religion or religious traditionalism, where socialist ideology has failed to offer minimal socioeconomic salvation, let alone indispensable political hope. These ideologies appear as the products of the crisis—not only of socialism, of course— though their proponents promise instead to offer the way out of the crisis and to salvation. The question is, who or what are the new nationalism, the old religion, and possibly other emerging ideologies likely to save? Like socialism before them, they appear as anti-status quo forces. Their supporters claim that they will be antisystemic; Wallerstein, Amin, and many socialists hope that insofar as they are so, these forces must ultimately be pro-socialist and therefore deserving of socialist support. But, as with the socialist states, it has not been demonstrated that these nationalist and religious forces must be antisystemic, as Wallerstein and Amin argue in this volume. It is at least possible that the proponents of these forces are at least half right in offering a way out of the crisis that will indeed lead to salvation—but of capitalism, even though it may cost hundreds of millions of lives in war along the way.

Thus a number of questions present themselves about the further development and resolution of these world crises (plural) or crisis (singular) and about the theory to guide their interpretation and the ideology to influence praxis. Here and now it is only possible to pose some of these questions and in some cases to offer some tentative answers for further reflection in the near future and perhaps for resolution or reformation on hindsight in the more distant future.

The development of these crises or this crisis poses the following questions among others in technical terms for political policymakers and the public in general: Are there numerous particular crises in many societies or aspects of life, or is there a general crisis—in the sense of the definition quoted in our opening paragraph—in a single world system, as argued by Wallerstein? Are the crises or crisis recurrent, occasional, or cyclical ones, and subject to possible resolution, or does the development of crises or crisis represent a step—or even the last step—to a general crisis that spells the end of the capitalist world system? Our observations and formulations above suggest that there is a single world capitalist system, which is undergoing another in a series of long cyclical crises from which it is likely to be able to recover through far-reaching and deepgoing economic, social, political, and cultural readjustments, as Wallerstein agrees, but that this crisis and its resolution also contributes to the cumulative degeneration and, after future long cyclical crises, to the ultimate dissolution of world capitalism in the still unforeseeable future, as emphasized by Wallerstein but not yet visualized by me.

Does—and if so why—the present crisis pose the economic alternative between increasing market demand (resolution of value in Marxist terms) to expand profitability and reducing costs of production through increasing exploitation (raising surplus value in Marxist terms) to deepen profitability? Arrighi thinks not, but I find that the crisis seems to pose this alternative in such a way as to oblige capital, labor, and the state(s) to opt for the second alternative of greater exploitation with less employment and public demand before the first alternative of renewed expansion can again become a realistic possibility as a result, precisely, of the prior rationalization and exploitation. This option of—or rather imperative for—world capitalist recovery implies or requires at least temporarily increasing capitalist exploitation or extraction of surplus value through the reduction of the work force, the reorganization and speed-up of the work process at lower real wages for the remaining workers, and reduced welfare for the population in general in favor of capital and its monopolization in the industrial capitalist countries. The same resolution of the capitalist crisis also involves the relocation of some industrial processes based on the increase in superexploitation in the Third World. Does the same resolution of the world capitalist crisis of capital ac-

cumulation imply or require the accelerated (re?)incorpora-
tion of the "socialist" economies and of "feudal" OPEC economies and virgin lands in the world capitalist economy, both as
sources of additional surplus value and as sources of demand
in part to compensate the demand restrictions in the developed and "developing" sectors of the world economy? This
process seems to imply the extension or intensification of the
operation of world market forces emphasized by Arrighi (*and*
of the law of value in Marxist terms) from the center of the
world capitalist economy into the socialist economies and to
populations and spaces (in the Middle East, Amazonia, Siberia,
the polar regions, the seabed, and even outer space) that
previously were effectively beyond the frontiers of the world
capitalist system. Does this process represent an "expansion
of the internal frontiers" of capital analogous to the expansion
of the "external frontiers" in response to each of the previous
major world crises of capital accumulation? Does this progressive change from expanding to deepening capital imply further
development and/or the beginning of the end of capitalism?

Arrighi doubts that the present crisis is one of a Kondratieff-
type B phase of overaccumulation of capital; and Wallerstein
and I, who see the present that way, believe that *this* crisis
phase is likely to be successfully overcome and to lead to a new
expansion of capital before the end of the century. Therefore,
we do not see *this* crisis as the end of capitalism and can even
visualize the regeneration of world capitalist development, in
part on the strength of this crisis. In this sense, I see, for the
foreseeable future, the continued development of capitalism,
economically aided and politically abetted by the participation
and collaboration of the Third World and the "socialist" countries. But to what extent is this continued development of
capitalism also a part or even a basis of its historic degeneration and its passage through a longer crisis of transition beyond
capitalism, as discussed by Wallerstein? This social transformation is still called the transition to "socialism," by analogy to
the transition that has been foretold for the past 130-odd years.
Yet even today it is still too early to foretell the timescale of this
process of capitalist development, degeneration, and transition.

It must be too early to answer the last question posed above by Wallerstein about the time scale, if only because the rise and fall of capitalism depends in part on the social resistance to its development and the generation of contrary or alternative political forces and developments. The political process has not yet run its course, even in the resolution of the present crises or crisis, let alone in the subsequent development or degeneration of capitalism and its alternatives. However, this political process already raises a number of further questions about prospects and policy for the immediate future.

The reorganization of the capitalist world economy to cut costs as between labor and capital, industrial sectors, and political-economic regions necessarily sharpens economic competition and political conflict among capitalists and their representative states as well. Some of this increasing competition and conflict was reviewed above in the discussion of U.S.-European-Japanese, East-West, and North-South relations. These conflicts may well lead to far-reaching economic and political realignments on the East-West and North-South axes, as well as to war. Therefore, this political economic process of capitalist crisis management may also generate periods of acute danger for world capitalism and suffering for its peoples, which on the other hand may also offer still unforeseeable opportunities for popular political forces to prevent the reorganization of capitalism and to hasten its degeneration and downfall. The latter, however, will require a socialist political organization that is quantitatively far greater and qualitatively very different from what we have so far known or can as yet foresee. For the time being, on the contrary, proletarian socialist ideology and organization in the West, East, and South, as well as among them, can only raise serious doubts about the prospects for socialism in the world for the foreseeable future.

I have already suggested that the politically reactionary, conservative, and social-democratic forces in the West and South (and perhaps the East) face crises of economic theory, political ideology, and social policy for which they themselves have as yet found no resolution(s). Pre-Keynesian neoclassical and monetarist economic theory, fascist political ideology, fundamentalist and evangelical religious culture or even cult religions, and nineteenth-century liberal social policy seem to offer renewed frames of reference and points of attraction (despite their mutual contradictions) in the absence of a viable alternative to the growing unreality of the U.S.-cum-Keynesian way of life. However, new situations will eventually require new theoretical, ideological, and political propositions, and who knows what combination of extant liberal, technocrat, and corporativist doctrines, as well as yet unheard-of new ones, will win the day—if any? The resistance to capitalist rationalization and reorganization from labor, socialist, environmental, feminist, ethnic, nationalist, religious, and rejectionist forces, among others, is considerable but highly divided and very confused. Neither individually nor much less collectively have they so far been able to formulate sufficiently attractive ideological alternatives. Viable resistance, let alone realistic alternatives, from the labor and socialist oppositions to contemporary capitalist reorganization seems to be decreasing rather than increasing. Certainly social-democratic and Marxist theory and ideology, and labor, socialist, and Communist Party policy throughout the world, face severe crises of direction and of legitimacy. Alternative environmental and feminist forces are growing, but the more they grow, the more their demands seem to become compatible with the exigencies of capital and the more is their leadership co-opted by or into the political establishment.

By far the strongest and most massive social mobilization in the West, South, and East has been taking place under ethnic, nationalist, and religious banners. Many of these movements are expressions of resistance to the present capitalist and socialist orders, and to attempts at their rationalization. Ethnic, regionalist, and nationalist movements in the West, East, and South have achieved greater mass mobilization and expressions of discontent with the economic situation than any directly "economic" or "political" challenges to the status quo. Demands for home rule through autonomy or sovereignty, and nationalist, chauvinist, and jingoist appeals to support one country's economic, political, and military resistance or challenge to one or all others have been finding increasing mass support. Yet many of these movements are manipulated by the capitalist right and divide the labor left; few challenge state power per se; and none reject participation in the international division of labor of the world capitalist economic system.

Religious conviction, combined with nationalist sentiment, as in Poland, Iran, and Afghanistan, have permitted the Catholic Pope John Paul II and the Muslim Ayatollah Khomeini to mobilize millions of people to a far greater extent and degree than other ideologies and leaders, although parts of Asia, Africa, and the Caribbean have also been experiencing progressive mobilization under socialist banners. All of these movements, which are likely to spread and intensify in the coming years, are expressions of growing popular frustration with political-economic policies in response to the crisis or crises and their social consequences in the developed, underdeveloped, and socialist parts of the world system. To that extent, these movements represent antisystemic resistance to the reorganization of the world system by capital and for capital accumulation. In all of these movements, the preponderant force in the mixture seems to be based less on orthodox socialist politics of anticapitalism, or even on religious convictions of integrity or rejection of competing ideologies, and most strongly on nationalist sentiments of identity in opposition to foreign interest and influence. The question remains how centrifugal these movements of opposition really are and how centripetal this system is to the efforts of these movements to destroy or even to dismember it, let alone to offer any alternative(s) to capitalism and its world system.

CRISIS, NATIONALISM, AND SOCIALISM

Samir Amin

1.   If we wish to see the present world economic crisis in the context of the history of the development of capitalism, we must resort to a theory of its development.

Such a theory of accumulation at the world level does not exist in the sense we too often give to theories—finite constructions which give a "perfect" account of reality. This type of theory would enable us to forecast the future, which would become completely clear. This possiblity does not exist in the social sciences—this is what distinguishes them from natural sciences. But there is, in my opinion, a set of fundamental concepts and a series of partial analyses of different aspects of this development that enable us to construct a coherent history of accumulation at the world level. Of course, we must refrain from the type of dogmatism that would consider that the set of concepts is finite and that there are never any "new" problems. It seems to me that the confusion stems mainly from a loose usage of a series of concepts and from a one-sided reduction of complex phenomena. This is why I intend to begin by defining the meaning of the concepts used to pose these questions, and by briefly outlining my point of view on each of them.

1.1   The expansion of capitalism—its relentless tendency to expand geographically and to tighten its hold on different aspects of economic and social life—is inherent in the capitalist mode of production. It is not a question of recognizing this, but of discovering whether this expansion results from an unchanging economic law (the search for profit), or from the class struggle. I answer this question in the following way: economic laws do not explain the concrete form the expansion takes. This is the result of the outcome of the results of class struggles (in the plural)—not only the struggle between the two main classes (bourgeoisie and proletariat) but also the struggle involving allies within the hegemonic blocs (land-owners, peasants, petty bourgeoisie) at the level of national and world alliances. It is because the concrete forms of expansionism are determined by class struggles, not by an economic law that is the same throughout history that the development of capital at the world level remains fundamentally unequal. Accumulation does not homogenize world society; it maintains and reproduces heterogeneity in new forms.

1.2   We can see three main stages of expansion: (1) mercantilism (sixteenth and seventeenth centuries); (2) competitive capitalism (nineteenth century); and (3) imperialism, or rather industrial oligopoly (from 1880).

We must then prove that the forms of expansion for each of these stages contain within each stage a certain number of decisive common features, and that these are not the same from one stage to another. We must prove, among other things, that the break in 1880 denotes a qualitative change. We must show that the same features characterize our own present stage (and therefore our crisis). We must explain the transition from one stage to another. But although the dates of the stages are significant, the "names" given them are not. The origin of some of the confusion, misunderstanding, and false debate on imperialism may well lie in the term chosen and in the dogmatization of the Leninist theses on "Imperialism, the highest stage of capitalism."

1.3 In all the stages, we can see a core and a periphery (cores and peripheries). In my opinion, the difference between core and periphery is qualitative, and has been insurmountable since the end of the nineteenth century. Until then, in the mercantilist and competitive capitalist stages, there were many semiperipheral situations (using the term as Wallerstein does) that could have risen to the rank of core. But by the end of the nineteenth century the extent of world domination of core capital was already such that it precluded this possibility from then on. In other words, there is not and there never will be a "new Japan" after Japan. This is why I insist on calling the whole of the contemporary epoch, from the end of the nineteenth century to the present, imperialist. To simplify, I maintain that the dynamic of the core is autonomous, that the periphery adjusts to it, and that the functions the periphery fulfills differ from one stage to another.

1.4   In all the stages, I distinguish between A phases of systemic growth and B phases of crisis or transition from one A phase to another. It is then necessary to show that the A phases are characterized by homogeneity (the elements of which must be defined) and that certain decisive characteristics in the process of accumulation change from one A phase to another. Similarly, it is necessary to show that in the B phases it was precisely these changes that were at stake. The stage of the crisis that gave birth to "imperialism" was a B phase. The question is whether we are not in a period of this type, during which both the characteristics of the A phase that has just finished (1945–70) and those of the imperialist stage are being questioned.

1.5   The problematic of a succession is different from that of an alternation of A and B phases. The succession of A and B phases is linked to historical materialism, by which I mean that it involves class struggle in all its breadth and complexity. The concept of alternation is mechanistic in the sense that it involves certain economic dimensions in their reciprocal relationships. Class struggle is a mere adjunct to this "model," which is reduced to simple economic terms.

However limited the concept of alternation may be, it cannot be denied. The cycle is the nineteenth-century form of this oscillation. Its very precision is a clear indication of the mechanistic character of the operation of economic laws in the period of "competitive capitalism." The alternation phases are a much less regular form (with the same underlying explanation) in the "imperialist" stage.

Obviously, the interweaving of the concepts of cycles, A or B phases, and stages 1, 2, or 3 restores to history all its concrete complexity.

1.6   Does phase A correspond to one type of hegemony and phase B to a conflict between candidates for hegemony? Yes— as long as the meaning of hegemony is made clear.

For example, from 1815 to 1880, during the stage of competitive capitalism, British hegemony was not shared. Future competitors were lining up, but they did not threaten the dominant position of Great Britain. In contrast, during the imperialist stage we can distinguish between: (1) An A phase (1880–1914) characterized by an equilibrium among several intensely competing cores some of which are aiming at a hegemonic position; (2) a B phase (1914–45) characterized by conflict between the cores; and (3) an A phase (1945–70) characterized by a new hegemony, that of the United States.

2.   Questions related to different problematics—stages of expansionism, the core-periphery opposition/complementarity, A phases of growth and B phases of crises (systemic, cyclical, conjunctural), hegemonies and conflicts of hegemony—interact in the unfolding of history.

Can one therefore, over and above a concrete analysis of these interrelated factors, hope to discover one, or several, fundamental "laws" of capitalist development, or better still laws of history itself (not simply of the capitalist mode of production)? Instead of a vain search for general laws, I prefer to list the questions that remain to be answered if we wish to further the materialist historical analysis of our era. We shall see that each of these questions is the subject of conflicting theses; hence the differing views of the present crisis and its possible outcome.

The first question is, what is the role of the "national" question? Historical materialism cannot be reduced to simply recognizing modes of production and social classes. What is the significance of the eventual recognition of this other "social fact," i.e., the nation? How is it linked to the existence of classes? If one opts for a hierarchy, deciding for example that classes are more fundamental than nations, what is the meaning of this decision?

The second question relates to the state and the state system (alliances and conflicts between states). If the state is not simply the agent that implements the will of the ruling classes (or even of the hegemonic bloc) or of the nation, how is it that changes in the economy imply transformations in the relation between the state and the economy (or between the state and civil society)? One postulate here, for example, is that the continual move toward the centralization of capital and of the organization of classes and social groups leads to "statism" (1984). This will be discussed below.

The third question is, what is the nature of the Soviet Union, and what is its perspective? Is it tending toward the "statism" mentioned above, or toward unequal development? In other words, does the Soviet Union represent the image of the capitalism of the future? Is it being reintegrated into the capitalist system as a sort of "second-class" imperialist country (or even as a dominated "newly industrialized country")? Is it in transition toward socialism?

The fourth question is, what is the nature of, and what is the outlook for, the countries of the periphery? Are they (at least some of them—the semi-industrialized countries) becoming "full-fledged" members of the capitalist system? Are others being "marginalized" or squeezed out of the system? Is the Third World a reality or is it breaking up? In other words, is the strategy of "delinking" and setting up self-reliant economies still possible or is it outdated in the present state of world interdependence?

The fifth question is, how does world politics function? What are the real conflicts? What is the perspective that the economic decline of the United States (if there is such a decline) opens up for Europe and Japan? Is the outlook one of increasing and violent confrontation? What are the strategic aims of the Soviet Union? Is it on the offensive? What are its means? How valid are the various geopolitical analyses about hegemony, "three worlds," etc.?

THE ITINERARY OF THE PRESENT CRISIS

The analyses of the crisis that I published in 1974, 1975, 1977, and 1978, while concentrating on immediate issues, use the general method outlined above. It is unnecessary to refer to these texts, all of which are available.[1] The periodization of the history of the expansion of capitalism since 1800, set out there, is based mainly on the nature of internal class alliances and the external ramifications that they imply (and therefore the function of the periphery). The dating of imperialism is considered fundamental and remains valid. I shall therefore examine the main conclusions of these analyses in order to set out those that still seem tenable and those that have become obsolete or demand revision.

1.   The long stage of competitive capitalism, from 1815 to 1873, is characterized by a twofold expansion of capitalism: First, internal expansion, marked by the development of new industries (still mostly family firms), which replace artisans, within the framework of a system of internal class alliances (with the peasants or with the landowners, for example) or external class alliances (between English industrialists and U.S. farmers, both of whom oppose English landowners, for example). This stage characterizes the development of the different core capitalist formations. Second, external expansion, mainly toward the peripheral regions of America and Asia (particularly India). Here British trade dominates, buying raw materials (cotton, foodstuffs) relatively cheaply, leading to a rise in the rate of profit. This external expansion functioned by means of an international class alliance (with the latifundistas and the compradors of the periphery). This twofold expansion is not the result of a "need for external markets," without which accumulation would be theoretically impossible; it arises from the drive to maximize profits, which is made possible by hegemonic class alliances.

British hegemony is unchallenged and is expressed in the form of a unified world monetary system, the gold-sterling standard, which moreover lasted until 1914, longer than the imperialist stage itself. This hegemony takes into account the European "balance of power" and respects the independence of the United States (and the Monroe doctrine). It therefore made possible the gradual emergence of new cores, although these were not able to challenge British hegemony until the end of the century. At this point, the role of the periphery was secondary in the formation of new core powers; the main raw materials (coal and iron) came from European national territories.

2.   The B phase of structural crisis, from 1873 to 1895, ensured the transition to the imperialist stage. The decline in

economic viability within the framework of the preceding period was the result of the process of accumulation itself. First, the organization of the working class and the threat that it represented (the Commune of Paris in 1871, for example) reduced the effectiveness of pressures to lower wages, particularly since the nascent competition between industrial firms (no longer between firms and artisans) and the rise in productivity it entailed acted to lower prices. Second, the internal class alliances (with landowners and the peasantry) necessary to meet this threat lowered capital's profit margin. Third, the new cores ousted England from its technological monopoly. And finally, local sources of raw materials became more expensive.

Capital's response to this unfavorable economic situation was to centralize and to export capital at a hitherto unprecedented rate. Centralization, which enabled the market for capital to become worldwide (thus complementing the market for goods), ensured that the new monopolies were able to exploit labor in the periphery, draining off any eventual ground rent or income from minerals and therefore raising the rate of profit. The export of capital was limited to financial flows through banks, intended for financing infrastructure (railways in particular) and for state assistance. It did not permit the implantation of capitalist production units dominated from afar. The "world penetration" of the system was effected only by trade between capitalist Europe and the periphery, whose products were produced for exchange in noncapitalist ways.

This structural change marked a new stage in the system. It therefore implied profound modifications in class alliances: First, the establishment of a world imperialist alliance, between the monopolies of the core and the ruling classes of the periphery (at this point the latifundistas and compradors), which henceforth fulfills essential functions in reproduction. Second, the neutralization of the working-class movement in the core nations. From now on, they conduct their struggle within the system and reject the alternative project of Marx's socialism. From the time of this new level of world penetration, there is no longer the possibility of new centers emerging.

These characteristics have remained true until now, which

is why I believe it is essential to recognize an "imperialist" stage. It is true, however, that the form of this imperialism alters, altering the allies in the periphery. Moreover, the stages in the development of imperialism set out here are based on the subordinate dependent allied classes (first the "feudal" strata, later the "bourgeoisie"). Without doubt, the dogmatic character of the Leninist analysis, with its refusal to recognize this change, is at the root of the ambiguities in the debate on the subject.

Let me make two additional remarks about this stage. First, it is no longer characterized by British hegemony but by a precarious balance between the powers (witness 1914); and second, monopoly power and the imperialist state coincide—whence, as Giovanni Arrighi has pointed out, the meaning of Lenin's analysis: economic competition becomes a conflict between states and leads to war.[2]

3. The B stage that follows (1914–45)—the thirty-year war for the British succession, as Arrighi aptly calls it—is a logical continuation of the preceding stage. British hegemony is completely ended; the world monetary system based on sterling disappears; and the chaos, fluctuation, and inflation that take its place reflect the intensity of the conflict between the claimants to the "throne." Two world wars win a victory for the United States over Germany. These wars, like the major crisis of 1930, result in state responses, either right wing (in the form of fascism), or left wing (in the form of the New Deal, social democracy, or the popular front).

The Leninist analysis of imperialism is set in this economic context. Arrighi is right to emphasize this and to remind us that Lenin calls this the "highest stage of capitalism" because he thinks that the conflict between monopolies leads to permanent war and to world revolution.

Moreover, the Russian Revolution tends to prove that this analysis is not unfounded. On the other hand, its failure to spread to the advanced parts of Euorpe shows that, if not Lenin, at least the Third International underestimated the effects of social-democratic working-class integration into the imperialist alliance. The discussions at the time on imperialism and the "collapse" (*Zusammenbruch*) shed light on this subject. This period also saw the emergence of the first national liberation movements in the periphery. Lenin transferred his hopes for the Western proletariat to the peasants of the East. The "Luxemburgists" declared that the eventual liberation of the East would force revolution on the West because accumulation could not continue without external outlets. The Keynesians showed that a reformist solution to the crisis existed, through a redistribution of income—just at the point when overexploitation could be transferred to the dominated peripheries.

All these theses are partly true and partly false. The social-democratic integration of the working class was based on imperialism, and the only capitalist solution left to Germany, once it had been deprived of its colonies, was therefore the aggressive expansion of Naziism. National liberation in the East usually remained under the control of the bourgeoisie, which was not so much engaged in "delinking" from the system as in increasing the integration of the periphery in ways that only accelerate accumulation at the world level. The capitalist mode of production could theoretically dispense with "external outlets," but in reality it cannot: maintaining its power demands continued hegemonic class alliances.

4.   It is true that, under these conditions, the U.S. hegemony that followed World War II reestablished, to use Arrighi's phrase, the predominance of the economy over the state. Globalization took the form of "free enterprise," just as under British hegemony it was based on "free trade." The dollar standard is proof of this hegemony.

This hegemony is based on a twofold international alliance: (1) with the bourgeoisie in Europe and Japan, subordinated politically (put under U.S. nuclear protection) on the basis of the Marshall Plan which, while aiding European reconstruction, offered an opening for the intensification of the exploitation of work through the modernization effected by U.S. capital and through competition; (2) with the bourgeoisies in the periphery, which U.S. imperialism supports against the old colonial forces, who finance their own accumulation (industrialization taking the place of imports) by increasing their export of raw materials—therefore by enabling the appropriation of agricultural, mineral, and oil income by monopoly capital (during a period of cheap energy).

5.   The crisis begins in the second half of the 1960s with the crisis of the dollar, and U.S. military intervention in Vietnam—the political-ideological crisis of 1968. The oil crisis of 1973 and the U.S. defeat in Vietnam in 1975 confirm this as a crisis in the North-South relationship—that is to say, a crisis in imperialism.

I have previously analyzed the oil crisis as both a crisis in the North-South alliance and an interimperialist crisis (the U.S. offensive against the rise of Europe and Japan). At the time—1974—it was not yet clear that Europe and Japan would successfully take up this challenge. Southern Europe seemed, therefore, to be a weak link in the imperialist chain: it is well known that the left's chances had never been better in this area (Italy, France, Spain, Portugal, and Greece).

In my earlier articles, I viewed the East, its chronic problems only worsened by the crisis, too one-sidedly. Its chance of integration into the world system—a theoretical solution to the crisis—was overestimated (and Soviet ambitions underestimated), and the tendency for the USSR and China to be reintegrated into the international division of labor were insufficiently explained. No clear distinction was drawn between those two countries, and there was no analysis of the specificities of the USSR and its aims.

In addition, I then saw the Third World as once again entering a stage of instability that threatened the international order. The New International Economic Order was analyzed as a symptom of a crisis in the alliance between the monopolies and the dependent bourgeoisies. But the two capitalist strategies—the restructuring of the monopolies and the new international economic order of the bourgeoisies of the Third World—are in conflict. The integration of the partly industrialized countries with the international division of labor, a process that is controlled by the monopolies, will not necessarily succeed. The aspirations of the Third World bourgeoisies are unrealizable, and reflect the historical incapacity of this class, as the collapse of the North-South negotiations has demonstrated. The vulnerability of the Third World is the beginning, therefore, of a stage of populist disintegration, and the only possible outcome is a national popular one (a new "national democratic revolution," a stage of the revolution which cannot be divided into subperiods). Can the concept of "interdependence" be saved in times of acute economic conflict? Is there a real danger of a financial crash? (These questions are set out in my last article cited in note 1.)

6.   An analysis of the present crisis as a crisis of imperialism gives to the date 1880 a meaning that is still valid.

6.1   Arrighi has defended the thesis that the fact that monopolies are linked to national spaces accounts for the transformation of competition between monopolies into interstate rivalries, and the nature of the reactionary hegemonic alliances of the period, which are aimed at reinforcing "national unity" around national monopolies (see the rise of fascism or of popular fronts).

This period fits Lenin's thesis—imperialism, the highest stage of capitalism. Monopolies lead to interimperialist wars and the latter to revolution.

A war took place, but what about a revolution? In any event, after 1945 we return to "peaceful competition" (characteristic of the nineteenth century) within the framework of the hegemony of free trade (the U.S. transnationals). This is a return to the market (the "economy") as the regulator of the growth and decline of the state. At the same time, capital makes up for its concessions to the working class by renewing its alliances (the social-democratic and technocratic alliance replaces the reactionary alliance).

World "peace" (the Pax Britannica of the nineteenth century or the Pax Americana of the post-1945 period) does not rule out local wars—for example, the nineteenth-century national wars during the making of new national states (Germany, Italy) and the twentieth-century wars during the formation of new states in the periphery.

Today's multinationals differ from the monopolies of the preceding phase in the sense that "mercantile, then financial, expansion acts indirectly on the international division of labor; the growth of the multinationals control it directly."[3] The growth of monopolies (the setting up of branches) is extensive whereas that of the multinationals is intensive (the division of labor within the firm itself) and transnational in its extent.[4] The problem of the transfer price is in this sense new (40% of world trade at the moment is intra-firm). This is, in my opinion, an undeniable sign of the globalization of the law of value—although this is denied by the main tendencies in Western Marxism.

According to Arrighi, we are not entering upon a new imperialist stage (characterized by world conflict, as was the period between 1880 and 1945) for the following three reasons: (1) We cannot go back on the widespread globalization of the transnationals (this is why the crisis will not lead to a protectionist reaction in the developed countries); (2) the East and the periphery, politically reinforced, cannot become the scene of a violent struggle to ensure the final domination of one or the other of the developed partners; and (3) the USSR, on the other hand, because it has not attained the level of development of the West, can only envisage growing by political and military means.

6.2   If this is a correct exposition of Arrighi's position, then it seems to me to underestimate the keenness of the competition between the United States, Europe, and Japan, which may well lead to a renewal of "statism." The suggested opposition between the market and the state is too bare. It underestimates the role of the state in the absorption of surplus (department III), which has increased continuously since 1930 and which the crisis may further (despite the current "neoliberalism"). (For a discussion of the departments, see my *Law of Value and Historical Materialism*.) It further underestimates the extent of state intervention necessary to ensure hegemony, including military force. Why should we exclude the possibility of Europe's acquiring military autonomy—was Brezhnev wrong in taking the threat of a European neutron bomb seriously? It underestimates the extent of state intervention in the development of new industries (research and development in the atomic field is largely done by the state, although this is not the case in electronics). Despite its transnational dimension, the national base thus depends heavily on the state. We have had British hegemony (a pseudo "superimperi-alism" before its time), which went when England lost its naval supremacy; conflicts over hegemony (corresponding to the anti-Kautskyist Leninist thesis—superimperialism is im-possible); and the hegemony of the United States (super-imperialism once again). Why deny the possibility of conflict among potential hegemonic powers? Why should we neces-sarily move toward the reconstruction of the world-economy rather than its break up? No doubt the existence of an aggres-sive Soviet Union would diminish the extent of interimperi-alist conflicts; but if indeed the Soviet Union is "in decline" and on the defensive, why will the contradictions not express themselves openly? In my opinion, then, Arrighi's position plays down the multipolar interaction that involves not only the West (or the three Wests: the United States, a united or disunited Europe, and Japan) but also the USSR and China. Will hostility to the USSR force the West to close its ranks? This is a moot point since, in opposition to the Peking/Wash-ington axis, Europe seems to have chosen the axis of détente—Moscow/Bonn/Paris.

Above all, this position sees the south too passively. Lenin's thesis of unequal development is not of unequal development between imperialist countries (which is admitted) but of the widening of the North-South gap. In my opinion, the substance of the Leninist thesis is there: the capitalist pattern of develop-ment (meaning the accession of the peripheral countries to core status) is closed to the countries of the periphery. This means that a socialist transition at the world level began with the breakaway of the South (the corollary of this position is the spread of "revisionism" among the working classes of the North). The substance of Lenin's thesis should not be sought in the specific situation of his time (the European war and possible revolution). My position is, however, rejected by the main currents of opinion in the West.

Of course, if one accepts Arrighi's position—which makes imperialism a conflict between states—the imperialism in question would not be a "new stage," still less the "highest stage" (leading to the stage of global socialist transition), but rather a moment that would reappear cyclically throughout the history of capitalism, as long periods of peace and conflict give way to one another.

Also, in my opinion, the development of the present-day peace economy is not necessarily permanent, in which case the Leninist thesis is not an outdated historical relic. However, even a tentative answer to this question demands a consideration of three questions: (1) what is the nature of the U.S. decline? (2) what is the outlook for the periphery in the present crisis? and (3) what are the strategic aims of the USSR?

THE AMERICAN DECLINE

1.   U.S. economic and political hegemony was based on the perpetuation of a particular set of conditions: (1) National liberation in the peripheral countries had to be "stabilized" at the bourgeois stage, with the U.S. military intervening if necessary to prevent it going any further. To this end, the United States was forced to intervene in Korea and Vietnam, and attempted to reconquer China in the 1950s and 1960s. It also attempted to avoid the "radicalization" of the Middle East by using Zionism as a bulwark. (2) Europe was both dependent on U.S. military protection and economically vulnerable. (3) The Soviet Union was confined to its territory and to the countries it dominated in Europe without any real possibility of expansion.

These conditions now seem to me at least partly out of date. First, the power of the bourgeoisie can no longer be stabilized in the periphery. In the East, U.S. intervention did not succeed in stopping the liberation movements; the United States finally had to recognize China in 1971 and to get out of Indochina in 1975. Elsewhere, the bourgeois ruling class is not directly threatened by revolutionary forces. In the Middle East, the United States succeeded in causing a decrease in Arab nationalism until a populist breakthrough, starting in Iran in 1979, loomed on the horizon. In Central America, although Cuba is isolated, it has been impossible to avoid a popular revolution in Nicaragua. Nor has it been possible to prevent people's movements in South-West Africa (Namibia) and East Africa from appealing to the Soviet Union for help. Finally, in Afghanistan, the United States has been forced to accept a *fait accompli,* even if perhaps only temporarily.

The defeat of the United States in the East is highly significant. It bears witness to the fact that this power has lost the ability to impose the reign of "free enterprise" by force which in turn reinforces the supremacy of the Third World states and gives them greater scope for maneuver. Had it not been for this, it is unlikely that the OPEC countries would have succeeded. It is also unlikely that the Third World countries would have been able to embark on the struggle for the "New International Economic Order" when they were not in a situation to impose a new, and more favorable, international division of labor.

The world-market-oriented development that has characterized the growth of the Third World is at the root of this weakness. This type of development characterizes both the newly industrialized and the less-developed countries; it remains fragile and the bourgeoisie that supports it is therefore in a vulnerable position. This is why the South remains the weak link in the world system, destined to become again a "zone of tempests," to experience crisis and increasing outbreaks of protest from the people.

This reversal was inherent in the reconstruction of Europe and Japan. Japan, and to a lesser extent Germany and the rest of Europe, have become competitive with—and sometimes even better placed than—the United States in the world market. Their growth has led to a reversal of the structure of the balance of payments: there is no longer the chronic U.S. surplus there was after the war. This is why the present crisis was first felt in international monetary relations. The collapse of the Bretton Woods system in 1971 marked the end of the U.S. era. We should not be overpreoccupied with the A and B phases, as expressed, for example, in the rise and fall of the dollar. Phases of deficit and devaluation give way to phases of improved equilibrium (with a rise in the dollar, as at the present), depending on the rise and fall of the political outlook. Similarly, the surplus of other countries is not permanent, as

Germany's current return to a deficit demonstrates. Further, it is necessary in any analysis to distinguish the relative competitiveness of the United States, Japan, and Europe. And above all one must bear in mind that Europe and Japan are still militarily incapable of facing the nuclear power and conventional weapons of the USSR on their own.

This final remark brings us to the question of the strategic aims and capabilities of the USSR, which seems since 1960 to have entered a new stage of development, characterized by development of a military sufficient for it to be competitive with the United States.

2.   For a long time the European "economic miracle" appeared to be a by-product of the worldwide growth of the "free enterprise" system characteristic of U.S. hegemony. Until 1973, this was effectively the case. The high rate of growth of the various countries (5 percent per annum on average), with almost full employment and limited inflation (3 percent per annum on average), facilitated a convergence of demand and production, not only among the six members of the EEC but also among the bordering regions, particularly Spain and Greece (and with the exception of the United Kingdom, which was unable to recover from its decline).

The results of this unequal development were due in part to the establishment of U.S. multinationals, but there is also little doubt that threats of nationalist reaction, at the time of De Gaulle, disturbed the United States. Furthermore, this brought with it—from the mid-1960s—a reversal in the trend of the balance of payments. It is thus legitimate to consider that the United States' benign neutrality toward the OPEC countries in 1973 was a U.S. counterattack, aimed at reminding Japan and Europe of the fragility of their growth.

Did this counterattack have the expected results? Japan and even West Germany managed to redirect their industrial exports (particularly toward the semi-industrialized countries and the East). Meanwhile, other European countries found themselves suffering not only the highly successful competition of Germany and Japan, but that of the semi-industrialized countries of the periphery and the East as well. In these circumstances, the enlargement of the EEC to include the chronically ill United Kingdom, followed by the still vulnerable Spain, Greece, and Portugal, has yet to be vindicated. The class alliances that characterize the various European formations have different historical origins, which limits the possibility of a common economic policy. In this respect the attitude of the EEC to the agricultural sector is characteristic: those in the north benefit from a common policy that supports cereals, meat, and dairy products, while those in the south, excluded from the hegemonic alliance at the European level, get no support at all for their products (wines, fruit, and vegetables). This is on the basis of a feeble "technical" pretext: these products are said to be unstockable. Will a stronger presence of the southern European countries in the Common Market force West Germany, for political reasons, to "finance" a common agricultural policy that will help Europe as a whole (and not just West Germany) to become competitive on a world scale? Will the European monetary system and the myriad common funds be acceptable and efficient?

3.   We can therefore see two divergent directions for European development.

According to the first, there will be a de facto "split" in Europe as a result of the dissimilarity between West Germany and the other European countries. These latter will be increasingly affected by competition from the semi-industrialized countries and those of the East, while rivalry between the three major powers (the United States, Japan, Germany) for the conquest of new and expanding markets will intensify.[5] Numerous examples bear witness to this rivalry: We have, for example, the increase in German investments in Brazil, at the expense of the United States (with open conflict in the nuclear industry), or the attempt by the United States to resist competition from Japanese electronics by moving its own electronics industry to Taiwan and Korea, an attempt thwarted by Japan's move to these same countries.

Seen in this light, the chances of Germany's "going it alone" are less clear than it is often thought. Germany's advantage in the leading industries is recent and still fragile. In effect, between 1958 and 1973 the German's share of world industrial production decreased (by 1.3 percent), as did that of the

United States (by 6.9 percent), Great Britain (2.5 percent), and France (0.7 percent). On the other hand, the socialist countries' share increased (by 6.3 percent), as did that of Japan (5 percent). Germany's advantage only began after 1973, and that of Japan is more assured. Moreover, if the winner of the competition between the United States, Japan, and West Germany has not yet been decided, it is not a foregone conclusion that the old industrialized countries of Europe can be reduced to the state of the semi-industrialized countries of the periphery. (I maintain, as I have before, that there is a qualitative difference between core and periphery.)

Given these conditions, Western Europe could opt for a second strategy: to reinforce its unity in order to benefit as a whole from the German "advance." The advantages are obvious, including of course the political and military ones. Furthermore, such a unity precludes neither the eventual emergence of a leader nor unequal development within an enlarged and extended Common Market.

Could Europe in this way become a real rival to the United States? Europe's advantages, which are perhaps even greater than those of Japan, should not be underestimated. First, on the strictly economic level, it does not appear that it will be easy for the United States to make up lost ground. Theoretically, if U.S. firms "wanted" to devote their research and development efforts to reversing the recent advances of European and Japanese industry, it would be reasonable to assume that they could succeed. But this does not take into account the structural effects of their decline in hegemony, which are difficult to estimate, for the sluggishness inherent in a situation of decline. Also, as Wallerstein has pointed out, the decline of a hegemonic power is not its own doing, but is the consequence of the more rapid rise of its rivals.

The United States now suffers from what was its historical advantage—its gigantic scale. The U.S. monopolies are less flexible than their European and Japanese counterparts. They have difficulty in dealing with the parasitism of their administrative hierarchies. This is why they lose so many battles in the intense competition that characterizes the present crisis phase. They are well equipped to compete in an oligopoly-type situation, typical of a favorable economic phase, by launching new products; they are poorly placed when it comes to dealing with the rapid reduction in costs that the crisis demands, and which Japan, and even more so West Germany, has managed to do.

Second, the wealth of the United States—it has on its territory a large part of the natural resources which it consumes, as well as a complete range of agricultural and industrial production—has become a handicap to its ability to compete in an increasingly globalized economy. The European countries can give up the less economically viable sectors of their economies; in the United States, these are defended by powerful interests. Oil is a good example. When Europe and Japan were getting oil almost free, the United States had to pay a tithe to its oil monopolies. The possession of natural resources may thus be a strategic and political advantage, but it can also make for added economic costs.

Third, on the political level Europe gains an advantage from being divided into States. This division enables the united front of capital to confront disunited "national" political forces. In this way, the European left was beaten repeatedly throughout the 1970s. Under these conditions, Europe can hardly be anything other than a Europe of monopolies—a Europe of the "workers" being an obvious illusion. Thus the rallying of all political tendencies, right or left, to the idea of Europe bears witness to the advantage this old continent has in its efforts to rise to a hegemonic position, at least on an economic level. This current focus on Europe recalls that of the Second International in 1914 when the working classes cooperated with "their" monopolies—these were, at the time, national ones. It marks a partial erasing of the local "national" contradictions that made southern Europe, in the middle of the last decade, into a series of rather weak links in the central imperialist chain.

Lastly, we should note that the strength of the working classes is not a major stumbling block to Europe's comeback, since they function within the framework of a political polarization that divides European society into two more-or-less equal forces, i.e., the liberals on the right and the social democrats on the left. The latter not only accept the rules of the political game but share an interclass solidarity—called the "national interest"—which has developed as a result of the access to the resources of the third world and of the over-exploitation of its labor force. The European left-right polarization thus fulfills the salutary function of imposing coherent policies, usually right-wing ones (especially at times of restructuring), with the possibility of a left-wing alternative acting as a safety valve. In contrast, U.S. political life has become an obstacle to the implementation of a coherent political plan. Given the lack of an autonomous working-class party, even a social-democratic one, it is hampered and fragmented by an emphasis on minor contradictions ("tempests in tea-cups," lobbies, etc.). The "irrationality" of this policy, and the pathetic aspect of presidential campaigns, are surely proof of this added difficulty. Nevertheless, the question remains whether the left-right political alternative in Europe can succeed in containing the contradictions inherent in the crisis, in making the working class accept a certain level of unemployment, and in making the petty bourgeoisie accept continuous inflation—all of which are necessary if any restructuring is to take place.

Our analysis of the rise of Japan and Europe, and of the consequent U.S. decline, is clearly not based on a comparison of breakthroughs in the sphere of avant-garde technology. To speak of a U.S. decline in this field would be to exaggerate. If we refer to microprocessors and robotization, Japan has no doubt already advanced definitively over its rivals, both qualitatively and quantitatively, by directing its efforts toward the mass production and installation of simple, strong robots, thus enabling big reductions in production costs. But the romanticism of the writings about this sphere ("the factory without a single worker") is belied by developments in Japan that prove that only partial robotization (in particular of the tasks of loading and unloading) is economically feasible. Further, there are no big secrets in this field and U.S. firms could quickly make up lost ground, particularly since scientific effort in the United States is directed along these lines. In other spheres—atomic and space research, the exploitation of the seabed, etc.—U.S. scientific and technical superiority remains considerable.

Any analysis of economic rise and fall that centers on technological breakthroughs ignores that it is not techniques that count, but the social capacity to implement them. Here again, the example of the use of robots in Japan shows that the new technology is aimed, just as Taylorism was, at subjecting the labor force even further to the logic of capital. It therefore implies social conditions that may not be as readily found elsewhere. It is not by chance that it is the rise of Germany and Japan that is the threat to the United States: they were both defeated in World War II, and not only did their industrial infrastructures have to be reconstructed on an ultramodern basis, but their working classes offered no resistance to their plans. By contrast, the decline of Britain and the difficulties in France are the result of efficient working-class resistance. And there is now much talk in right-wing U.S. circles of the "re-industrialization" of the country. Moreover, the flow of Japanese and U.S. capital is facilitating this renovation in the United States, which started in the south and west and is aimed at the old northeast and its AFL-CIO unions. The question remains as to whether it be rapid and efficacious.

The economic decline of the United States is clearly relative. The advance of Europe and Japan has just begun and is still tenuous. The superiority of U.S. multinationals remains overwhelming. But it is permissible to suspect that the growth of investment controlled by the U.S. multinationals *outside* the United States, far from demonstrating the vitality of U.S. capitalism, is on the contrary a sign of its decline. The U.S. monopolies are avoiding the task of restructuring their national base and instead seeking easy profits abroad. Great Britain made this same choice at the end of last century, and it is the reason for its marked decline. Thus decline began in the 1880s, and at the time was barely visible; the same may thus be equally true for the United States—at least it is a plausible hypothesis. History will tell us whether the United States will be able to reverse the trend or whether it will react slowly and in fits and starts, at times even attenuating the decline without stopping it completely.

There is no doubt that the sphere in which the United States can react the most efficiently is the military one. The setback after its defeat in Vietnam is almost certainly temporary. But the military recovery, while obviously likely to pose again the question of the relationship with the USSR, will have no direct effect on the economic competition with Europe. Furthermore, Europe, concentrating on its economic aims, has adopted an attitude of extreme détente toward Moscow—tolerating, for instance, the events in Afghanistan. The Russians have succeeded in facing a Peking-Tokyo-Washington axis with a Moscow-Bonn-Paris axis—one based on détente, moreover—thus defusing the U.S. attempt to blackmail Europe with the argument of the need for an atomic umbrella. This European choice demonstrates, *a posteriori,* that European construction, far from being in response to a U.S. strategy for regaining hegemony (one is reminded of the analyses of the "Germano-American Europe"), is, on the contrary, based on economic competition. Naturally, the future is, in the last analysis, a matter of relations between the United States and the USSR. But that is another question.

4.   Japan in the East is not the mirror image of Europe in the West. In the sphere of economic competition, Japan remains in a better position than Europe. But it has been forced—geopolitics do count—to link its fate with that of the Sino-American alliance, therefore allying with a socialist country that does not intend to give up its autonomy and with an economic rival. This is why analyses that emphasize the "capitalist and brilliant" future of the "zone of Confucius" (China, Japan, Korea, Vietnam, and any eventual dependencies in Southeast Asia), which will take over from the West, are not only based on an unrealistic view of the Chinese system but also joyfully leapfrog over the problems and contradictions of the next few decades.

5.   Is interimperialist economic competition being modified by the emergence of new problems outside the "traditional" framework of the problematic of capitalism and imperialism?

It is certainly necessary to emphasize the new aspects of the development of the forces of production, in particular: (1) the real scarcity of cheap natural resources on the planet, both in energy and other spheres; (2) the added cost that ecological constraints will impose on economic activities; and (3) the relative autonomy of the dynamic of technological progress and the outlook for the development of robots (based on the spread of microprocessors), with all that these imply in the way of renewed contradictions (jobs, further restructuring, etc.).

Nevertheless, it is my opinion that these new elements will not prevent interimperialist competition; they will merely determine its context. On another level, they might act to encourage an increased demand for "statism," but we should not attribute to the "administered economy"—whether administered by the state or by para-state institutions, if private legal forms are respected—the ability to suppress interimperialist conflict.

THE CRISIS OF CAPITALISM IN THE PERIPHERY

1. My firm opinion is that the crucial aspect of the present crisis is that it is a crisis in the international division of labor, that is, a crisis of the "North-South relationship," a crisis in the imperialist system. In the last resort, it is the international division of labor that conditions the evolution of interimperialist relations, although the evolution of the East-West relationship remains largely independent of the North-South relationship. The view that this is a crisis of imperialism is contrary to the view that sees the origin and central aspect of the crisis in the relationship between capital and labor specific to the advanced capitalist countries. The difference between the two positions is not a question of dogma, but of observing the reality of the conflict. What conflicts fashion the development of the contemporary scene, are the basis on which alliances and camps are organized, and therefore condition the outcome of other conflicts? I maintain that the transformation of the capitalist system into an imperialist one at the end of the nineteenth century and its major results (social democracy in the West, the struggle for national liberation in the periphery) have transferred the main contradiction from that between capital and labor to that between imperialism and the popular forces in the periphery.

2. A first hypothesis, while recognizing the important role of the periphery in the development of capitalist accumulation at all stages, emphasizes the adjustment of the periphery to the exigencies of the expansion of capital.

2.1 In principle, this is so. The defining characteristic of the periphery is in fact the way in which it is "indirectly" subordinated to the domination of capital. This subordination works by way of the conservation and/or reproduction of precapitalist modes (or noncapitalist modes) of production, and therefore through the forms of "formal subsumption"—as opposed to the "real subsumption"—of labor to capital. These forms are based on a superexploitation of labor in the periphery that enables the transfer of value for the benefit of dominant capital, and thereby reinforces the class alliances on which this dominance is based. The "interclass" solidarities known as "national interest" have no other basis. All our hypotheses about "unequal exchange"—the form assumed by this global organization of exploitation—have their foundation here. Therefore, the charge of "circulationism" is dogmatism pure and simple, in that it obscures the real problems of imperialism.

Not only does capital know how to "reap the profits" of precapitalist relationships and subject them to it; it can even create, out of nothing—and for its profit—noncapitalist relations, such as slavery in the Americas, the second serfdom in Eastern Europe, the slave trade in Africa, the reserves in South Africa, etc. It is in fact on the basis of this observation, particularly as far as South Africa is concerned, that in the early 1960s I was led to raise questions about the domination of capital in the contemporary imperialist period.

Can we extend this argument and see the eventual integration of the Eastern European countries into the international division of labor as a form of future growth? In this sense the state mode of production would be subordinate to the capital that dominates the world system. We shall come back to this point later.

2.2 The political forms this articulation and/or subordination takes obviously depend upon the content of the underlying international division of labor and on all sorts of conditions. Underneath the extremely varied historical forms, it is possible to see a correlation between "colonial" forms—by which I mean forms characterized by the direct intervention of the ruling political power, with conflict between several core powers for hegemony—and "neocolonial" forms—which are characterized by the political independence of the periphery and the hegemony of a single core power that is able to dominate by economic means alone. I therefore see, in turn, (1) a mercantilist era, during which Spain, France, Holland, and England quarrelled over American empires; (2) an era of British hegemony, between 1800 and 1880, and the independence of the Americas; (3) an era of conflict between Great Britain, Germany, the United States, and France, between 1880 and 1945, and colonial imperialism; and (4) an era of U.S. hegemony, between 1945 and 1970, and the neocolonial independence of Africa and Asia. Can we imagine that a period of open conflict between the two superpowers will now call for a renewal of direct military and political intervention?[6]

2.3   In times of conflict over hegemony, the struggle for the control of the periphery becomes particularly acute. On the economic level, the competing core powers attempt to move certain activities to those peripheral countries they control in order to reduce costs; at the same time, as Wallerstein correctly points out, metropolitan capital tends to go to the state for protection and support. And even its metropolitan opponents (the working class, for example, or small-scale production sectors) also turn to the state for similar assistance.[7]

These trends are obvious today. Competition between the three major powers for access to the markets in the new semi-industrialized countries of the South and East and in the former core powers, which I already mentioned, is proof of this. If we consider that the desire of the Third World countries to participate in a New International Economic Order is somewhat unrealistic, can we therefore conclude that the North will succeed in dividing the South, in integrating the semi-industrialized countries, and in neutralizing the "fourth world"? This is one possible scenario, but it presupposes that the internal contradictions of the South can be overcome—which is far from certain.

2.4   The argument that the "recuperation" of the semi-industrialized South is inevitable is based on a rigorous analysis of various models of development in action in the periphery. Nevertheless, it assumes that there is no other possibility, even in theory, and thus takes its place alongside views that development is a series of necessary successive stages.

The countries that are at present semi-industrialized have chosen models of development which, in addition to their variety (import substitution, exports based on subcontracting, etc.), are all based on giving priority to the consumption patterns of the middle classes. The result is that the path on which they have embarked is more of an impasse than a stage of true development at the end of which they will find themselves in the situation of the developed capitalist countries of the core. Either at the level of the structure of production and its relationship to the distribution of income and the structure of consumption, or at the level of autonomy vis-à-vis the outside world, these countries merely show the present mode of development in the periphery—in other words, one stage in a general model of expansion through the homogenization of the field of capital.

Here we have, in my opinion, a basic qualitative difference that is denied by those who see only unqualified "capitalist" development. This real difference leads us to make a radical critique of development models, whether they be bourgeois models or models with Marxist pretenses, such as those favoring "industrializing industry," which is merely an adaptation of the Soviet model for the use of the underdeveloped countries.[9]

The final result of this strategy, which has inspired the most radical attempts in the capitalist Third World (in Nehru's India and Nasser's Egypt), has already been shown to be a form of subordination very different from any other. It is diametrically opposed to the Chinese model, based on the "Ten Great Relationships," where priority is given to agriculture and industry plays a supporting role ("walking on two legs"). This path alone afforded the chance of autonomous development ("self-reliance"), but it implied a leveling of incomes, independent of the productivity of each sector (equality, therefore, between town and country, and reduction of large wage differences in the towns), thus ensuring a parallel advance in modernization and in the standard of living of the entire population. This is both an authentic transition to socialism and a form of national liberation (a delinking from the imperialist system). It obviously implies a type of power whose class content is different from that of the capitalist peripheral countries, even if they are of a radical bourgeois type. Thirty years of the Chinese experiment demonstrates that there is an alternative choice and that it is possible to have development untied to the demands of accumulation in the world system.

The argument that this possibility does not exist is based on two sets of reasoning: (1) that globalization is irreversible, and (2) that the countries of the East (including China) will be forced, after an autarkic transition, to become reintegrated into the international division of labor.

The first set of arguments is based on a "technicist" vision of historical development. The technological gap is such that if a country wishes to acquire advanced technology at once and on a mass scale, then it must import it. Therefore, it must be paid for with (1) agricultural exports, which only increases local food scarcities while providing no guarantee of autonomy, given the West's enormous production capacity and its use of food as a "weapon"; (2) mining exports, but for countries rich in resources the temptation to live off their income is very real; or (3) industrial exports, but this means the acceptance of delocalization, dominated by capital, and the concealed sale of cheap labor that this implies. On the other hand, if the gradual narrowing of the technological gap is seen from a point of view that corresponds to other class interests, it is not inevitable that a strategy of dependent development that accepts subjection to capital will be adopted.

2.5   A final point deserves some clarification. The hypothesis that development within the world system is inevitable is based on a confusion between "peripheral" and "dependent." A comparison of examples from the periphery (Brazil and South Korea, for example) and examples of "backward core powers" (Spain, Portugal, Greece), or of "nonperipheral dependence" (Canada) is necessary to clarify this.

The "peripheral/dependent" confusion has gradually led to the obscuring of the main point of the analysis, the internal class relationships that underlie peripheral development. The comparison between Spain and the Third World is enlightening. During the 1950s and 1960s, Spain developed rapidly, largely as a "dependent" zone: development implied an opening to the outside world that increased the country's integration into the international—and especially the European—division of labor, mainly financed by foreign capital. This was accompanied by an almost parallel increase in the real wages of workers and employees, and in the real incomes of small-scale peasants (with large regional and sectoral differences, however). Parallel increases of this sort do not exist in any example of rapid growth in the Third World—neither in Brazil, where growth has been accompanied by a fall in wages and rural pauperization, nor in South Korea, where incomes have at best stagnated (Iran is a similar case), nor in such radical bourgeois experiments as Egypt. This contrast therefore forces us to distinguish between the social dynamic of the backward core powers and that of the peripheral countries.

This same distinction applies to Canada, which although totally dependent economically, in the sense that it is simply a province of the United States and its growth is almost exclusively due to accumulation within the U.S. monopoly system, is not "peripheral." Workers' incomes increase in the same way they do in the United States.

3. In opposition to the premise that development within the global system is "inevitable," I take a position that emphasizes the contradictions of unequal development.

3.1   The present crisis, like any crisis, contains one solution that is inherent in it—that is, there is an imperialist solution. The current crisis of imperialism has revealed the following changes in the balance of power: (1) intra-West changes, expressed through the international monetary system; (2) changes between the West and the USSR (mainly military, and since 1960); (3) changes among the West, the USSR, and China (China having succeeded in the 1970s in asserting itself as an autonomous force); and (4) as an addendum, North-South changes (too much was made of the success of OPEC, when it was in fact limited to this group of Third World countries, as the failure of the North-South negotiations over the New International Economic Order have shown)—but this in no way means that the most acute contradictions in the world system are not to be found within the North-South relationship. On the contrary: the weakness of the states of the South—or of their ruling classes—is the result of the contradictions of the system.

This weakness opens up the possibility of a capitalist "solution," which would lead the way to a new stage in the globalization of the system. We have seen the internationalization of commodities (in the nineteenth century) and then of capital (1880–1945), and now we are seeing the beginning of a globalization of the labor market with the spread of the multinationals and massive immigration (since 1945). This could intensify during the decades ahead.

But this is not the only possible solution, or even the most likely one. In all likelihood, neither of the two solutions outlined—the noncapitalist one of the radical bourgeoisie, or the New International Economic Order of the Third World states—is a realistic alternative.

3.2   I have already stated that the "noncapitalist direction" has a class content that prevents its being radically opposed to the more classical strategies of dependent development. The fact that this direction is recommended by the USSR tells us more about the USSR's strategic ambitions than it does about the Third World countries in question. For the weakness of the bourgeoisies in the periphery (even the "radical" ones) creates a vacuum that encourages the intervention of the superpowers. The issue therefore demands an analysis of the USSR and its ambitions. Let us pose a series of questions about this:

(1) Is the USSR "imperialist" in the sense that it would pursue objectives in the periphery similar to those of the Western monopolies? Or are its aims different because the laws which control the state mode of production are different? What are these laws and to what specific contradictions do they respond?

(2) Is the aim of the USSR to subordinate specific peripheral countries or to find a means of changing the USSR-West relationship? If COMECON is not an alternative for the un-

derdeveloped countries, one that they can oppose to their participation in the capitalist international division of labor, is the USSR aiming, through the triangular relationship East-North-South, at changing its relationship with the West in its favor?

I have already looked at the strategies and limitations of the New International Economic Order. If the Third World states do not succeed in asserting their conception of a New International Economic Order, they are no doubt capable of proposing compromise solutions which could put off the day of reckoning for some time.

The condition of the newly industrialized subcontracting countries, such as South Korea, may well decline in the next decade. South Korea is now caught between an insufficient internal market (international subcontracting is based on low salaries, and there is no "growth with redistribution"—despite the praises of the World Bank), the attraction of North Korea (of the nation and of the people), and the pressure from U.S. and Japanese monopolies, which demonstrates the fragility of this strategy and the difficulty of converting it into a more self-reliant one.

Is the outlook of those countries with mining resources any better? The effort to have more local transformation of raw materials may result in partial success and some local redistribution of income. But these transformation industries in fact only make the countries more dependent, because they reinforce the pursuit of this kind of production instead of attempting to convert further the economies by absorbing considerable investment (which ultimately profits the core countries), and because they integrate the local economy further into the market for products controlled in the last analysis by the monopolies.

As for those "half-solutions" that involve industrialization based on import substitution, while maintaining participation in the international division of labor, these do not solve the fundamental question of the aims of this type of industrialization. It is worth noting that agrarian reform—in the Arab world, for example—while it has modified the distribution of income within the better-off quarter or half of the population, has in no way changed the share of the poorest strata. In the last analysis this kind of reform, while progressive, has only contributed to enlarging the market in the periphery (for durable consumer goods, etc.). Its effect has therefore been no different from that of the reactionary policy of Brazil, which based its industry on the demand for durable consumer goods while lowering wages, to the benefit of the middle classes. These policies in no way lessen the violent social contradictions that are characteristic of development in the periphery.

Resort to greater cooperation between the countries of the South may ease the difficulties. Its "collective autonomy" is theoretically possible—three-quarters of the imports of the underdeveloped countries consist of products using simple technology which the semi-industrialized countries could supply. But we may doubt the political practicability of such a policy, at least on any significant scale.

Many countries in the periphery will prefer to play the easier game, choosing a development strategy that impoverishes the weakest—easier because it will be supported from abroad by one country or another. Are there not regional subimperialisms (an unfortunate term), "expansionism," or "mini-hegemonisms" in Latin America, the Middle East, Africa, and Southeast Asia that prove the attraction of this easy choice to local dependent ruling classes? Perhaps the only thing we can hope for is that in those domains where a collective interest exists, and which are threatened by the strategies of the North, common policies will make some progress. For example, will the OPEC group, confronted with the World Bank-IMF duo, be able to invent a financial strategy that is aimed at supporting a greater degree of autonomy? The search for, and the financing of, new sources of energy for the countries of the South (solar, for example), the tripartite organization of the metallurgy industry (financed by one country, using raw materials from a second, for the markets of a third), and short-term financial support to help those countries the IMF is trying to force into abandoning attempts at autonomy (Tanzania and Jamaica, for example)—all these could be the aim of policies of "collective self-reliance." But it is obviously necessary to do more than simply to "collectivize risk," which threatens the financial investments, in particular of the oil countries, in the West (as the blocking of Iran's credits demonstrated).

Finally, will a new set of special links be associated with those pragmatic "half solutions," this time between the Third World countries and those of the "second world," and will they mean greater negotiating power for the former? I used to think so. But the results to date are minimal; neither Lomé II nor the EEC-Maghreb association have been equal to the problem. Does another possibility exist, then? If Europe fails to consider anything other than its economic competition with the United States, there is a strong risk of its attempting to impose unfavorable conditions re the Third World. This would be an expression of Europe's blinders, its obsession with its own economic outlook to the point of forgetting political conditions. Europe, preaching détente with the USSR, the victim of a short-sighted view of the Third World, runs the risk of failing in its economic project just because of its inability to take part in the world level discussion aimed at enlarging the area of autonomy between the two superpowers.

3.3   Therefore, it does not matter how the questions are formulated. The only true resolution of the contradictions that increasingly characterize the societies of the periphery is a national and popular one. This is the only way in which these societies can avoid the disintegration that has already begun—a disintegration that bears witness both to the local ruling classes' inability to impose a re-sharing of world surplus value to their advantage, and demonstrates the absence of an immediate revolutionary challenge. This in turn is the result of the opportunism of the left wing of the national liberation movements which, for almost three decades, have endorsed the strategy of the "noncapitalist path." Disintegration is the fatal result of a bourgeoisie incapable of really implementing a bourgeois revolution. It means that the task of a national democratic revolution, seen as a necessary stage in a continuing revolutionary process, remains an objective need.

The national democratic revolution, which some feel is no longer needed once independence is achieved, in fact only changes in form. It can no longer be aimed primarily at "feudal" and "comprador" elements, as was the case in the 1930s, but must be aimed at the bourgeoisie (even if it is a state bourgeoisie), which has become the main means of transmitting imperialist exploitation. This is why I believe that we are still in the imperialist stage of the world system.

Disintegration is perhaps necessary, in the sense that fundamental social upheavals can scarcely erupt in "calm" situations. Neither electoral nor terrorist tactics, nor that of "foco"-ism (starting a civil war by intellectual decision) can substitute for the consolidation of a revolutionary alliance during the process of disintegration. Would the Russian and Chinese revolutions have been possible had it not been for the disintegration of the USSR during World War I, or the disintegration of China that followed the miscarriage of the bourgeois revolution of 1911, which delivered the country to the warlords?

At the outset, disintegration has the appearance of "populist revolt" in the sense that it is the revolt of a large grouping of popular forces with undifferentiated objectives. At this point it is more a refusal of what is than the expression of a positive strategy for constructing a different society. This is why the ideologies that bind this kind of revolt are based on the past: ethnic groups, religions, and castes provide the basis for uniting popular social forces. But these ideologies do not have the consolidating power of communism, which is why they create confusion and must finally give way, either to capitalist restructuring or to the crystallization of a revolutionary alliance.

The decade of the 1980s sees the Third World entering into this phase of disintegration. The fall of the Shah at a time when the modernization of Iran was accelerating, the collapse of the South Korean model, the renewal of Islamic integralism, the collapse of the interclass, interethnic and intercaste structure that the Indian National Congress had managed for half a century, the collapse of a number of non-national states in Africa (from Chad to Uganda)—do these not provide evidence of this disintegration?

Naturally, the form the populist disintegration takes depends on the economic and social infrastructure of each society. A typology is useful in differentiating between the form characteristic of non-national societies without bourgeoisies

(Chad, etc.), those characteristic of semi-industrialized countries dominated by a dependent constituted bourgeoisie (Egypt,
India, etc.), and those characteristic of totally dependent semi-
industrialized economies (South Korea, etc.).

In the short run, populist disintegration creates a vacuum
that tempts external forces, particularly the superpowers.
Moreover, the partners in the conflict are themselves the first
to invite intervention, to make up for their weaknesses. The
superpowers are pursuing their own objectives, motivated
mainly by their conflict at the global level. Whether they act
directly or through the intermediary of the local hegemonic
aspirations they are encouraging (Iran, Iraq, Indochina, etc.),
they can offer no solution to the contradictions of the local
society. What is more, they have already lost the aura of ideological power that characterized them in the preceding phase.

The populist revolt that again makes the Third World a
"zone of tempests" in the world system poses two fundamental
questions: (1) what form, if any, will the transition to socialism
at a world scale take, and (2) is delinking a necessary stage,
one that makes sense of a strategy of nonalignment—the
creation of autonomous spaces for peoples vis-à-vis the global
hegemonies in an attempt to avoid the tragic choice of Chile
versus Afghanistan?

THE CRISIS OF THE SOVIET SYSTEM

1.   The political disappointments of the last few years have
led to fewer analyses of the dynamics of particular societies and
their interaction at the world level. A frequent hypothesis
results from this lack of analysis: the countries of the East (the
USSR, Eastern Europe—Yugoslavia and Albania included—
China, Korea, Vietnam, Cuba) are not "socialist" but "statist"—
a term that describes a form of expansion of capitalism specific
to our times—are being reintegrated into the world system
(the capitalist one, or course), and their momentum, like that
of other countries, especially in the Third World, is based on
"nationalism." This is therefore a stage of integration into the

world system of societies not (not yet?) capable of exerting a hegemonic influence.

This hypothesis seems to me to misread the nature of the statist mode in question—is it in transition, or is it the culmination of a mode, and why?—and to place the USSR, the Soviet satellite countries, Yugoslavia, Albania, China, and Korea too hastily in the same category.

My position is the following: The Soviet experience has taught me that "transition" does not necessarily lead to a classless society. An analysis of the nature of Soviet society has led me to suggest that it is a new class society and not a "degenerated working-class power" or a "restoration of capitalism," because the statist centralization of capital amounts to a qualitative shift. But the Soviet experience is not the only one at issue. The dominant demand expressed by the Western working classes (social democratic or communist) also calls for a gradual advance toward the statist mode. There are forces at work which explain this convergence. My analysis of the "technocracy" and "labor aristocracy" (at the world level) in terms of a rising new class indicates that the contradictions of contemporary capitalism could be overcome through a nonsocialist development of the system.

My analysis of the USSR is based on a conception of the transition as a stage of intense class struggle—a reflection of the struggle between the forces of reproduction of class exploitation and those aimed at ending it. The capitalist mode does not therefore "naturally" lead by way of revolution to either a classless or statist society. The latter is possible but not inevitable. The statist mode ("socialist," or "real existing socialist"), frozen, subject to "economic laws," can no longer evolve of its own accord toward a classless society. To argue that it could, it would be necessary to presume that it develops under the aegis of "objective" forces, i.e., the development of the productive forces (the "scientific and technical revolution").

The historical conditions that explain the consolidation of the statist mode in the USSR must be sought in two complementary areas: (1) At the level of social facts, in the breakup of the worker-peasant alliance as a result of collectivization in the 1930s. This was seen as a means of financing "primitive socialist accumulation," and was the origin of the despotic state. Primitive socialist accumulation became in turn the basis for the formation of a new exploiting class. (2) At the level of ideology, in the weaknesses of Leninism, which did not succeed in breaking cleanly with the positivist economistic concepts of the Second International and the Western working-class movement (see the discussions of the neutrality of technology, the centralization of the party, etc.).

What is termed "revisionism" is really nothing other than these developments taken as a whole. They led to the reconstruction of a class society instead of the pursuit of the transition toward a classless society. True, the very term revisionism remains open to discussion because the analysis of this evolution is still insufficient. In effect, the term refers to the fact that Marx's theses would have had to be revised to allow for this negative development. It was used by Lenin to describe the working-class parties in the Second International which, in their abandonment of internationalism in 1914, "revised" Marx (as the Bernstein current of opinion admitted). It was used again by Mao Zedong, to describe the Soviet system and policies, as well as those of the parties that supported it, although the Chinese Maoists did not backdate Soviet revisionism to the 1930s. Similarly, Lenin did not go back to the roots of the "first revisionism," since up to 1914 he considered Kautskyism nonrevisionist!

This revisionism, then, which is manifested in a despotic type of exploiting and oppressing state, was not founded on para-capitalist economic development (both by resorting to market processes and opening up to the outside world). On the contrary, it was based on development relatively closed to the outside and on the administrative management of the economy; it sought its legitimacy in the theory of democracy and in the party. It was, as we know, exported to Eastern Europe and elsewhere.

On the other hand, China has not (not yet?) questioned the peasant-worker alliance (the peasantry had no compulsory role in the financing of industrialization), has not (not yet?) questioned the centrality of its aim of basing industry on a maximum egalitarianism (a limited range of salaries, equality of salaries with peasant incomes), and has not (not yet?) opted to open to the outside world to any great extent. And while the reforms under consideration at the moment, based on the autonomy of the firm, will reassert the role of value in economic management, this does not prevent the elaboration of a plan aimed at maintaining town-country and intra-urban parities. Of course, China may still develop in a revisionist direction, but that will depend on its social dynamic and will not be determined by technical and economic factors. Soviet revisionism can, after all, be contrasted with a revisionism based on extensive use of the market (but on the basis of collective rather than private ownership of capital) and a very considerable opening to the outside world. In Yugoslavia these conditions aided in the consolidation of a new class, which is also para-statist, but which, given the nondespotic character of the state, operates in a more flexible social climate. China could also undergo this type of development.[10]

2.   If we refuse to accept the concept of "revisionism," we must accept that there is no development pattern other than that inaugurated by the Soviet Union and the countries of the East, which have been described as "socialist despite everything" (a development viewed as "positive on the whole"). According to this point of view, the "faults" are specific to historical situations and do not alter the fundamentally socialist character of societies in which the private ownership of capital has been abolished. If we believe that the development of the forces of production necessarily implies a statist-type management of the economy, then we confuse socialism and statism. Those who are not enchanted by this prospect see the arrival of 1984 (referring to George Orwell's novel). But is this inevitable? The "Amin-Frank" position on this is worth a brief exposition at this point.[11]

Our position is that "1984" is a polemical way of describing the statist mode of production. Its adherents see the rise of this mode as a response to capitalist contradictions, either within the framework of a superhegemony or of the division of the world between several superpowers. But the question is not whether this is likely, but whether it is possible, and here the desire of the working classes and technocracies of the West for a statist form of government is more significant than the projection of pseudoeconomic and pseudotechnical trends— for example, the increasing socialization of the productive forces. The fact that the form of statism envisaged does not have to have the primitive character of that of the Soviet Union is only an additional argument in favor of the thesis that statism is superior to capitalism, and is therefore one possible outcome, given the contradictions of capitalism. The analysis of these ideologies is therefore important, even if it is imperfect and intuitive. I have in mind here the analysis of the ideology of organizations (the Frankfurt school), of the decline of the bourgeois way of life (the crisis in the reproduction of the bourgeoisie, inheritance and the family, schooling, etc.), of the capital-labor alliance (which might seem unavoidable given the absence of a "socialist" revolution), and of the criticisms of the socialist experiences in the advanced industrialized countries.

Seen from this angle, relations between statism and the market are more complex than is often suspected. Is a system of "administered prices" not half way between these two theoretical systems? Is it not rather one-sided to put the question exclusively in terms of markets (equals capitalism) or administrative management (equals statism)? What is the real difference between a system of prices administered by the monopolies and the system in the Soviet Union, which is said to be statist but may increasingly be a reflection of the relationship between monopoly groups? Are administered prices reflecting market forces or overriding them?

It is also confusing to link simplistically the tendency to statism and the perspectives of the international division of labor. The distinction I drew earlier between the 1984 A scenario (the transfer of all classical industry to the periphery and the concentration of the quaternary sector in the core) and the 1984 B scenario (no transfers to the periphery, which is condemned to disappear) was aimed at separating these two questions. The tendency toward A is the result of powerful spontaneous forces, particularly the search for profit. There is nothing in the least felicitous about its possible result (the South African model), with or without the "market." But this tendency nonetheless comes up against obvious difficulties: if the transnationals do not decide to raise the price of raw materials, following the example of oil, it is precisely because they are not sure of being able to keep the profits resulting from this increase (in the case of oil, the oil states kept them). The success or failure of A will therefore depend upon the outcome of all the conflicts of our time combined. In the meantime, we are progressing toward a combination of A plus B: the newly industrialized countries are emerging at one pole and the Fourth World at the other. The populist revolt of the Third World (the newly industrialized countries plus the Fourth World) is the main force that could bring about the failure of the A or B alternative, or of a combination of the two. It gives us no information as to the other question, whether the direction will be that of statism or socialism.

3.   The thesis of relentless "capitalist degeneration" is based, as we know, on the supposed inevitable consequence of the "underdevelopment of productive forces." This will bring about a deterioration of state power (which nevertheless is still controlled by the working class, according to the Trotsky-ists) and lead to attempts at reintegration into the world system. Why?

According to this thesis, the statist mode of production is in effect incapable of ensuring continual growth. There is a crisis as soon as a country has to go from extensive accumulation based on the absorption of excess labor to intensive accumula-tion based on improvements in productivity. It is at this point no longer possible to avoid turning to the outside world, in order to import on a large scale the technology that cannot be produced locally. To pay for this, the country will be forced to export, emphasizing the advantages it gains from its cheap labor force. The Soviet Union will thus be gradually forced to accept the dictates of the law of value at the world level and become integrated into the system as a sort of industrialized semiperipheral power or a second-class imperialist power. In effect, the true centers in the world system are characterized by the advanced form of wage labor and the peripheries by semiforced forms of labor (slavery in the nineteenth-century United States, the second serfdom in Eastern Europe, Soviet administrative constraints, forced labor under colonialism, etc.), all of which imply the direct intervention of the state. In these circumstances, the Soviet's "advantage" in competing with the capitalist peripheries and the declining centers (e.g., Great Britain) will only lead to the reproduction of unequal development, to its ultimate disadvantage.

4.   Neither the postulate of a "1984" fatal for the entire world, because the development of the productive forces must lead to this end, nor that of a fatal degeneration of those countries whose insufficiently developed productive forces will force them to reintegrate into the world capitalist system as semiperipheral countries seems to us convincing.

The crisis of the East is nevertheless real and structural. The 1930–35 break created in the USSR an irreversible situation characterized by the consolidation of a despotic state class. The result is that the system is, in the last resort, governed by the maximization of the incomes of the state class and its growth through the integration of the middle classes. This hypothesis should be linked with that of the Hungarian sociologists who put forward the hypothesis that the law of the system would lead to the maximization of state-controlled products, and not of the national product.[12] It is easy to understand that the income controlled by the state forms the basis of the income of the state class, and that the maximization of this controlled income can conflict with that of the national product. We can then understand the depth of the crisis in the Soviet system, which makes the transition from extensive to intensive accumulation difficult. But how will the USSR react to this crisis? By "capitulating" to the imperialist system? By an expansionist advance using the military means at its disposal?

We reject the possibility of capitulation and gradual peaceful integration into the capitalist system. In effect, whatever opinion we may have about the origin, nature, and outlook for Soviet military power, that power is a reality. Further, this reality and the self-centered nature of the economic structure—the result of a history that started with the socialist revolution—exclude, in my opinion, the possibility of the reduction of the USSR to the state of a semiperipheral country dominated by world capital, at least for the next few decades.

The participation of the USSR in the international division of labor can in no way efface the autonomous character of the Soviet system. No doubt the middle classes' aspirations to an improved level of consumption can work in the direction of unequal and dependent integration. But these classes are only the subordinate allies of the state class, which retains a monopoly over the political direction of the state.

As for China, there is no question of its having chosen to subordinate its development to the demands of the accumulation of capital at the world level. China remains self-reliant and, given this outlook external relations are subjected to the logic of its internal development. The threat of deviation as a result of a too wide opening to the external world coinciding with unfavorable developments in internal social relationships to the benefit of the middle classes certainly exists. But this is still far from the Yugoslav situation, if such is even conceivable in such a huge country.

5.   How will the structural crisis of the statist system in Eastern Europe develop during the present decade? There are unlimited possibilities. What seems undeniable is that the crisis will deepen, and that it will probably end in the disintegration of this system. The explosive situation in Poland reminds us of this.

Some think—and even hope—that this disintegration will lead to a reintegration, pure and simple, into the capitalist system and to the restoration of classical production relations. This seems to me unlikely; the abolition of private ownership of the means of production seems to me irreversible. The revolt of the workers in the East should be seen as a socialist attempt to get out of the contradictions of the statist system, not as a return to the past. Moreover, the aim of the revolt is the recovery of elementary rights for the working class (freedom of association and expression, the right to strike, etc.), but these will be difficult to achieve because the link between Soviet despotism and socialism has put a worker revolt under a banner whose meaning is questionable. In this sense, the disintegration of the East takes on an aspect of populism characteristic of the South.

The path of this disintegration cannot be predicted. Order

may be restored by violence, as in Hungary in 1956 and Czechoslovakia in 1968. On the other hand, the West may profit politically and ideologically if the Yalta system and the Warsaw Pact collapse. The calculations of the USSR and Europe concerning détente are ambiguous. No doubt the USSR sees détente as the strict observance of the Yalta partitioning; Europe, however, may see it as the means whereby the East can be peacefully "integrated" into its expansion—although this does not at the moment seem to be Europe's strategy, which in fact accepts the Soviet point of view. Will the revolt spread from Eastern Europe to the USSR itself? There the system seems more stable. Dissidence is limited to the intellectuals, who are usually reactionary and heartsick for traditional Russia. The masses are mute, the result of despotism and of the "human face" of neo-Stalinism, which has renounced blind repression; the middle classes are satisfied with the improvement in their material situation; and the Russian nation is proud of its military power. But what will be the outcome of the centrifugal forces that will result from the nationalism of the oppressed Muslim, Caucasian, and Baltic nations?

Whatever happens in these peripheries, my opinion is that the 1980s will see an increase in all these processes of disintegration, which opens up new perspectives for the development of the socialist movement in the East and West. This movement may be faced, for the first time in half a century, with the prospect of emerging from the impasse in which it has been locked by the opposition between the capitalist and so-called socialist states. If this new situation is created, I would return to the basic discussion of the "two revisionisms," i.e., that of the Second International and that of Soviet communism. The problems of the former were not really overcome by Lenin. History has proved that he did not deal adequately with the problematic of socialism in the West, as Rosa Luxemburg and Antonio Gramsci, among others, suspected. We cannot reduce the impotence of the Western working-class movement to its complicity with imperialism, even if this is an essential aspect of the question. Similarly, we cannot attribute the non-communist working-class movement's impotence to policies that involve the mere "management of capital" by a corrupt bureaucracy. Along with social experiences of this type, there has also developed a social reformism that has profoundly modified the question of social transformation. Nor is it possible to consider the self-management (*autogestion*) trends either as vestiges of "anarchism" or as neocapitalist means of integration. The move of certain Communist parties toward Eurocommunism, as opposed to the freezing of others in fixed "pro-Soviet" positions, is an indication that the divisions inherited from World War I and from the Russian Revolution are beginning to be questioned. The construction of Europe—a strategy being implemented unilaterally by capital—could, were there to be a revival of the working-class movement in the West as there is in the East, and if this movement were to become aware of the effects of imperialism on the societies of the West, open new perspectives. But it must be remembered that in the short run right-wing reactions are possible: the whittling away of the democratic state by "new-style" pseudoliberal authoritarianism and the development of anti-Third World racism are evidence of this. In my opinion, this development, which would sentence the working-class movement to another long night of retreat, will depend primarily on the direction in which imperialism develops.

Will the 1980s see, as a result of this profound crisis in the statist East, the de facto beginning of the end of the "revisionisms"? In my opinion, the question remains open.

THE NATURE OF THE ISSUES AT STAKE IN THE CRISIS: AN ATTEMPT AT SYNTHESIS

The components of the system analyzed in the preceding sections (the decline of the United States, the economic success of Europe and Japan, the crisis in development in the peripheral capitalist countries, and the crisis in the Soviet system) must now be brought together into an overall hypothesis about the nature of the conflicts of our time and of the issues at stake in the crisis.

To do so, I shall examine the present world conflict, in terms of the two superpowers, interimperialist conflict, China, and the capitalist Third World; the demand for "delinking" and "nonalignment"; and the contradictions of the socialist transition at the world level. I shall then offer an interpretation of the subjects in question—crisis, nationalism, and socialism—and discuss the developments that seem most probable in the next decade.

1.   The necessary starting point for this attempt at synthesis is an analysis of the "international situation."

1.1   In effect, an analysis of the conflicts of our time, whether they be "internal" or "international," "ideological," "social," "economic," or "political," must be set in their world context, for they interact and take on significance in this setting.

Now, there are two opposite theses here. One interprets these conflicts as an open struggle between the socialist and capitalist camps. I reject this idea because I believe that the statist mode of production is not socialism, and that the principal forces on the left (at the world level) have not put the abolition of social classes on their agenda. They are struggling for other things: an improvement in the situation of the working classes in the imperialist system (this refers to some working-class forces in the West), a move toward the state mode of production (referring to other working-class forces), an improvement in the situation of the peoples in the periphery, within the framework of a renewed world economic system (referring to movements for national liberation).

The other thesis begins with a recognition of these facts, and then analyzes the world situation as one where nations and the states predominate. In this context, hegemonic class alliances formulate their strategy in terms of the actions of the states they govern, while blocs of oppressed classes formulate their strategy within the framework of the nation-state, using the political forces of the left at the world level. This is why the struggles of our times do not appear as struggles between "socialism" and "capitalism" but as national struggles. This is also why nationalism seems to be the predominant force everywhere. I have published my interpretation of this second thesis, which seems to me correct, elsewhere, and I refer the reader to it.[13]

1.2   The elements to be considered are therefore as follows:

(1) The question of socialism is not on the agenda of class conflict in the developed West, where the decline of the United States and the economic growth of Europe and Japan are in the forefront.

(2) The development impasse in the USSR, the uprisings in Eastern Europe, and the assertion of Soviet military power, coupled with the U.S. setback (even if momentary with regard to military power), and with détente in Europe, create an unsettled situation and a real danger of escalation.

(3) The Third World, although weak and incapable of forcing a redealing of the cards to its benefit, is, precisely because of this, in acute crisis. The West and the USSR, called upon to intervene, have nevertheless lost control of events in the face of a rising tide of populism.

Conflicting hypotheses exist around the increasingly crucial question of war or peace. The first hypotheses, that of the Soviet Union and its allies, is that only "imperialism" can envisage war. The USSR, a socialist country and the "natural ally" of the people, is simply resisting imperialist aggression with the means of dissuasion at its disposal. This hypothesis is purely ideological. War is simply the pursuit of political objectives by other means. There is nothing that a priori precludes that a society will resort to this method in the absence of any other.

Diametrically opposed to this hypothesis is the one that states that militarization is inherent in the state mode of production, and that this militarization leads inevitably to expansionism. According to this point of view, the state mode of production, based as it is on the exploitation of labor, demands a continual reinforcement of the means of oppression, and therefore militarization. But if this requirement were inherent in the system, its existence would date back to the 1930s; in fact, until 1960 this was merely a potential tendency. The military inferiority of the USSR forbade any expansion beyond the zones tolerated by the compromise with imperialism (as the partition at Yalta proved). Whatever the nature of the Soviet system may have been, it was still on the defensive—the Cold War and McCarthyism were not invented by Stalin. But as of 1960, military parity between the superpowers altered the possibilities for the USSR.

This view merits discussion. First, it is based on an obvious fact: the military aspect of the Soviet empire. The USSR has never succeeded in exporting its system or its influence by economic means; it has instead used military means to install a state class in its own image and made this class dependent on it, politically and militarily. But did we not see a class of this type assert its independence as soon as circumstances permitted (in Rumania)? Do we not see that the influence the Soviet Union has been able to exert on the Third World has remained fragile (the Middle East) until the time when it has intervened directly (Afghanistan)? This fact is thus, in my opinion, more a proof of the weakness of the Soviet Union than of its strength.

However, whether the resort to military intervention is a sign of strength or weakness, whether it is motivated by the expansionist nature of the system or "defensive" (the last resort in avoiding the disintegration of a zone of influence), are not the fundamental questions. In either case, the USSR is clearly capable of envisaging military intervention. After all, what was the invasion of Czechoslovakia in 1968 but military aggression, even if it was "defensive" in the sense that the country might otherwise have escaped the clutches of Soviet influence?

The same is true of the relationship between the USSR and the West. Why should we a priori reject the Chinese position, according to which the USSR may coerce the world system into a more favorable collaboration? It could, for example, put pressure on the policy of détente in Europe by threatening supplies from the Third World (see the policy of intervention in Africa, the Middle East, and the Indian Ocean). What the Soviet Union is really seeking in the Third World is not exploitation in the classical sense, which it is in any case not really capable of, but a strategic position gained by means of alliances.

In order to argue the likelihood of Soviet aggression, it is not necessary to postulate that expansionism is inherent in the state mode of production, just as it need not be said that imperialism necessarily brings war. No social system is aggressive in itself. War is a means that is not specific to any system, but that becomes a reality in a given economic phase, as Alexander Faire has reminded us.[14] Nor is it necessary to claim that the United States is a declining superpower and the USSR a rising one that sees an opportunity to extend its domination to the whole of the planet. On the contrary. In my opinion, it is the *weakness* of the Soviet system that leads it to be aggressive. The dual "decline" of the United States and the USSR, along with the weaknesses of Europe (economically expanding but militarily vulnerable) and of the Third World (which cannot escape the domination of imperialism without appealing for Soviet support) creates this extremely dangerous situation. It encourages the USSR to expand both directly and indirectly (Afghanistan and Kampuchea) and could lead it to accelerate its plan to force the West to accept a "Finlandization" by putting pressure on its supplies from the Third World, before the United States has finally recovered military supremacy. The Soviet Union is encouraged in this direction by appeals from petty bourgeois national liberation movements in the Third World and by détente in Europe, which encourages a tacit left-right alliance (by keeping alive, in the left and in the working-class movement, the illusion of Soviet "socialism").

1.3   The theory of Soviet aggressivity matured during the Sino-Soviet conflict. This conflict is central to our times, although its source has only gradually come to light. The difference between the "Maoist" and "revisionist" lines was certainly apparent in the 1950s (Mao Zedong's "Ten Great Relationships" signalled the Chinese Communist Party's awareness as early as 1956), and situated the conflict in its basic setting, the construction of socialism. The conflict broke out, however, as a result of a difference of opinion as regards the international situation. The USSR was accustomed to having only vassals (Yugoslavia's desire for independence meant excommunication in 1948) or situational allies (the Western Communist Parties and the radical bourgeois national liberation movements). Its attitude was only accepted by the left throughout the world because until 1960 it seemed to be a fortress under seige. But China would not accept a vassal position—at a time when, having caught up with the United States on the military front, the USSR was becoming increasingly arrogant and questioning the United States about the division of the world (see the Camp David interview between Khrushchev and Eisenhower).

It would be a mistake to forget these circumstances and the very real threat the USSR poses for China. In effect, how could the Chinese ignore Khrushchev's proposal to Adenauer that there be a common "European" front to ward off the "yellow peril"? How could they forget the ruthless withdrawal in 1960, when all contracts in progress were broken in an attempt to subjugate China? How could they forget the constant anti-Chinese racist hysteria in the Soviet press, which is evidence of greater preparation for war on the Eastern than on the Western front—toward which Soviet language is pacifist? How could they forget that the USSR has in fact foreseen an atomic attack on China and the annexing of Sinkiang? How can they forget that Mongolia, with less than 2 million inhabitants, is the stronghold of a Soviet army of 1 million, with rockets trained on Peking a few hundred kilometers away?

The conflict therefore brings to light a fundamental reality: the emergence of a modernized China (whether it be capitalist, socialist, or even revisionist like the USSR) is basically unacceptable to the USSR, which already has its work cut out dealing with the West. All Chinese tendencies agree on this. Further, whatever its future development, it will continue to be threatened by the USSR, although it may not always be the number one target (nor do those in power in Peking believe this to be so). On the other hand, since China may feel equally threatened by imperialism, a tactical reconciliation with the USSR cannot be excluded. It is a game for three players, not two.

In effect, the Soviet threat does not rule out imperialism. During the 1960s, China thought itself capable of opposing the two superpowers simultaneously (both Soviet pressure on the frontier, and its support for India in the war for the frontier, and U.S. support for Taiwan's aggression) by relying on the "zone of tempests." China recognized Cuba as a socialist country when the USSR was still hesitating, and encouraged all revolutionary Third World liberation movements: Bolivia, Algeria, the Congo, the Portuguese colonies, Vietnam, Palestine. China also relied on the Western working classes, which it believed were in no way revisionist. During the 1970s, however, it was forced to relinquish these hopes. It is understandable then, that China, anxious to safeguard the independence of its development, chose an alliance with Washington. Moreover, it was the United States that after twenty years of attempting to "reconquer" China (beginning with the Korean war, between 1950 and 1953), was forced to admit its failure and recognize China (in 1971), before being hounded out of Indochina in 1975.

Nevertheless, this alliance could "spin the top in the other direction," that is, conceal the fact that imperialism too is aggressive and can resort to war in pursuit of its policies. We might then forget that in other areas of the world the main, and real, enemy is not the Soviet Union, but omnipresent Western capital. On the other hand, the uprisings in the Third World and the USSR's difficulties in Eastern Europe (Poland) may lead to a rapid change in the balance of power. The development of a popular reaction to the crisis in the West (see, for example, the rise of the right in the United States) means that there is an element of the unknown in these disturbances. In these circumstances, the most effective response to the danger created by the interventionism of the two superpowers is to reinforce the truly nonaligned countries. If this is not done, the peoples of the Third World, in their rebellion against imperialism, may well be thrown into the Soviet bloc. In that case, the Peking-Washington axis might not suffice to counterbalance the USSR's advantages on other fronts. On the other hand, it should not, therefore, preclude support for nonalignment, which is the only way to create an autonomous space between the two superpowers and is a precondition for the development of autonomous socialist forces.

1.4   Given present international conditions, there is no question of treating all countries that call themselves socialist as if they were identical by describing their conflicts as simply expressions of the nationalism of statist regimes.

The conflicts in Eastern Europe are confrontations between the hegemonic Soviet power, the regimes modelled on it, and the people of the region. Here the aspiration for "Europeanness" is all the stronger because it coincides with the interests of the middle classes created by revisionist development. The fact that this aspiration is partly associated with a desire for European working-class traditions and partly with the attractions of capitalism is obvious, particularly when we consider that Yugoslavia—the only country in the region aside from Albania, to have undergone an authentic socialist revolution— was unable to resist many of the effects of Western integration. But whatever the immediate outlook—and these countries do not benefit from the active support of a Europe which is preoccupied with détente—these conflicts nevertheless weaken the USSR and refuse to take the despotic state mode of production for granted.

The conflicts in Indochina must also be seen in this global context. There is no doubt that the USSR has found an echo in Vietnam, where the struggle for national liberation— exemplary as it was—did not create the most favorable conditions for socialist construction. But it is not only that Soviet aid has maintained an illusion; from the beginning to end, the struggle for liberation had a foreign power as the main enemy, thus retarding the growth of class consciousness. This is what distinguishes the Chinese Communist Party from the Indochinese. The invasion of Kampuchea, facilitated by the conduct of the Pol Pot regime, was not the result of Vietnam's atavistic desire to expand. It resulted from a convergence of the impasse in which Vietnam found itself (the beginning of a statist revolution) and Soviet encouragement (aimed at keeping a closer hold on Vietnam and incorporating it into its plan for encircling China).

In this light, we must return to a discussion of that badly phrased choice: support for the revolution versus the primacy of the state's interest.

Proposition 1: The "egoism" of the revolutionary and socialist forces (and states) that attempt to subordinate the strategies of their allies to their own immediate aims is natural. This is because such "self-centeredness" has its origins not in a basic opportunism, but in the unequal development of the socialist revolution (a revolution that is not, and cannot be, global). This explains why the USSR sacrificed the German revolution of the 1920s (which was to a great extent a myth anyway) and the revolution in the West of the 1930s (the "popular fronts," another myth). It also explains why the Vietnamese Communist Party attempted to subordinate the Kampuchean Communist Party to its alliance with Sihanouk, why Yugoslavia gave up supporting Greece in 1948, and so on. This policy did not prevent authentic revolutionary movements, all of which "disobeyed," from asserting themselves—examples include China's refusal to obey the orders of the Comintern, Vietnam's refusal to obey its allies in 1945, the Communist Party of Kampuchea, and even the Cuban revolution, which succeeded almost by chance. On the other hand, external aid has never been a substitute for internal revolution and correct strategy. Vietnam did not win because of Soviet and Chinese aid; nor was Kampuchea's victory due to aid from Vietnam. The "domino" theory has never been proven: geographical proximity did not pull Thailand or Burma along the road to socialism.

Proposition 2: The hegemonism of the superpowers and future local hegemonisms will not be of the same nature. It is probably true that they have their origins in the same impasse, and that in this sense we could say that expansionism is inherent in the state mode of production in the same way that imperialism is inherent in capitalism. But the analogy stops there because each form of expansionism has a logic and aims of its own. To say that they both originate in a form of "nationalism" that is characteristic of all peoples and all times, and in the expansionist desire (or desire for world hegemony when this appears a possibility) that this nationalism presupposes, advance us no further than any poor philosophy of history would. Any superpower has global pretensions and aims either at the exclusive domination or partition of the planet (and thereby deserves to be called "social imperialist"). It may be "defensive" in the sense that it feels threatened by the hegemonism of its adversary, which might attempt to exploit its crisis, and that its response is to take the initiative. Local hegemonisms are forced to locate themselves within the limits drawn by the conflict of the superpowers. The same, moreover, is true for the Western bloc. "Sub-imperialist" desires, aimed at smoothing out local contradictions at the expense of weaker neighbors, are necessarily accomplished in the context of the global strategies of capital.

Proposition 3. We should be wary of arguments invented for the occasion that usually conceal the nature of the aims. Arguments of this type can be classified as follows: (1) The argument for exported revolution is an ideological by-product of the French revolution (where it concealed the aspirations of the French bourgeoisie, which Napoleon was to reveal) but alien to Marxism. (2) The "humanitarian" argument of saving a people from barbarism (used in Kampuchea, Afghanistan), which Stalin exposed. ("Between the Afghan emir, and the English worker, the forces of progress are on the side of the former, who is attempting to escape foreign exploitation and oppression."). This argument has been used by colonial powers from time immemorial. (3) The argument of "defense," which diplomats fall back on (Afghanistan threatening the USSR, Kampuchea and Vietnam, etc.).

If these propositions are accepted, it should be obvious that the best "support" for the "peoples" is to leave them to settle their contradictions themselves. The need to respect national sovereignty is not based on an a priori belief in their divinity, but in an analysis of the real dynamics of social change. It is obvious that the problems of the Afghan people will not be solved by the Russians, any more than those of the people of Kampuchea will be by Vietnam (the concept of Indochina, which is not based on the nations of the region but only on French colonial history, has no meaning).

2.   "Delinking" is therefore a strategy applicable both to socialist transition and to national liberation at every stage, even at the outset. The two are inseparable. Further, it is a strategy that takes note of the popular response to the crisis.

2.1.   The "traditional" belief of the working class and of the socialist movement (and of the "evolutionist" social democrats) is that socialism will first be built in the advanced capitalist core states, because of the level of development of the forces of production. The "globalization" of production implied by this level of development is the basis for postulating a "world revolution" (or at least a European one). Lenin and Bukharin replaced this belief with the concept of unequal development within the imperialist system, which was divided between core states, where the socialist transformation is retarded, and peripheries, where the convergence of the movement for national liberation, the peasant revolution, and the working-class movement enables capitalist relations of production to be overcome earlier, even though the level of development of the forces of production remains low. The concept of "rupture" is then inseparable from the concept of unequal development and socialist construction, based on a "country" leaving the capitalist-imperialist system. The concept of "rupture" is already present in the "socialism in one country" thesis, which therefore still seems to me to be fundamentally correct.

However, the concept of "rupture" does not have any scientific status. It refers to a complex empirical reality (or an aim), which is why it is helpful to retrace the history of its development in order to analyze its various elements.

Any revolution is, by definition, a rupture—the Paris Commune, Russia in 1917, the Chinese Revolution were all ruptures. Within Marxism, however, rupture specifically (1) concerned those relations of production that were transformed after the abolition of private ownership of the means of production—this abolition was the outcome of a radical change in the nature of political power; and (2) was believed to operate in the already developed capitalist spaces. The question of the relationship between these spaces and those ruled by capitalism (economic, technical, cultural, political, and military relationships) is not made explicit because it is assumed that the space in question is "strong" enough that its transformation will not be vitiated by the maintenance or suppression of these external relationships. Moreover, it is obvious that it is the forces of production/relations of production and base/superstructure oppositions that dictate the nature of the rupture in question.

There are therefore two distinct, yet linked, sets of questions: (1) What is the "change" or rupture, and (2) what is the relationship (or absence of relationship) with the outside world? One good way to look at these questions is to look at how we interpret past historical ruptures and compare this with how they were interpreted, particularly by their actors.

The Paris Commune effected a decisive rupture at the level of political organization, and Marx drew certain conclusions from it. But the Commune had no time to be confronted with a reorganization of the relations of production, and the only relationship it had with the outside world was the armed confrontation when Paris was surrounded.

The Russian Revolution began by effecting a rupture at the same level—political—and of the same type. Faced with the issue of the relations of production, the initial response was a spontaneous and radical revolution. Not only was private ownership of the means of production abolished, but so were trading relations (during the period known as "war communism"). The situation created by the war—both the civil war and the war with the outside world—reduced relationships with the outside world to those of military and ideological confrontation. However, the Bolsheviks believed that the Russian Revolution would be the spark which would set off a European, if not a worldwide, revolution. The result would be a rapid transition to socialism; the problem of the relationship between the socialist and capitalist zones would be solved de facto in favor of the socialist zones.

But the extension of the revolution never occurred. Some have not been willing to learn the lesson from this and give up the a priori schema of a world revolution. Such people are not concerned that their "theory" reduces them to complete impotence; they can always take refuge in academic or sectarian Marxism. But those who are concerned with the transformation of the world should learn the lesson of history: imperialism has made the socialist transformation of the core states unlikely, while this transformation is a burning topic in the periphery. This changes the terms in which the two questions listed above are posed.

In Russia, after the war communism period, the NEP re-established both trading and economic relations with the outside world. This should not lead us, however, too rapidly to the conclusion that the USSR was thereby reintegrating itself into the world capitalist system. External exchanges remained limited and very much under control, while political power remained in the hands of the worker-peasant alliance. Later negative developments can thus in no way be explained as the inevitability of "socialism in one country," or by the effects of equally inevitable external exchanges. The explanation lies in the shortcomings of the Marxist outlook of the time (shortcomings shared by the opposition and the main tendency)— the "technicist" ideology of Bolshevism, the distrust of the peasants, etc. In these circumstances, imported technologies play a part in vitiating the strategies of transition, but only because the question of the development of other forces and relations of production is not even raised.

In these circumstances, when the worker-peasant alliance broke down after 1930, and the country started on an accelerated program of state industrialization, a class society was gradually built up. But here again, the relationships with the outside world play only a supporting role in this reconstruction. Moreover, the imported technology is disconnected from the world market by the administrative planning of prices and is reconnected to a new mode of production—the state mode. It is therefore not an integral part of any "return" to capitalism.

The Chinese experience has made it possible to analyze further the question of rupture. During the long period of civil war, "delinking" was practically total. In this repect, Yenan provides a lesson that it is essential for any Third World country setting out in a socialist direction to learn. Moreover, the Vietnamese and Cambodians reproduced this model and had to go through the same stages. This was not an accident. After 1949, the autarky of Yenan was extended to all of China, largely by force of circumstance (the Western blockade). The importation of Soviet technology during the 1950s had the same effect as the import of Western technology would have had, but the question of international strategy had more to do with the Sino-Soviet break than with the negative effects of this technology on the relations of production. The subsequent development of the class struggle on the basis of the worker-peasant alliance enabled further advance in practical response to the problems posed.

The cultural revolution emphasized the first question (what rupture?) and subordinated the second (what relationship with the outside world?). The commune as a way to integrate agriculture, industry, education, administration, and politics propelled the social tranformation further than anything we have seen to date. At the same time, the cultural revolution reduced China's contacts with the outside world to a minimum. The present reforms may enable the forces of production to continue to develop along the lines of socialist construction despite a wider opening to the outside, but they also create the danger of going astray. In my opinion, however, given these possible developments, the main elements are political power and the relations of production, any relationship with the outside world being subordinate to these.

If, as historical experience seems to indicate, the important elements are the class struggle and the transformation of the relations of production, and if the intensity and type of relation with the outside world only has the effect of reinforcing the orientation toward development that is defined by the relations of production, why speak of "rupture," "delinking," or "self-reliant development" instead of simply of the "socialist transformation of the relations of production"? There are two opposing answers to this question.

The first argues that the only question is that of the transformation of the relations of production. This transformation is difficult because the forces of production are insufficiently advanced and have been developed by capitalism, in the framework of a system of exchange at the world level. Given these conditions, ending relationships with the external world becomes an additional handicap to the development of the productive forces and, because of this, makes the transformation of the relations of production still more difficult, if not impossible. This argument is closely linked to the idea that technology is neutral. If this were so, socialism would be impossible because, given the existence of imperialism, it could not be envisaged in developed countries. If socialism in one (backward) country is impossible, socialism itself is impossible.

The other argument is that the transformation of the relations of production must and can be effected, even if the forces of production are less developed. There is no other choice. What is more, if the forces of production are to be developed, it is on the basis of these new relationships, which will in turn direct development in directions that differ from those taken on the basis of capitalist relations of production (for technology is not neutral).

Two questions then arise. The first is whether "socialism in one country" is possible. My answer is yes. Is it certain? No. Another possible outcome, one to which history bears witness, is the state mode of production. But is there not a third, classical "capitalist" development? My answer is that it is probably impossible. This is where the concept of self-reliant development comes in: a type of development where relations with the outside world are subordinated to the demands of internal accumulation—as opposed to extroverted development, where the accumulation (which is dependent) comes from relations with the outside world and is shaped by them. The socialist revolution in the periphery makes self-reliant development possible (and necessary). The extroverted economy and society are extremely vulnerable to the pressures of imperialism, both externally and internally (through social classes shaped by imperialist domination). The concept of self-reliant development obviously does not apply to a socialist revolution in a developed country which is already self-reliant. But this is not the issue. "Normal" capitalist development within the world system demands this change in the character of the economy and society, from outward-looking to self-reliant. Imperialist domination makes it impossible.

In the case of self-reliant development, were a society to direct itself toward the transformation of the relations of production, the question as to which of the two strategies—suppressing relations with the outside world or maintaining them—is most conducive to the success of this transformation arises. My position is that a reduction in external relations is the better choice because the technology that would be imported, were these relations to be maintained, is not neutral and is in fact a hindrance to social transformation. Nevertheless, the stagnation of the forces of production is also a disadvantage, so that it is possible that a certain amount of technological importation is useful and necessary. A certain balance must be found; it is a question of political pragmatism. It may be that in some circumstances too brutal a rupture of external relations will have negative consequences. Is that not the difficulty at the moment in Vietnam and Cambodia, and was it not the case with the cultural revolution? The (correct) (re-) discovery that technology is not neutral has led us to forget the necessary development of the forces of production. A more refined analysis of the role of technology is therefore needed.

Two remarks can be made on the basis of this analysis. The first is that countries in the periphery that have not undergone a socialist revolution have never really embarked upon a self-reliant type of development and have not delinked. This is why these fragile experiments (Egypt under Nasser, Tanzania, etc.) are reversible, even though certain transformations (agrarian reform and nationalization, for example) might not appear to be so. But where development remains outward looking, these "irreversible" transformations are easily won back by monopoly capital, whereas this is not the case with self-reliant development.

The second point is that delinking would probably be necessary even for a developed country that embarked on a transformation of its social relationships. In fact, external relations—which would then be relations of imperialist exploitation—are the basis of a class structure that is opposed to transformation. If, therefore, the underdeveloped countries appear to be at an impasse, faced with a real contradiction, the developed countries are even more so. Rudolf Bahro is perfectly aware of the nature of this problem, which makes him unusual. The main lines of thought, even the most progressive ones, do not admit it, either in the developed capitalist or in the Eastern European countries. This analysis therefore implies, among other things, that the European working-class movements must renounce the temptations of the "European" option. For yielding to demands to "develop the forces of production" means postponing socialist transformation in those places where it could be begun by breaking the weak links in the European system.

There is one conclusion to be drawn from this analysis. If things are as we claim, a rupture of the world system is the only way out of the difficulties of the contemporary world, then the model for the transition to a classless society would resemble that of the "transition from antiquity to feudalism." By this I mean that it would be a model of "decadence," rather than a model of "revolution," which was the case for the transition to capitalism.

2.2   Delinking is not only a precondition for national liberation and the transition to socialism; it is also a precondition for eliciting a response from the people to the intervention of the superpowers and imperialism, and for encouraging their attempt to control change to fit their own aims, which are diametrically opposed to those of imperialism.

Delinking is thus the only way to recreate an autonomous space suitable for liberating the dynamics of fundamental social conflict. There is no doubt such a withdrawal risks developing a vision of the nation as a confined space within which internal class domination is legitimate. Revisionists do try to justify their acts in this way. It is useful to view the questions relating to comparative situations of quasi-autarky or opening to the outside from this point of view: Albania and Yugoslavia; Rumania and Poland; Burma; Ethiopia, Yemen, Afghanistan, etc. Similarly, it is useful to discuss European problems in this framework, examining the ambiguities of European "nationalism" and infranational regionalism. But conversely, unqualified "internationalism" has become a means of supporting local systems of exploitation that have their niche in the global hierarchy. Yesterday's justification of colonialism is today's justification for the servile strategy of a bourgeoisie dependent on imperialism.

If there is a possibility for delinking, it is to be found in the Third World. This is the only way in which nonalignment can be interpreted. Keeping a distance is the absolute minimum these countries can undertake, given the present accentuation of even secondary contradictions.

3.   Finally, our epoch is one of struggle between a nascent socialism and a capitalism that is still very much in command.

3.1   Of course, this struggle is not between two "clans," corresponding to two groups of states. Socialism has made its way mainly by severing weak links in the periphery. These ruptures, whatever their middle-term perspectives and their possible setbacks, deal a blow to the system of global centralization specific to contemporary capitalism. They therefore create the condition for the eventual construction of a globalization based on different relations of production.

What relations of production? Perhaps those of a classless society at the world level, or perhaps those of a society based on the state mode of production, one either united or divided into several (or many?) states. The analysis of these possibilities is not based on a mechanistic forecast of economic trends—seeing, for instance, the tendency to the centralization of capital as the ultimate motive force of history. On the contrary, it is based on a close examination of the fundamental questions relating to the functioning of society: the nature of the relationship between the forces of production, the relations of production, and ideology (the relative importance of economism, of merchant relations, the question of alienation, etc.).

Is such an examination not the object of the present study? Let me say simply that the prospect of an inevitable socialism is closer to the prophetic tradition of the Golden Age than to the Marxist method (even though the latter is colored by the ideological climate of the culture into which it was born). Once again, let me draw a parallel with the passage from antiquity to the modern world: European feudalism appears, looking back, as a stage in the break-up of the early Roman tributary centralization, freeing local forces of production and preparing for the rapid birth of capitalism; this again centralized the surplus, but at a much higher level of development, by means of the globalization of the modern economy. Today such a development seems inevitable, but such was by no means the case in the year 200, in the year 1000, or even in the year 1700! Moreover, why should our future necessarily tread a similar path, from capitalist to communist globalization via transitional national socialisms? The military and technological balance of power of our epoch have not only had the effect of accelerating history, but also of imprinting upon it unforeseeable developments. Can we exclude the possibility of the East and South being engulfed by the West, or of the West and South being engulfed by the East, or of the destruction pure and simple of the South, at least in part?

3.2   What I have attempted to do here is to set out some of the "big questions" facing the working-class and socialist movements, as well as the movements for national liberation. We have seen that as regards each of these questions—whether it be strategic and tactical choices, or theoretical and practical ones—the various tendencies are contradictory and hesitant. The fact is that this "crisis," which affects not only communism but the social democracies and the national liberation movements, is coupled with a real crisis in the world imperialist system and in the Soviet state mode of production. We can therefore see this positively as a time for rethinking— required by the evolution of the imperialist system—of the socialist revolution and national liberation movements.

In my opinion, the questions are fundamental. It is impossible to define a strategy aimed at the abolition of the class system without a clear analysis of the tendencies at work that favor a new class system, of the state mode of production type, within the advanced capitalist societies. These are tendencies that express the class interests of the labor aristocracy and technocracy. We must also draw conclusions from an analysis of the Russian Revolution (in terms of the social nature of the Soviet regime), and of the imperialist system ("global" revolution, or a series of ruptures starting with the weak links, particularly in its periphery). We must also analyze the world equilibrium and the aims of the Soviet superpower. A correct analysis of these questions implies certain fundamental theoretical ideas concerning the relationship between the base, ideology, and social dynamics, and the nature of unequal development in a society and in the contemporary system. I have tried to make the foundations of these ideas explicit.

Unfortunately, none of the major tendencies in the Western working-class movements—be it social democratic or communist—nor any of the major tendencies of socialism and national liberation in the periphery have clear positions on these questions.

Criticisms of Soviet autocracy are always from a liberal point of view, whether it be that of the social democrats or of the Western Eurocommunists. The "socialist" character of the USSR is not fundamentally questioned. At the same time, the project of the Eurocommunists is not clearly differentiated from that of the traditional social-democratic or new socialist (and left-wing social-democratic) projects, or from those of orthodox communism as regards internal class alliances (the question of the conflicting aspirations of the exploited classes on the one hand, and of the labor aristocracies and technocrats on the other). All these points of view share a state mode of production conception of the society that is to be built. They also pay no attention to the profound effects of imperialism on society or to its prospects in the advanced countries of the West. Finally, if they are at times reserved about the demands of Soviet diplomacy, it is for reasons of national autonomy without any understanding of the world game. (The idea of "polycentrism," put forward by Togliatti not long before his death, went further than those of the currents predominant at the time.) In these circumstances, Eurocommunism in no way appears up to the task of renewing the working-class and socialist movements in the West. Far from supplying an alternative to the present impasse, it merely creates a new myth.

The fundamental reasons for the present impasse are in the crisis of the socialist and national liberation movements. They are equally incapable of criticizing the "petty bourgeois" state mode of production, of understanding the implications of delinking and of the worker-peasant alliance in the transition, and of understanding the nature of the conflict between the superpowers. As we can see, the peoples of the periphery are responding in their own way to this impasse: by "populist" uprisings and the renewal of "traditional" ideologies.

4.   To confront "nationalism" with "socialism" is therefore to fail to understand the nature of the real issues at stake in the contemporary conflict.

4.1   To a great extent, a theory of the nation must still be constructed. We are dealing with a social reality that is not independent of social classes, but is not Marx's hypothesis that when social classes disappear, nations will also cease to exist an extension of the European cosmopolitanism of the Enlightenment and the nineteenth century, which believed that the globalization of the economy would do away with national realities?

Similarly, a theory of the state and of power must still be elaborated. The socialist transition shows that not only does the state *not* disappear, but that it even fulfills a central function. Either the state becomes the rallying point for the new class (revisionism), or it becomes the means by which the people (workers and peasants) express their alliances and their contradictions. Therefore the issue is not between classes confronting each other "in vacuo" but between them and the state, a necessary means for the expression of their will and strategies. Does the persistence of the state during the transition correspond, then, to the reality that Wallerstein has depicted, that what exists is not a state but a system of states—it being the latter that may eventually disappear? And should we not agree with Wallerstein that it is not the nation that is at the origin of the state, but that the state created the nation, by asserting itself as a national state within the world-economy?

As long as we are unable to answer these questions, it will be probably difficult to know whether new national states can be formed when the world-economy has already reduced them to peripheral states. It will be still more difficult to estimate whether the nation will outlive the eventual disappearance of a system of states.

4.2   The issue is therefore not "internationalism" (which is assimilated to socialism) or "nationalism" (assimilated to a form of "capitalism"). It is even possible to speak of "proletarian nationalism" and "bourgeois internationalism" without playing with words. The capitalist mode of production is based on the search for profit, quite outside any discussion of "nation." The bourgeoisie is therefore not a priori either nationalist or internationalist. It uses or subordinates its attitude about this to its strategy, guided by its search for profit. But in so doing it forces other classes to define their strategies as responses to its own.

History therefore shows that the hegemonic bourgeoisies are "internationalist." Some striking examples include the ambiguity of the nationalism of the French Revolution (defensive or offensive?), the cosmopolitanism of Victorian England (accompanied as it was by a feeling of superiority tainted with racism), the cosmopolitanism of the U.S. transnationals after World War II, the Soviet "internationalism" referred to in Eastern Europe, and contemporary "Europeanism." Rising bourgeoisies, still weak, are not even necessarily nationalist (they are sometimes, of course, as in nineteenth-century Europe). Do not dependent bourgeoisies frequently rally to the flag of cosmopolitanism in the name of universalism, both in the Third World and Eastern Europe? It even happens that the people rally to bourgeois universalism—for example, the adherence of the working classes in the West to colonialism. Finally, are not "nationalist" reactions common in the ranks of the very people struggling against the principal enemy— universalist imperialism or social imperialism—with whom the local bourgeoisie has allied, betraying the nation? The importance of national liberation in the Third World (and Eastern Europe) is, in my opinion, fundamental to the advance of socialism.

5. The contemporary crisis has a place in the long transition from capitalism to socialism. It is not only an economic crisis in the advanced capitalist countries, or even a crisis in the North-South international division of labor. It is a crisis of two hegemonies—that of a declining United States (even if this decline is theoretically reversible), which makes it therefore a crisis of the imperialist system, and that of the USSR, to deal with the aspirations of the people of Eastern Europe and yet is incapable of overcoming the weaknesses inherent in the state mode of production. But the crisis in the East is not a crisis of socialism, because the state mode of production is not socialist.

If I dare to make a few forecasts for the present decade, I would sum them up as follows: The political crisis of peripheral capitalism will worsen, giving rise to a long period of populist uprising and disintegration. The crisis in Eastern Europe will also worsen. These two crises will not lead to the development of a new stage of capitalism, however; on the contrary, they will open the way for a possible socialist alternative. The transition to socialism could continue, as it has up to now, through national democratic revolutions in the weak links of the imperialist system. But there could also be a beginning, in the West and in Eastern Europe, of a working-class renewal. The form is difficult to predict.

The political situation created by this decline of the two hegemonies bears with it the danger of war. This was less likely, appearances to the contrary, when the two blocs confronted each other between 1945 and 1970 without a crack showing. War occurs most often when the major forces on the international scene feel their positions threatened, both by their own decline and, as a result, by the danger they represent to each other. In these circumstances, it is essential to maneuver to enlarge the space for autonomy between the two superpowers. This is why nonalignment is a centerpiece in a strategy which, beyond its immediate contribution to reducing the danger of war, offers the most propitious way to develop the forces of national liberation and socialism. And this nonalignment of the Third World countries would be still more efficacious if it were to find true support in Europe and China.

CONCLUSION: A FRIENDLY DEBATE

It will not have escaped the reader's notice that, although the four of us started from common commitments and premises, we did not therefore arrive at identical conclusions. Nor is there any simple line of division among us. Rather, as is to be expected given the complexity of the object of study, many differences of emphasis have emerged, some of them reasonably important. The result is in fact a friendly debate about what is really happening, and may therefore be done about it. It is this debate that we wish to make explicit here.

The debate centers around three main problem areas, each related to the "crisis": (1) the patterns of capitalist development, (2) the balance sheet of the antisystemic forces, and (3) the prospects for the future. We shall treat each in turn.

We have rather important differences on the way in which the so-called long waves of capitalist development fit into the contemporary picture. We are speaking of those waves of expansion and stagnation, approximately fifty years in duration, that are sometimes called Kondratieff cycles. None of us doubt they existed in some sense in the "classical" period, from the late eighteenth century until World War I, for which they were originally described by Kondratieff, Schumpeter, and others. For some of us, they have a far earlier starting point, but that is not the issue here. The issue is whether the capitalist world-economy has entered its structural crisis, and to the extent that it has, whether the Kondratieffs continue to exist in a form comparable to those of the nineteenth century.

For Frank and Wallerstein, the long waves represent part of the recurrent pattern of the functioning of the system, one of its basic outward expressions. The pattern has remained substantially the same despite the structural crisis; indeed, it may be seen as one of the elements determinative of the crisis. One can project from this regularity the likelihood of another expansionary phase beginning in about 1990. This prediction is not only objectively based but enters into the subjective evaluation of economic actors.

Amin and Arrighi are more impressed with the specificity of each so-called wave than with the recurrence of a pattern. Even if there were such a pattern in the nineteenth century, they say, what one means by a structural crisis of the system is that the old "rules" no longer apply. They consider, therefore, that using such a concept tends to make analyses dangerously abstract. They also fear the excessive "economism" of Frank and Wallerstein, who in turn fear the others' excessive "voluntarism." It is, we all agree, a matter of emphasis, but an important one.

The same debate repeats itself on the question of "waves" of "hegemony." For Frank and Wallerstein, we can learn much about the decline of U.S. hegemony from observing its parallels (however limited) with the earlier declines of Dutch and British hegemony. Amin and Arrighi consider the specificities of the present situation so different from those associated with the "decline" of the British in the late nineteenth century as to render any such discussion specious.

A secondary issue here is the nature of the economic stagnation of the 1970s and 1980s. On this, Amin, Arrighi, and Frank all believe that one of the specificities of this most recent stagnation is that, unlike many previous stagnations, it is in no sense the result of a "deficiency of demand" but rather is motored by a significant fall in the rate of profit, triggered in part by the post-1945 strength of labor in the core countries (rising real wages) and perhaps by the ability of some peripheral countries to assert some market strength (e.g., through OPEC). Since demand is not the problem, they expect the efforts of capital to center on ways of reducing costs. For Wallerstein, the whole distinction of deficiency of demand versus fall in the rate of profit is without great importance. Both are part of a single imbricated picture which can be called the discrepancy between global supply and global demand. Stagnation is the result of this discrepancy, in which there is a constant back-and-forth between demand deficiency and the fall in the rate of profit. Neither "causes" the other in the sense of a temporal priority. In a period of stagnation, therefore, both the reduction of costs and the increase in effective demand are interacting parts of a single "solution."

There is a further difference among us on the subject of "imperialism" and its utility as an analytical tool. For Frank and Wallerstein, imperialism is a term that covers any use by core states of their political strength to impose price structures that they find favorable on the world-economy. Sometimes this takes the form of conquest and political overrule; at other times, it takes the form of "informal imperialism," called by others "neocolonialism." They consider this phenomenon so endemic to the functioning of the capitalist world-economy from its beginning that they doubt the utility of a separate word. In any case, they do not rule out the possibility that the "colonial" form of imperialism, which has now been virtually liquidated, might recur. They note, however, the political importance of the existing liquidation.

Amin is closer to the traditional position of Hobson and Lenin. He believes that imperialism is a phenomenon which, in the sense he uses the term, came into existence in the late nineteenth century and to some extent continues even now. He believes that this stage of capitalist development represents a qualitative leap forward in the crystallization of the world system. Arrighi thinks that Hobson's and Lenin's concept of imperialism (a transformation of competition from market competition among enterprises into military competition, i.e., war, among core states) has been relevant throughout the first half of this century. He thinks, however, that the concept has lost much of its relevance because of the structural transformations of the world-economy unleashed by U.S hegemony in the 1950s and 1960s. The term should, therefore, either be used to designate a transitory phase in the development of the capitalist world-economy (roughly from the 1880s to the 1940s) or, as Frank and Wallerstein suggest, not be used at all.

Our views are also diverse when we discuss the antisystemic forces of the modern world, which for convenience we shall divide into the socialist states, the socialist movements, and the nationalist movements.

Let us start with what is for many the keystone of the arch, the USSR. None of us doubt the historic importance of the October Revolution, both as an event that transformed world political reality and as one with worldwide symbolic importance. The question, however, is how to assess the historic significance, the present importance, and the future trajectory of this state structure.

First of all, what is it? Let us start with that upon which we can agree. We all agree that the USSR by its very existence and by its intermittent support for national liberation movements has, to an important degree, been a force that has undermined world capitalism. We all agree that its internal regime has been repressive and that it has often failed to support socialist and national liberation movements in other countries, movements worthy of support. We all agree that however impressive the increase in the military and industrial strength of the USSR (as compared to tsarist times), it is nevertheless far less strong than both it and its hostile critics assert and, for this reason if for no other, has only a limited capacity for direct imperial expansion. Finally, we all agree that it is less stable internally and vis-à-vis its close associates than is sometimes thought, and that nationalism in Eastern Europe and the nationalities question inside the USSR are serious Achilles heels of the present political structure.

We disagree rather importantly on how to describe the USSR's economic structure. For Frank and Wallerstein, it remains, despite all the internal changes, an integral part of the world division of labor governed by the rules of the capitalist world-economy and therefore fundamentally subject to its vicissitudes. While neither Amin nor Arrighi consider the USSR to have a socialist economy, as they define the term, they do feel that it is substantially outside (Amin), or weakly incorporated into (Arrighi), the capitalist world-economy, and that it has markedly weaker tendencies to overproduction. They agree that the Soviet polity and economy are relatively weak, but they tend to feel that this weakness is an element that provokes a certain expansionist tendency. Frank and Wallerstein, but especially Frank, are skeptical of this last inference.

Finally, there is a point of agreement which places the views of the four authors in opposition not only to Establishment views but to those of most of the world's left. Insofar as the political system of the USSR can be considered to be open to change, whether gradual or sudden—insofar, that is, as the present structure might in some sense "break down" (either internally or vis-à-vis Eastern Europe)—most analysts (of the right, center, and left) believe that this would mark a significant setback to world socialism. We do not believe that this is necessarily so. The contrary might well be the case. Insofar as the rigidities of the USSR are a barrier to the progress of the world socialist movement, such a "breakdown," far from bringing about a counter-revolution in the USSR and weakening world socialist forces, might well strengthen these forces everywhere, including inside the USSR itself.

This brings us quite naturally to the question of Eastern Europe. It is clear that, aside from Yugoslavia and Albania, none of the governments, members of COMECON, came to power through a mass popular movement; and therefore in none is the force of nationalist sentiment one of the pillars of the existing regime. Quite the contrary, as the rise of Solidarity in Poland has exemplified, the workers have asserted their class interests under the banner of the Holy Mary and historic Poland. It is clear, too, that these workers see this as their only way to be antisystemic, at least at present. Therefore we place their efforts in the family of world antisystemic—that is, anticapitalist—forces.

What, then, shall we say of socialist states elsewhere—China, to be sure, but also Vietnam, Korea, Cuba? Unlike the regimes of Eastern Europe, most of these non-European socialist states did indeed come to power as the expression of large popular movements. Most of them were able to be simultaneously the expression of socialism and nationalism. But once in power, have these regimes been fundamentally different from the others? Here we have some differences among us. In terms of their relationship to the capitalist world-economy, the same division of views exists vis-à-vis China as exists vis-à-vis the USSR. Frank and Wallerstein see China as more deeply involved than do Amin and Arrighi. There, however, the agreement stops. For Frank, the movement in China has been "recuperated," more or less in the same sense as the movement in the USSR has been. For Amin and Wallerstein, and largely for Arrighi, this is simply not so. Amin sees China as a basically socialist state, whose fundamental worker-peasant alliance has not changed through the many ups-and-downs of internal politics. Wallerstein and Arrighi emphasize the civilizational factor, the degree to which China, a non-Western country, is governed by a popular regime that incarnates a sense of historic resistance to world capitalism and a renaissance of other peoples. *Pari passu,* the argument applies to Vietnam and to Cuba.

The discussion of socialist states merges rapidly into a discussion of socialist movements. There is no question in any of our minds that there is a "crisis" in Marxism as an explanatory model, as well as a crisis in socialism as a world-historical movement, in the sense that the orthodoxies (plural, because there are several) have proven in error, not totally but in important ways. Our separate essays indicate some of the ways in which each of us would restate or reformulate the theoretical issues and the practical conclusions. For example, it is clear that workers often assemble today to defend proletarian class interests under banners other than socialism. Frank draws from this a sense of regret, if not of unease. Arrighi sees it as a reflection of the workplace strength of the labor movement (especially in the core) and its ability to pursue the reality of labor's interests. Amin and Wallerstein see it as a sign of increasing strength of workers' class consciousness throughout the world-economy, enabling them to pierce any ideological veils (even those that call themselves Marxist or socialist), and thereby pursue their interests effectively.

One of the historical phenomena on which Marxist and socialist thought was clearly deficient was the importance given to nationalist and/or populist movements. There seems little doubt that they were historically underestimated. But how should we formulate a better estimate? For Amin, nationalism today cannot develop significantly in the absence of a socialist content. For Arrighi and Frank, it is the other way around. Wallerstein believes both statements are largely true.

Frank takes a largely negative view of the spread of populist nationalism (including movements grouped around religion, race, or language). Frank believes that the nationalist element ultimately overcomes any socialist perfume, and that therefore nationalism is ultimately bourgeois and not antisystemic. Indeed, he argues that the contrary might be true, that nationalism is the optimal mode of bringing the rebellious back into the system. Amin, Arrighi, and Wallerstein disagree. For them, anything that prevents world capitalism from using more primitive forms of exploitation is good, both in itself and because it deepens the contradictions. While not every movement that might be called nationalist fits this category, a large number of movements, especially outside of the European zone, are basically anticapitalist in spirit and social base, unlike most nationalist movements of the nineteenth century. While their ideology may be confused and unoriginal, their overall impact has been positive and quite unlike the racist, xenophobic movements that are constantly reemerging in the core countries.

The variation in the analyses of the dynamics of world capitalism and of the world antisystemic movements naturally leads to somewhat different predictions and prescriptions for the future, whether we look at an immediate future (the 1980s) or a longer term one.

Two immediate questions are on most people's minds when they think about their expectations for the 1980s. Will there be a "crash," and will there be a world war? The answer to the first depends in part on what one means by a crash. If one means a serious financial collapse followed by a price drop and a significant increase in world unemployment, then Amin, Frank, and Wallerstein all think that there is a reasonably high probability of this in this decade. Arrighi rather strongly disagrees. He feels that the forces pushing against such a deep downturn are very great. He puts particular stress on the structural strength of the labor movement in core countries (which will rule out the serious collapse in prices, output, and employment that occurred in the 1930s), and on the likelihood of multiple intra-Third World wars (which will serve as a fillip to world effective demand). While the other three do not deny these factors have retarded the collapse, they are skeptical that they will continue to do so in the face of the logic of the continuing anarchy of world production.

When it comes to the question of war, opinion is more diverse. On the likelihood of a world war, there is a gamut of views, from Amin who believes it is at least a serious possibility (resulting from the same kinds of "miscalculations" that will cause a "crash") to Arrighi who believes it is virtually inconceivable in this coming decade. Wallerstein and Frank are in between and in that order. All, however, agree on the likelihood that the 1980s will be a decade during which the number of wars in and among Third World states will grow. It is indeed out of such wars that a larger conflict is most likely to grow. Where there is disagreement is on the pattern of world alliance structures that will serve as the matrix within which these conflicts will occur. As previously suggested, none of us believes that the NATO/Warsaw Pact confrontation, which dominated world politics from 1948 until recently, is in fact the correct description of potential military battlelines, however much ideologies in both camps may believe it or want it. We all agree that the Washington-Tokyo-Peking axis has become in a brief period fairly solid and will continue to crystallize. Amin, Frank, and Wallerstein all believe that, counter to that axis, there will emerge, and is already emerging, a Bonn-Paris-Moscow axis of "détente" which could crystallize faster than one imagines. Arrighi doubts this. He believes rather that Western Europe is moving toward neutrality, toward becoming a big Switzerland. None of us believes that Western Europe is likely to engage militarily on the side of Washington-Tokyo-Peking, should the issue arise.

For the three who see the development of this new Europe-USSR axis, the basis of such a "deal" would be both economic (arrangements between Western and Eastern Europe on the one hand, and joint arrangements with the Arab world on the other), and political ("liberalization" in Eastern Europe and relative social peace in Western Europe). Arrighi is skeptical about the likelihood of such a "deal" because he rates higher than the others the likelihood of Western Europe getting the purported advantages of this "deal" without having to make it.

There is further disagreement about prospects beyond the

immediate future. Two strategies have been central to social-ist movements since the nineteenth century. One is to seize state power to establish a "socialist" state. In contemporary jargon, this strategy is aimed at "delinking" from the world capitalist system. The second is to gain significant state power through the ballot box and parliamentary reforms—what has come to be called social-democratization. Since our assess-ments of the past history of these two strategies differ, our appreciation of their future history differs as well.

Delinking as a strategy gets high marks from Amin. He believes it has been relatively successful and quite positive wherever it has been tried. Sometimes it has established a socialist state, as in China; even where it has not, it has at least established a noncapitalist one, as in the USSR. Socialism in one country, for Amin, is not only possible but will remain the central strategy of world socialist movements over the next fifty to one hundred years because it provides the optimal mechanism to arrive at a world socialist order. Those "radical" regimes who have not delinked (e.g., Egypt under Nasser) have not survived.

Frank could not disagree more. Delinking has never worked to any significant extent (with the possible exception of North Korea and Albania), since the delinked states have all been in one way or another reintegrated into the capitalist world sys-tem. Frank points out that most "delinking" was not self-started but was imposed on revolutionary regimes by "de-stabilization" through embargoes by core powers, and was therefore forced as much as it was voluntary. How efficacious, then, can voluntary delinking be? He also asks why "older" socialist states constantly counsel "younger" ones not to de-link (the USSR to China and Angola, China to Vietnam, Cuba to Nicaragua), if it is so advantageous to one and all.

Wallerstein agrees with Frank that delinking has neither been successful nor by and large voluntary. Furthermore, he sees a negative impact on the world socialist movement through successive disillusionments. He considers delinking to be simply the avatar of mercantilism in the twentieth cen-tury and that therefore, even as a tactic, it is primarily possible for large states, such as the USSR or China. He tempers this

view with the note that delinking has had positive mobiliza-
tional effects, and that a comparison of the fates of Nasser,
Nkrumah, etc. on the one hand, and Castro on the other must
give pause. Nonetheless, even if the tactic has some positive
effects, he wonders if its day is not done and whether the world
socialist movement should not now—will not now—seek alternative strategies.

Arrighi agrees that delinking is essentially mercantilism,
but mercantilism with a new content. As noted before, he sees
less reintegration into the world-economy than do Frank and
Wallerstein, if less creation of socialisms than does Amin. For
Arrighi, as for Frank and Wallerstein, the question is what the
strategy of the future will be.

On the strategy of social-democratization, none of us is
impressed with it as a model of the liberal polity. All believe it
has masked important repression, which has however been
combined with substantial economic gains for the proletariat
in the core countries during the post-1945 expansion. For
Amin and Frank, the present crisis will lead to increased
repression in the core states. They call this "1984," referring to
the vision of George Orwell. Amin feels the states will begin to
approach the Soviet model. Arrighi also thinks this trend will
grow, but he sees it as quite different from the Soviet model.
He calls it "liberal corporatism." All of us believe this is a model
only for core countries and is not a mode of transition to world
socialism. Quite the contrary. If this view sounds a bit like
Milton Friedman's assessment of social democracy, it is—
except that for us it is capitalism itself that has bred this social
form, and far from being in opposition to capitalism, it is its
most sophisticated product. Amin draws from this the conclusion that revolutionary forces are today located primarily in the
periphery. Wallerstein makes a distinction between the United
States and Western Europe in this regard, and believes that in
the United States, both because of its internal social structure
and because of the effects of "decline," there will be serious
social unrest in the 1980s.

Perhaps one of the most fundamental differences among us
is our long-run vision. Amin, Arrighi, and Wallerstein are
long-run optimists, seeing the demise of world capitalism as

virtually certain. They believe this to be so, not because of errors in judgment that will be committed by capitalist forces, for errors are reparable or even preventable. They believe this to be so because they believe, as did Schumpeter, that it is capitalism's successes that will breed its failure; that the more capitalism expands, recuperates oppositions, and adjusts difficulties, the more it is led into impasses from which there is no exit. They see Frank as pessimistic because of his exaggerated emphasis on these "successes" and his impatience for more consistent policies on the part of antisystemic movements. Frank denies he is pessimistic. Although he does not believe capitalism to be eternal, he cannot yet foresee when the demise of world capitalism will occur. But if Amin, Arrighi, and Wallerstein all agree on the virtual certainty of the demise of world capitalism in the next century, they vary in their degree of certainty about what will replace it. None believe a socialist world order is inevitable; a new class society is certainly conceivable. But Amin thinks world socialism is highly probable, and Wallerstein is close to this view. Arrighi is more skeptical.

All four of us, however, continue to believe that human social action to transform the world is still possible, desirable, and urgent. All believe the world is indeed in a long-term structural "crisis," and that intelligent reflection is a priority to which we must all give allegiance.

NOTES

A CRISIS OF HEGEMONY

1. A few remarks on terminology: "capitalist world" and "communist world" refer to geopolitical entities, that is, to the two political blocs (also euphemistically referred to as "free world" and "socialist world") into which the world was divided at the end of World War II. By "Third World" I shall understand the geopolitical entity that emerged in the 1960s with the growing political independence of the peripheral regions of both "worlds."

   "Capitalist world-economy" or "world-economy," on the other hand, designate the single world system defined by the world division of labor (see Immanuel Wallerstein, "The Rise and Future Demise of the World Capitalist System: Concepts for Comparative Analysis," *Comparative Studies in Society and History* 16, no. 4 [1974]).

   "Empire/imperial" refer to the classical meaning of empire as a hierarchical order of states guaranteeing universal peace. In this sense, they are opposites of the terms "imperialism/imperialist" introduced at the beginning of this century to designate a situation of anarchy in core interstate relations, tending toward universal war (see G. Arrighi, *The Geometry of Imperialism* [London and New York: Schocken, 1978]).

   "Market/market-like" refer simply to multilateral systems of exchange of goods/services against money in which prices are not mere accounting devices. As we proceed, it will become clear that in using the term I never imply the existence of "pure competition" or of a "self-regulating" market economy.

2. By "core capital" I shall understand those capitalist enterprises that because of their product mix and forms of organization of production and distribution have strong competitive advantages in the world-economy. The adjectives U.S., German, Japanese, West European, etc., refer to the country of origin. They will be used whenever this is considered to be of some relevance.

3. I seem to be in some disagreement with my co-authors about the status of Germany and Japan in the world-economy immediately

after World War II. My co-authors hold the view that Germany and Japan occupied a core position throughout the postwar period. I maintain, on the other hand, that the technological, and above all organizational, superiority developed by U.S. core capital in the interwar years (particularly the potential for transnational expansion through direct investment) had the effect of "degrading" countries such as Germany and Japan to semiperipheral status. This is the reason why I say that they *moved* to a core status.

4. Karl Marx, *Capital,* Vol. I (Moscow, 1959), p. 332.
5. Ibid., p. 361.
6. I have dealt with the analogies between "imperialism" and "mercantilism" in my *Geometry of Imperialism.*
7. "Notes on Exterminism, the Last Stage of Civilization," *New Left Review* 121 (May-June 1980): 3–31.

CRISIS OF IDEOLOGY AND IDEOLOGY OF CRISIS

1. This essay draws on and extends the analysis in the author's recent books *Crisis: In the World Economy,* and *Crisis: In the Third World* (both Holmes & Meier in New York and Heinemann Educational Books in London, 1980 and 1981) and *Reflections on the World Economic Crisis* (Monthly Review Press in New York and Hutchinson Education in London, 1981).
2. For Wallerstein's analysis, see his *The Modern World-System,* volumes I & II (New York and London: Academic Press, 1974 and 1980) and *The Capitalist World Economy* (Cambridge and New York: Cambridge University Press, 1979). For Frank's historical analysis, see his *World Accumulation 1492–1789* and *Dependent Accumulation and Underdevelopment* (New York: Monthly Review Press, and London: Macmillan Press, 1978/1979). Logistics are introduced by Rondo Cameron in "The Logistics of European Economic Growth: A Note on Historical Periodization," *Journal of European Economic History* 2, no. 1 (Spring 1973). The history of long cycles and trends is discussed in a special issue of *Review* 2, no. 4 (Spring 1979).
3. The analysis of Keynesianism, monetarism and supply-side economics and their future is extended in my "After Reaganomics and Thatcherism, What?" in the special issue on the "World Capitalist Crisis and the Rise of the Right," *Contemporary Marxism,* no. 4 (Winter 1981–82).

4. My analysis of the experience with and prospects for delinking and self-reliance is extended in my "Crisis and Transformation of Dependence in the World System" in *Mode of Production or Dependence? Alternative Perspectives on Peripheral Social Formations*, ed. Dale Johnson and Ronald Chilcote (Beverly Hills and London: Sage Publishers, forthcoming).

5. E. H. Carr, "The Russian Revolution and the West," *New Left Review* 111 (September-October 1978), pp. 31–36.

6. Régis Debray, "Marxism and the National Question," *New Left Review* 105 (September-October 1977).

7. The political implications of recent developments in socialist Asia are further explored in my "Kampuchea, Vietnam, China: Observations and Reflections," *AMPO Japan-Asia Quarterly Review* (Tokyo) 13, no. 1 (Winter 1981) and in a prelimary version in *Social Praxis* (Amsterdam) 7, nos. 3/4 (1980).

8. Eric Hobsbawm, "Some Reflections on 'The Break-up of Britain,'" *New Left Review* 105 (September-October 1977).

9. Paul M. Sweezy, "U.S. Foreign Policy in the 1980s," *Monthly Review* 31, no. 11 (April 1980). Sweezy cites a careful study by the Center for Defense Information in Washington, D.C., entitled "Soviet Geopolitical Momentum: Myth or Menace—Trends of Soviet Influence Around the World from 1945 to 1980," *The Defense Monitor* (January 1980). For a similar conclusion, see the Washington-based Institute for Policy Studies publication by Alan Wolfe, *The Rise and Fall of the "Soviet Threat."*

CRISIS, NATIONALISM, AND SOCIALISM

1. See: "Toward a New Structural Crisis of the Capitalist System," *Socialist Revolution* 1 (1975); "The Crisis of Imperialism," chap. 5 of *Imperialism and Unequal Development* (New York: Monthly Review Press, 1977); "Self-Reliance and the New International Economic Order," *Monthly Review* 29, no. 3 (July-August 1977); "Collective Self-Reliance or National Liberation?" in *Dialogue for a New Order,* ed. K. Haw (London: Pergamon, 1980); "Du Rapport Pearson (1970) au Rapport Brandt (1980), ou la crise de l'idéologie du développement," *Africa Development* (1980).

2. Giovanni Arrighi, *The Geometry of Imperialism* (New York: Schocken, 1978).

3. Ibid., p. 143.

4. Ibid., p. 134.

5. This is the thesis of Isaac Minian, *Intercapitalist Rivalry and Industrialization in Underdeveloped Countries* (1979).

6. See Albert Bergesen and Ronald Schoenberg, "Long Waves of Colonial Expansion and Contraction, 1415–1969," in *Studies in the Modern World-System,* ed. A. Bergesen (New York: Academic Press, 1980), pp. 13–23.

7. Immanuel Wallerstein, "The Future of the World Economy," *Processes of the World-System,* ed. Terence K. Hopkins and Immanuel Wallerstein (Beverly Hills: Sage, 1979), pp. 167–80.

8. Pierre Jacquemot, "Modèle théorique d'accumulation en économie, semi-industrialisé à base exportatrice," *Cahier No. 76* (UER Sciences des organisations, Université de Paris, Dauphine, 1979); P. Jacquemot and M. Raffinot, "Politiques industrielles et développement périphérique," *Cahier Economie du Développment* (Université de Paris, Dauphine) 3 (1978).

9. I refer here to the bourgeois models of W. Arthur Lewis, Fei and Ranis, and to those of F. Perroux, G. de Bernis, and A. Hirschman, criticized by Jacquemot.

10. As far as these questions are concerned, I can only refer the reader to my study of the concept and nature of value, and the ways it functions in various relationships of production, both social and statist. See Samir Amin, *The Law of Value and Historical Materialism* (New York: Monthly Review Press, 1978).

11. Andre Gunder Frank and Samir Amin, "Let's Not Wait for 1984: Discussion of the Crisis," in Andre Gunder Frank, *Reflections on the World Economic Crisis* (New York: Monthly Review Press, 1981).

12. G. Konard and I. Szelenyi, *La marche au pouvoir des intellectuals* (Paris: Editions de Seuil, 1979).

13. Samir Amin, *Class and Nation, Historically and in the Current Crisis* (New York: Monthly Review Press, 1980), pp. 218–24.

14. Alexandre Faire, *L'Economie, le marxisme, la crise, la guerre,* mimeo (Paris, April 1980).